John Graves, Writer

John Graves, Writer

EDITED BY MARK BUSBY
AND TERRELL DIXON

UNIVERSITY OF TEXAS PRESS, AUSTIN

Mark Busby's introduction updates and revises his entry on John Graves in *American Nature Writers*, edited by John Elder, Scribner's, 1996. Portions of Rick Bass's tribute appeared in his introduction to the 2002 SMU Press reprint of *Hard Scrabble*. Bill Wittliff's essay was originally published as the foreword to the 2004 SMU Press reprint of *Notes on a Limestone Ledge*. The essays by Terrell Dixon, James Langston, and Dickie Maurice Heaberlin were originally published in *Southwestern American Literature* 29.1 (Fall 2003). Used by permission.

Printed in the United States of America
First edition, 2007

∞ The paper used in this book meets the minimum requirements of ANSI/NISO Z39.48-1992 (R1997) (Permanence of Paper).

LIBRARY OF CONGRESS CATALOGING-IN-PUBLICATION DATA

John Graves, writer / edited by Mark Busby and Terrell Dixon. — 1st ed.
p. cm.
Includes bibliographical references and index.
ISBN-13: 978-0-292-71494-6 (alk. paper)
ISBN-10: 0-292-71494-7 (alk. paper)
1. Graves, John, 1920– 2. Authors, American—Texas—Biography.
3. Authors, American—20th century—Biography. 4. Texas—In literature.
I. Busby, Mark. II. Dixon, Terrell.
PS3557.R2867Z75 2007
813'.54—dc22 2006023533

Contents

Preface

MARK BUSBY AND TERRELL DIXON

THIS COLLECTION BEGAN converging as the result of several events. The Southwestern Writers Collection (SWWC) at Texas State University–San Marcos held a symposium called "The Writer John Graves" in September 2002, bringing together friends, acquaintances, and scholars of John Graves' work. The next fall, when the Western History Association (WHA) met in Fort Worth, organizer Ron Tyler planned a session on Graves' work that included Mark Busby, Terrell Dixon, Don Graham, and Stephen Harrigan, with Graves commenting on the discussion and announcing that his memoir would come out in 2004. As that session ended, Jim Lee, now of Texas Christian University Press and a longtime faculty member at the University of North Texas, joined us, as the idea for collecting essays on John Graves began to take shape. Mark Busby and Terrell Dixon agreed to begin the process, using the presentations at the San Marcos symposium and WHA as the beginnings of the collection. This book is the culmination of those events.

We decided early that we would not necessarily plan a Festschrift, which is usually a celebratory volume with contributions by an academic's colleagues and former students. We wanted to have essays that celebrate Graves' life and work, but we also planned to include other analytical essays that offer insight into his life and career by writers who may or may not have ever met John Graves but who have examined his work carefully. And we believe that this collection fulfills our goals.

WE HAVE DIVIDED THE COLLECTION into three parts after our preface and coeditor Mark Busby's introduction. The first part includes the transcript of a session at the John Graves' symposium in San Marcos, with Sam Hynes, Graves' longtime friend, fellow student at Columbia, and a distinguished writer and scholar, and Dave Hickey, Graves' former student at TCU and later a MacArthur Fellowship winner for his art criticism. Graves commented on and responded to these two friends' observations about their experiences with him at two distinctly different periods in his life. The symposium commentary is followed by an interview by Dave Hamrick, the 2004–2006 president of the Texas Institute of Letters and editor of *John Graves and The Making of* Goodbye to a River.

Part 2 is perhaps the Festschrift portion of the book. Here six of John's friends provide personal responses to their close connection to John and his work. Bill Wittliff has had a long and close personal relationship with Graves for many years, back to the 1960s when Bill and Sally Wittliff ran Encino Press. Next, Rick Bass notes the strong influence that Graves has had on Texas literature and on his own work. Then Bill Broyles pays tribute to Graves' work. Broyles was the founding editor of *Texas Monthly* and enticed Graves to write a regular column for the magazine early in its existence, bringing literary prestige to *Texas Monthly* before it was the established publication that it has become. There is a strong connection between these two former Marines, one from World War II and the other from Vietnam. Next John Erickson tells of visiting Graves early in his writing career, before Erickson created the now-famous Hank the Cowdog series, and how the relationship he established with Graves helped him find his way as a writer. The next essay in this section is by Bill Harvey, who was drawn early to Graves' trip down the Brazos and sought his advice before setting out on his own canoe trip forty years after the classic journey. Finally, a seasoned observer of Texas letters and of Graves' work, James Ward Lee, examines Graves' career in light of the 2004 memoir *Myself and Strangers.* Lee gains insight into the importance of Graves' Fort Worth experiences in the making of the writer, as well as the significance of rejection in his journey to becoming a writer.

Part 3 turns to specific examinations of Graves' work. Alex Hunt's essay explores how Graves' writing often has provoked discussion about the relationship of literary art with activism and about what properly constitutes the categories of "nature writing" and "environmentalism." He then argues for Graves' work as its own uniquely Texas hybrid. Terrell Dixon looks at the place of *Goodbye to a River* within American environmental literature; he observes how the sometimes misunderstood subtleties of Graves' style and structure develop the themes of the book and at how the book alternates between acceptance of and argument with some of Thoreau's beliefs.

James Langston and Betsy Berry treat one of the issues that always produces heated discussions among students—the question of gender in Graves' work. Langston argues that in *Goodbye to a River,* Graves presents a strong female character, Davis Birdsong's grandmother, Maw, whose strength provides the model for a kind of life that Graves himself later pursued. Berry approaches the issue by also demonstrating how Graves strongly influenced another Texas writer, Beverly Lowry. Berry evaluates the strong similarities between Lowry's character, Will Hand, in *The Perfect Sonya* and Graves and analyzes Lowry's critique of the Texas "masculine mystique." Dickie Maurice Heaberlin points to similarities between John Graves and E. B. White, particularly both men's attraction to dachshunds (often pronounced "dash hounds" in rural Texas) and the two writers' styles, especially their fondness for the em dash (—).

In her essay, Lisa Slappey looks at the writing of *Goodbye to a River* as both a rite of passage for its author and a study of how "an ethnocentric, aggressive, colonial culture" imposed itself on indigenous inhabitants. Barbara J. Cook demonstrates that Graves' initial three major works, *Goodbye to a River, Hard Scrabble,* and *From a Limestone Ledge,* constitute different aspects of a single, continuing narrative about our right, human relationship to the land. Graves' essays for *Texas Monthly,* the glossy magazine of an increasingly urbanized state, are the focus of Cory Lock's contribution. She explores the place that his Country Notes essays had in the magazine and how the successive editorships of Bill Broyles, Greg Curtis, and Evan Smith viewed the importance of Graves' writing about rural subjects.

Finally, Don Graham, who has long observed Texas literature, examines Graves' main body of work. Graham evaluates Graves' memoir, pointing out how Graves, unlike some other memoirists, chooses to concentrate on sketches of relatively unknown figures. He also points out the numerous literary insights the young Graves had during his writing apprenticeship. Graham links how Graves' return to Texas at the end of the memoir signaled the beginning of his real writing career, with the publication of what for Graves became "the book"—*Goodbye to a River.*

The three sections, we hope, offer a full picture of John Graves, writer. Our title echoes the symposium on Graves at Texas State University in 2002, and we would like to thank SWWC curator Connie Todd and her staff, especially Steve Davis, for the help and inspiration. Mark Busby acknowledges the help of his staff at the Southwest Regional Humanities Center, especially Sharon Pogue, Christopher "Twister" Marquiss, and Tammy Gonzales. Terrell Dixon also thanks the Martha Gano Houstoun Endowment in the English Department at the University of Houston. And, without doubt, we'd like to thank the *dos Lindas,* Linda Busby and Linda Walsh, for all their help in moving us on down the river. Finally we acknowledge John Graves, writer, for working with us on this project and for showing all of us the way.

As a young boy.

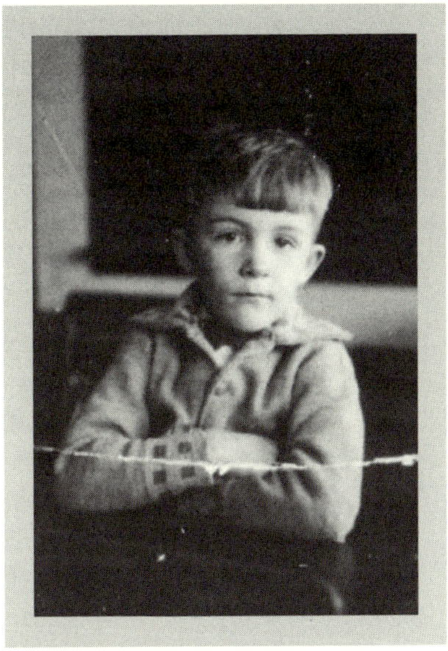

In the first grade.

With his father in Cuero, Texas, 1930s.

With a flattop haircut.

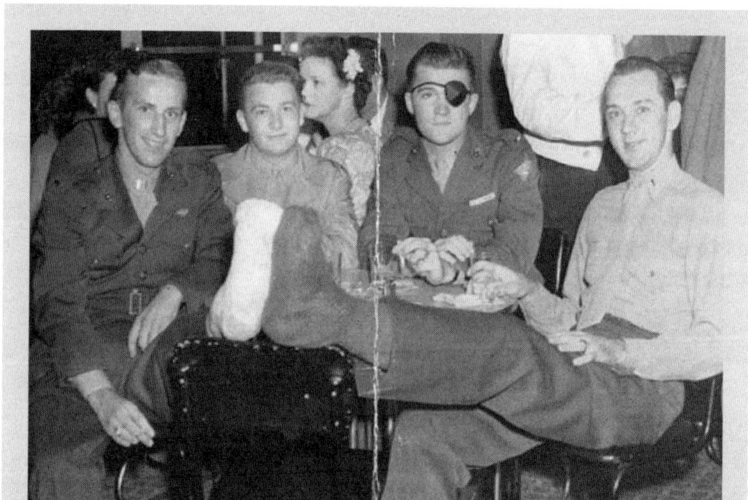

Relaxing with friends. Graves with his eye patch.

In Europe, 1949.

In a Madrid café, circa 1954.

In Europe.

With Watty in his canoe. Photograph by Jane Cole.

With his dog on the Brazos River at start of the Goodbye *trip, 1957. Photograph by Jane Cole.*

Fishing on the Trinity River, circa 1957 or 1958. Photograph by Jane Cole.

With his wife, Jane, 1960s.

At Hard Scrabble, 1960s.

As a mason, 1962.

On his hardscrabble ranch. Photograph by Bill Wittliff, © 1971.

Wearing his hat.

On his porch. Photograph by Bill Wittliff, © 1971.

In his barn office.
Photograph by Bill Wittliff,
© 1977.

In 1986. Photograph by
Bill Wittliff, © 1986.

Fishing on White Bluff Creek.

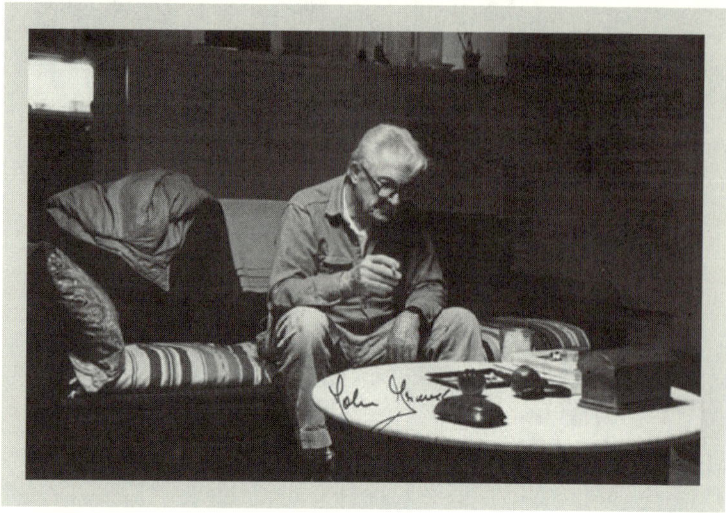

At home. Photograph by Bill Wittliff, © 1991.

John Graves Day, 1995.

At the dedication of a statue in his honor, 2004.

John Graves, Writer

Introduction

MARK BUSBY

READING TEXAS WRITER John Graves' major works, *Goodbye to a River* (1960), *Hard Scrabble* (1974), *From a Limestone Ledge* (1980), and the memoir *Myself and Strangers* (2004) makes you feel as though you have made a friend. After riding down the river in his canoe and listening to him ruminate about the virtues of hard-scrabble farming or the disappearance of his dog Blue, you have spent much quality time with the kind of writer who gets inside you, who speaks with a clear, personal voice so that when you are through with a book you know you have met a man—a man who understands the light and the dark of his world and a writer who helps you see the grays of it, too.[1]

In his best-known work, *Goodbye to a River,* Graves points to the two dimensions of his life and work:

> If a man couldn't escape what he came from, we would most of us still be peasants in Old World hovels. But if, having escaped or not, he wants in some way to know himself, define himself, and tries to do it without taking into account the thing he came from, he is writing without any ink in his pen. The provincial who cultivates only his roots is in peril, potato-like, of becoming more root

> than plant. The man who cuts his roots away and denies that they were ever connected with him withers into half a man. (145)

It is the masculine language of the time, and Graves' work indeed concerns the traditionally masculine worlds of canoeing, camping, and building fences, but the double vision of this quote indicates that Graves resisted narrowness, particularly the provincial jingoism that Texas regionalism has sometimes encouraged. Throughout his work Graves has looked clearly at where he came from, digging deeply into the roots sunk into Texas soil, and has also traveled widely. As a result, his work reveals his strong sense of the integral relationship between the particular and the universal.

His keen sense of the differences among places resulted partially from Graves' growing up in two distinct places, the newly urban Fort Worth, Texas, and the richly varied South Texas town of Cuero, where his grandparents lived. Born in Fort Worth on August 6, 1920, he explored the Trinity River bottom before it became layered with Coors cans. From a cattle town on the fork of the Trinity River along the Chisholm Trail, Fort Worth had evolved into a city with a central, downtown business district and a ring of homes circling it. As a boy, Graves would take the streetcar down Camp Bowie Boulevard to visit the men's store his father operated, "where oilmen in tan gabardine suits and Borsalino hats would gather around a big table in the rear and tell good profane stories about oil towns with names like Desdemona and Ranger and McCamey, and muse about the big-money game they played and the personalities of those with whom they played it" (*Growing Up in Texas,* 66–67).

This city life was complemented by the boy's venturing out into the nearby Trinity River bottom, where deer, quail, rabbits, and squirrels still abounded, and he and his friends took their scrappy hounds out there to hunt. Back in the city, he hung around at the drugstores and hamburger joints with other lank-haired youths and lived a typical life for someone growing up during the Depression. But this average life was marked by several influences that affected this boy who was vaguely aware that he wanted to know more of the wider world. Through his varied reading, some teachers, and an educated, cosmopolitan neighbor, Graves was led to imagine life outside his surroundings:

> I went through the mélange of best-sellers and classics and leftover 19th-century sentimentality that was on the shelves at home, and stuff dragged down out of the attic of my grandfather's house in Cuero or sought out at the public library downtown. It made for a fine stew in the head, that mingling of Conrad and Fielding and Scott with the Southern soupiness of authors like F. Hopkinson Smith and the Reconstruction virulence of Thomas Dixon and the British Empire heroics of G. A. Henty and the farflung enthusiasm of roving Richard Halliburton. It was further flavored by reading on special subjects that seized me from time to time—Texas and Western lore, the Civil War, fly-fishing, horses, how to make buckskin out of rabbit hides and brew tea out of sumac. . . .
>
> But I remember also three or four first-rate teachers along the way who cut through my hangdog dislike of school and showed me what poetry consisted of, and a few other people like the bachelor surgeon who lived with his brother-in-law and sister a couple of doors from our house. He smoked Edgeworth tobacco in the finest-smelling pipes I have ever been around, and had a Yale education and the literate feel for language that many of the old-time Texas Methodists used to have. During long summer evening lawn conversations he could dip up out of memory, without self-consciousness, tags from Shakespeare or the Authorized Version or the whole long lovely flow of English poetry to suit almost any point, ironically more often than not. So despite all the hodgepodge reading I did, I had an early chance to see that good books were sense and language woven together, and that the weaving mattered greatly. (*Growing Up in Texas,* 69–70)

Reading books and listening to stories of the world beyond Fort Worth led him to think about the variety of the world, and this awareness was enhanced by the second major life influence as he grew up: regular trips to visit his father's family in South Texas. Graves' grandfather had run away from his Missouri home in his teens, settled in Cuero, along the Guadalupe River, shortly after the Civil War, and married into a ranching family. Although Cuero is only 250 miles from Fort Worth (a short distance in Texas terms), it seemed like a different world from the growing commercial city dotted with elm, sycamore, and bois d'arcs. In Cuero, "big dark liveoaks hung with Spanish moss stood around the houses and sometimes in the middle of the streets, the soft Gulf air working through them and beneath, with always somewhere the frenzy of mockingbirds and the sad low fluting of doves" (*Growing Up in Texas,* 72). South Texas also offered a variety of cultures and languages as Germans, Czechs, and Mexicans lived, worked, and spoke among themselves and interacted as needed with the English-speaking Texans from British and Scotch-Irish stock.

> South Texas was more than Grandpa and that house, even if the memory of them sums it up for me. It was friends I still have, when I see them, and camping and trotlining with them on the slow green Guadalupe, and racing ponies down dusty roads, and quail-hunting at Christmas with uncles to whom shooting and fishing and good dogs were a big part of what life was about, and Mexicans from whom I first got the taste of soft Spanish on the tongue, and elders' bloody tales of Reconstruction days and the Sutton-Taylor feud. It was a lot of things that Fort Worth was not, but mainly for me, I think, it was the past. Not as you find the past in books, even good books, but as you find it to touch. South Texas was where I could reach back to the things, good or bad, that my own people had been, and comprehend a little bit about what other people had been in relation to them. Like all human pasts—and all human presents and all human futures—it had vast imperfections, but I am glad I got to touch it.
>
> Because if you are a backward looker, you need something to look back to. (*Growing Up in Texas,* 75)

So these two areas of Texas profoundly influenced Graves, and he continued to carry with him the sense of place and history that he learned growing up. He took the influences to Rice Institute (now Rice University) in Houston, graduating Phi Beta Kappa in the class of 1942. At Rice he studied with George Williams, who also would teach William Goyen and Larry McMurtry. When his graduating class went directly into the war, Graves into the Marine Corps, he carried his influences beyond Texas. After completing Marine Officer Candidates School, he served in the Pacific as a first lieutenant. Seriously wounded on Saipan, he was waiting to be evacuated from an army field hospital when a wounded young soldier next to him asked where he was from. When Graves told him Texas, the young marine asked Graves to hold his hand and said he was glad to have a marine from the South next to him because the wounded soldier could understand what he said. And then the boy "clenched my hand harder still, and died" (*Hard Scrabble,* 92). As a result of his wounds, Graves lost the sight in one eye and received a Purple Heart. Later, he was promoted to captain and served as a Marine Reserves officer for many years.

After the war, Graves lived for a while in Mexico, and then with the GI Bill, he began graduate work at Columbia University in New York City. He took a writing class from Martha Foley, who edited *The Best American Short Stories* and *Story* magazine for many years. He sold one of the stories he wrote for her class, "Quarry," to the *New Yorker* in 1947. His master's thesis subject was William Faulkner.

After receiving a master's degree from Columbia in 1948, he taught at the University of Texas in Austin for two years. Then the wanderlust got him, documented in *Myself and Strangers,* and he left the country and traveled around France and Spain, where he lived for a while, and then to Tenerife in the Canary Islands, and to New Mexico, before he came back home to his blood's country in 1957 when his father became ill. He took a canoe trip down the Brazos River that fall and wrote a magazine article about the experience, which was published in *Holiday* that year. After joining the English faculty at Texas Christian University in Fort Worth in 1958, he expanded his river article into his first book, *Goodbye to a River.*

With some of the money he made from the book, Graves purchased a plot of land in Somervell County, Texas, near Glen Rose, about an hour southwest of Fort Worth, beginning a relationship with the land that eventually inspired his second major book, *Hard Scrabble.* He received a Guggenheim Fellowship in 1964 and then left TCU in the mid-1960s to work for Stewart Udall, who was then the secretary of the interior. He concentrated on water issues in Washington, D.C., and wrote "A River and a Piece of Country: A Potomac Essay" for the *Potomac Interim Report to the President,* a collection of essays by a task force to which Graves was assigned. The report was eventually published as *The Nation's River* in 1968.

His interest in water issues then led to his being one of three major contributors to *The Water Hustlers,* an analysis of water issues in specific parts of the United States published by Sierra Club books in 1971. Graves' essay, "Texas: 'You Ain't Seen Nothing Yet,'" provides an analysis of what he saw as the ill-conceived Texas Water Plan of 1968. The book demonstrates Graves' careful research and clear understanding of ecological issues. However, Graves has dismissed the work, saying:

> I guess I undertook it because I had so recently been doing that work for the Interior Department. I was really up on hydrology and the ins and outs of the water bureaucracy at the time. . . . What I did was all right, I guess, but the state water plan collapsed. Essentially any polemical writing is devoted to an evanescent problem. If it's solved, it disappears, and if it's not solved, it goes away. Polemics are self-destructive in that sense. They're not very satisfying. (Bennett, "John Graves," 71)

On his return to Texas in 1970, after ten years spent building the house on the land he called Hard Scrabble, Graves moved to the 380-acre place with his wife, Jane, whom he had married in 1958, and their two daughters, Helen and Sally. Working on the land also led to Graves' becoming a regular contributor to *Texas Monthly* magazine and to the writing of his third book, *From a Limestone Ledge,* which is a collection of these magazine articles. He continued writing, including the text to accompany photographs for a coffee-table book, *Texas Heartland: A Hill Country Year;* and contributing prefaces, forewords, and introductions to *Landscapes of Texas: Photographs from Texas Highways Magazine; Gringos in Mexico: One Hundred Years of Mexico in the American Short Story,* edited by Edward Simmen; *Digging into South Texas Prehistory: A Guide for Amateur Archaeologists,* by Thomas R. Hester; *Cowboy Life on the Texas Plains: The Photographs of Ray Rector,* edited by Margaret Rector; and *Vaquero: Genesis of the Texas Cowboy,* with photographs and text by Bill Wittliff. Additionally, he has lectured and commented widely, especially on Texas literature and the environment.

Two of Graves' publications, *The Last Running* (1974) and *Blue and Some Other Dogs* (1981), are short pieces expanded with photographs and drawings into fine-printing books published by Bill Wittliff's Encino Press. Wittliff, who is also a screenwriter and film director, has been one of Graves' closest friends and supporters over the years. *The Last Running* was originally a short story published in *Atlantic Monthly* in 1959 and included in *The Best American Short Stories* in 1960. *Blue and Some Other Dogs* was first published as one of his *Texas Monthly* pieces and was included in *From a Limestone Ledge.* It is a poignant story about the disappearance of Graves' ten-year-old mixed-breed sheepdog, described as the best dog he ever had. A third fine-printing book, *Self-Portrait with Birds: Some Semi-Ornithological Recollections* (Chama Press, 1991), was first published in *Of Birds and Texas* in 1986.

Graves' most significant work is *Goodbye to a River,* based on his canoe trip down the Brazos River in 1957. Graves had written a number of magazine pieces for various publications at that point, and he had a contract with *Sports Illustrated* to do a piece on the canoe trip. (The piece became more philosophy than sport and was published in *Holiday* instead of *SI.*) Graves' strong sense of history was inspired by his South Texas experiences and merged with his keen feelings for the natural world, developed during the time he spent in the Trinity River bottom. He knew that if the five proposed dams were built along the Brazos, the area would be irreparably changed. The Brazos is the third-largest river in Texas and the largest between the Red River and the Rio Grande. Called El Rio de los Brazos de Dios (the River of the Arms of God) by the early Spanish explorers, it flows for 840 miles from its source until it empties into the Gulf of Mexico near Freeport, just south of Galveston Island.

Drawing from a long tradition of nature writing about rivers—such as Henry David Thoreau's *A Week on the Concord and Merrimack Rivers,* the Rivers of America series, and Paul Horgan's *Great River: The Rio Grande in North American History*—and from the elegiac pastoral tradition, Graves brings his own unique approach and concerns to writing, much of which reveals a deep ambivalence about his being identified as a nature writer in the Thoreauvian tradition or being perceived as an ideologue single-mindedly pursuing a temporal agenda. In "On the Desirable Reluctance of Trumpets," a 1963 article published in *College Composition and Communication,* Graves articulated his concerns about hard-nosed persuasion, the article's title revealing Graves' persuasive strategy. In it Graves states that polemical writing "is preachment, a trumpet-note for good action, an exhortation boiling up out of a vision of present wrong and possible right" and that it "arises from a belief that something can be done about almost anything" and is based on "the principle of action that will produce change" (210). He then asks, rhetorically, if it follows that writers should "tootle our built-in trumpets frankly in favor of whatever cavalry charges against evil we see as desirable [and] encourage the conscripts to do the same" and answers by saying:

> No, sir, not for a good many of us, it doesn't. Those who like to tootle are going to keep on tootling; their number is legion and they will be with us always, and bless their good hearts one and all. But the fact that even those who don't want to are forced by their own humanness into reluctant or unconscious music of this sort does not invalidate detachment as an ideal, any more than democracy as a concept is invalidated by the fact that it has nowhere ever quite worked, and never will.
>
> The fact is that detachment is in spite of everything probably the best general ideal that a writer can hold to. First-rank writing whatever its form is concerned with expressing human truth. All-out tootlers are apt to confuse truth with facts . . . The facts of human existence are mostly obvious, and if they are evil facts they can often be changed; they are susceptible to cavalry charges. The truths the facts add up to, though, are neither obvious nor very susceptible. (212; Graves' ellipsis)

These comments clarify some of Graves' basic assumptions underlying his approach to writing persuasively. Both his desire for detached rather than polemical persuasion and his acute awareness of the complexity of human truth lead him to approach writing about damming the river with subtlety. His trumpeting is muted, a reluctant persuasion that takes the form of presenting human truths that are attached to the history of places and objects and therefore instill in those places and objects a value beyond and beneath the surface.

The detached position Graves stakes out leads to subtle persuasion in *Goodbye to a River*. He adopts a rhetorical stance similar to the one Shakespeare's Mark Antony takes in his famous eulogy for Caesar, saying he comes just to bury Caesar, not to praise him, and then setting about to move his audience in his subtle praise. That is what Graves does with his piece of the Brazos, and it is profound persuasion. As the book begins, for example, Graves seemingly disarms a reluctant reader by saying that he holds no bitterness about the proposed series of dams:

> In a region like the Southwest, scorched to begin with, alternating between floods and drouths, its absorbent cities quadrupling their censuses every few years, electrical power and flood control and moisture conservation and water skiing are praiseworthy projects. More than that, they are essential. We river-minded ones can't say much against them—nor, probably, should we want to. (8)

The clue to his real position here is the placement of water skiing in the last and emphatic position and saying, tongue firmly in cheek, that it is "essential." He then goes on to announce that it is not his fight and that he is just going down the Brazos to "wrap it up" before the river and "Satanta the White Bear and Mr. Charlie Goodnight" disappear under "the Criss-Crafts and the tinkle of portable radios" (9). This contrast between the high significance of Texas history and the brittle inconsequence of skiing to the sounds of portable radios heightens his position through verbal irony and allows him to achieve the detached position he seeks.

Goodbye to a River, like many Texas narratives, uses the journey for structure, and the journey takes on symbolic significance as well. This journey is a personal process, a trip to recover a wanderer's sense of history and place. By returning to places that have meaning, the persona-narrator demonstrates how one regains a rootedness that gives life meaning. Although the narrator does not mention Ishmael's water journey undertaken during a "damp, drizzly November in my soul," by leaving on a gray, threatening November day, Graves connects *Goodbye to a River* to *Moby Dick,* another work that uses the water journey of escape and return to suggest the powerful personal insights that the experience provides.

While *Goodbye to a River* enacts the escape-and-return pattern on a small scale as the writer-narrator leaves on November 11, 1957, for a 175-mile journey that ends with return to civilized life on December 2, the return to Texas after Graves' decade as a sojourner abroad also underpins the book. Particular and general pulse like systolic and diastolic in Graves' work, intertwining into a whole. This individual experience represents the possibility of understanding available to everyone, because "one river, seen right, may well be all rivers that flow to the sea" (254).

Still, it is the vividness and intensity of Graves' observations presented in his recognizable style that make the book memorable. This casual and folksy yet philosophical and literate canoeist with his Dachshund pup, Passenger, spins out stories connected to the history of places like Poke Stalk Bend, Old Painted Campground, Thorp Spring, Mitchell Bend, and others. By revisiting these places and recovering the stories the countrymen and women tell and by examining the natural history of the area, Graves constructs and dramatizes how a single individual can "know" a river, understand himself, and symbolize the process of achieving awareness of self through valuing place.

With the river journey to provide the structure, Graves moves back and forth from the river to the larger world through references to his own wandering past and through epigraphs and allusions to Sir Gawain, King Arthur, Laurence Sterne, William Butler Yeats, Thomas Hardy, Thoreau, Thorstein Veblen, T. S. Eliot, and one of Graves' favorite writers, the Spanish philosopher Juan Ramón Jiménez, who provides a quotation that buttresses the book: "Foot in one's accidental or elected homeland; heart, head in the world's air" (254). From these and other references to the "the world's air," Graves shifts to stories of the homeland, recalling the times he and his friend Hale and their massive black companion Bill Briggs spent on the river in their youth (with echoes of Huck Finn) to stories about the Comanches, who called themselves "The People"; the Mitchell-Truitt feud that ended with Cooney Mitchell's hanging in Granbury; the time the hermit Sam Sowell was almost burned up by thoughtless kids and was saved by Graves' friend Davis Birdsong; and the time Birdsong tried to impress a French diplomat by putting his leg behind his head. The human history is complemented by careful examination of natural history, as Graves observes the plants and animals along the trip, musing on the firewood quality of cottonwood, willow, cedar, ash, mesquite, live oak, and walnut, and reproduces in hieroglyphic the birdcall of redbirds and Carolina wrens.

Along the way Graves returns to several important concerns, such as his relationship to Thoreau, to hunting, and to the persistent puritanism of the people who live along the river. Anticipating that critics would note Thoreau's influence, Graves attempts to provide some distance between himself and his strong forebear. Graves makes it clear that he finds Thoreau too rooted in the world's air, too transcendently "ascetic," and consistently refers to him as "Saint Henry." The Texan's distance from his river-traveling ancestor is especially clear when it comes to hunting. Graves notes that even though "Saint Henry had impulses to gobble woodchucks raw," he eventually concluded that "blood sports were for juveniles" (53–54). Although Graves wavers along the way, he ultimately aligns himself with "Prince Ernest Hemingway" and asserts that

> killing itself can be reverent. To see and kill and pluck and gut and cook and eat a wild creature, all with some knowledge and the pleasure that knowledge gives, implies a closeness to the creature that is to me more honorable than the candle-lit consumption of rare prime steaks from a steer bludgeoned to death in a packing-house chute while tranquilizers course his veins. (167)

At one point late in the book Graves apparently decides to hunt no more—only to grab his gun when a good shot presents itself, suggesting that the persona the writer has created is inconsistent. Yet it is just such wavering that is significant. His repeated references to the country's Puritanism reinforce his emphasis on his shifting awareness of varying positions. Nature itself confirms his point:

> Sunshine and warm water seem to me to have full meaning only when they come after winter's bite; green is not so green if it doesn't follow the months of brown and gray. And the scheduled inevitable death of green carries its own exhilaration; in that change is the promise of all the rebirth to come, and the deaths, too. . . . Without the year's changes, for me, there is little morality. (119)

Later considering the puritan outlook of the people who live along the river, Graves makes a similar point, noting that if "wrong is sharply wrong enough, its edge digs deeper down into the core of that sweet fruit, pleasure, than hedonism ever thought to go" (191). Later he makes the same point symbolically, when he has Davis Birdsong tell a story about following Sam Sowell through the shin oak brush one day and finding a coiled diamondback rattlesnake. As Birdsong raises his ax to dispatch the snake, Sowell stops him and acknowledges the human connection to the snake's symbolic evil. Good and evil intertwine in Graves' world, and his trip down the river reinforces this knowledge for him in personal, historical, and natural ways.

This awareness suggests how Graves differs from some other Western nature writers. Graves' world is ultimately a "fallen," Manichean world with good and evil intertwined, unlike the innocent world that Thomas Lyon describes as the terrain of other Western nature writers in "The Nature Essay in the West." The function of the nature writer, Lyon suggests, is "to reforge a fundamental continuity between inner and outer, so that for the reader the world is alive again, seen precisely for what it is, and the mind is alive to it." Lyon continues:

> To have known the beauty of the world, seen with unclouded eyes the sheer wonder of a clear river or a mesa or a cottonwood tree, is to be in some sense and for that time, psychologically whole. The deepest attraction of the nature essay, probably, is this basic rightness of gestalt. Good nature writing is a recapturing of the child's world, the world before fragmentation, the world as poets and artists can see it. (221)

Although the elegiac tone of *Goodbye to a River* suggests nostalgia, Graves does not look back to an innocent world devoid of evil. Rather, his piece of the Brazos reinforces and becomes the vehicle for his understanding of human complexity.

In an insightful observation of Graves' style in 1981, Larry McMurtry, who taught with Graves at TCU in the early 1960s, points out that "one of his most frequent rhetorical devices . . . is to undercut himself: questioning a story he has just retold, doubting an observation he has just made, twisting out from under a position. Often he simply reverses his field and abandons whatever line of thought he has been pursuing" ("Ever a Bridegroom," 29). This technique highlights the complexity and mystery of human truth rather than clarifying it. McMurtry explains:

> He is popularly thought to be a kind of country explainer, when in fact he seems more interested in increasing our store of mysteries than our store of knowledge. He loves

> the obscure, indeterminate nature of rural legend and likes nothing better than to retell stories the full truth of which can never be known. If nature continues to stimulate him it may be because it too is elusive, feminine, never completely knowable.
>
> Certainly he is not looking forward to becoming the Sage of Glen Rose. His best writing is based on doubt and ambivalence—or at least two-sidedness; he is not eager to arrive at too many certainties, or any certainty too quickly. The persona he adopts most frequently is that of the man who *considers.* He may choose to consider a goat, a book, an anecdote, or some vagary of nature, but the process of considering is more important to the texture of his books than any conclusions that may get drawn. (29–30)

Goodbye to a River demonstrates clearly the reluctant trumpeter *considering,* in this case the human and natural history of a small piece of the Brazos River. Through his emphasis on using the natural world to consider the human history associated with it and his own consciousness, Graves provides a clear example of the process Scott Slovic describes in *Seeking Awareness in American Nature Writing.* Slovic notes that the tradition of nature writing from Thoreau through Annie Dillard, Edward Abbey, Wendell Berry, and Barry Lopez reveals an emphasis on the relationship between nature and the considering writer's mental state: "Nature writers are constantly probing, traumatizing, thrilling, and soothing their own minds—and by extension those of their readers—in quest not only of consciousness itself, but of an understanding of consciousness" (3).

Graves' consciousness results from a combination of personal experience, history, folklore, nature, and philosophy—a unique mixture that led to numerous positive reviews. Paul Horgan in the *New York Herald Tribune Book Review* hailed Graves as a new talent: "This highly original book bears witness to the appearance of an excellent literary talent not previously seen in book form." Wayne Gard in the *New York Times Book Review* called it "a memorable saga . . . a warm, moving book with many rewards for the reader." And Edward Weeks in the *Atlantic Monthly* pointed out the connection between the specific and the general, saying that "as you read, you have the feeling that the whole colorful, brutal tapestry of the Lone-Star State is being unrolled for you out of the biography of this one stream."

The book was selected as a finalist for the National Book Award for 1960 and won the Texas Institute of Letters Carr P. Collins Award for nonfiction that year.

By considering the complexity of human experience, Graves uses numerous themes and techniques that demonstrate how he senses more than a simple attitude. Those same concerns recur in his second book, which follows logically from *Goodbye to a River,* recounting a wanderer's return to a region that provides understanding about the profound value of knowing place. *Hard Scrabble* takes the commitment to place further than the first book and dramatizes Graves' attempts to recapture a worn-out piece of land. But this seemingly simple purpose takes on varied meanings and demonstrates Graves' awareness of simple complexity. One technique that he uses to achieve this purpose, for example, is to adopt several terms that on the surface seem simple and clear. One is the term "Tonk Nation," which initially seems to refer to the Tonkawa Indians who lived in Central Texas at the time of first contact with European explorers but whose numbers decreased until they disappeared from the state. Graves soon broadens the term from its specific reference to a band of native people, explaining that it can be applied "to the hard-bitten whites who settled and lingered there." He then adopts it as a generic term that is "quite descriptive of the country itself," noting that "as erosion and agricultural ruin spread down through the lower hills, Tonkishness spread with them, and in later days the name came to fit the whole hill zone, including Hard Scrabble. I use it that way in my mind. The Tonk Nation wherein we dwell . . ." (27; Graves' ellipsis).

Another term that contains layers of meaning is what Graves calls the Ownership Syndrome, shortened usually to the Syndrome. Initially negative, referring to the narrow vision of people who own and work land, the term shifts meaning and indicates the kind of concern for land and property that ownership instills. The Syndrome usually is in conflict with the Way, shortened from the natural Way, or "sacred Way," of preserving nature for wild things. Held together, both terms achieve a creative tension that adds complexity to seemingly simple ideas.

Another term that seems uncomplicated but achieves complexity is "O. F.," which Graves applies humorously to the Old Farts like himself who putter around "reading magazines about making compost and how to build things out of hunks of busted concrete," as his lawyer friend comments (8). But Graves quickly tells the lawyer that the O. F. is "a friend of mine—kinfolks, sort of," and makes it clear that he identifies with the O. F. In the fictional chapter 10 of *Hard Scrabble,* the O. F. becomes the major character as Graves traces his leaving home, coming to the area, marrying, and having children. The O. F., in his dealings with his wife and daughter, becomes a young and later an old father. Although Graves never translates O. F. as "Old Father," in his connection with the fictional character's problematic relationship with his daughter Midge, the story emphasizes the fatherly relationship, and the O. F.'s connection with husbanding the land gains more emphasis throughout the rest of the book. Finally, Graves asserts:

> If much of a future remains to mankind on this planet—a good moot point, of course—it probably rests largely in the hands of Old Farts, of whatever age or size or color or sex or wealth or class or profession or level of educational bliss. For the mark and sign of a true hydrogen-sulfide Old Fart is this: that while he knows men must use the earth, he knows too that it matters for its own sake and that it must stay alive, and therefore according to such understanding as he may have he tries to keep his dealings with it right and gentle, and only thereafter reflects on fiscal gain. (230)

It is just such a reconciliation that *Hard Scrabble* is about, for Graves takes as his major theme the process of *recovery.* Ostensibly, working this hardscrabble farmland is an attempt to recover the land itself from the unproductive state it has reached because of relentless cotton farming and mindless overgrazing by his thoughtless forerunners in the Tonk Nation. But it is also largely about recovering a sense of balance between human and natural worlds that the seeming warring camps of nature lovers and economic Darwinians obscure. Just as *Goodbye to a River* concerns reclaiming a balance between a concern for the particular and an understanding of the general, larger world, *Hard Scrabble* emphasizes that both the Way and the Ownership Syndrome have competing truths.

The book's structure largely derives from the pull of these opposite positions, as thesis and antithesis, and then points toward the synthesis that the writer—the O. F., the Head Varmint—ultimately achieves:

> So that he can no longer truly find the dividing line between his more or less useful country self, who plows and sows and builds and fences . . . and that other less pragmatic self, older in time but younger in spirit, who sips with bees and envies trumpeting cranes, and is restless when the plover flute from beneath low clouds on their way . . . and runs in his mind with Evetts Gilliver's hounds and with the fox they chase as well as with all honest chasers and all chased beasts now and in all times past. . . .
>
> Queerly, they are the same man. (248)

Throughout the book, Graves moves easily from one seeming opposition to another as his book leads toward its final reconciliation. In the first part of the book, Graves traces the history of the region, explains how he came to buy his plot in Somervell County, and considers the trees, shrubs, grasses, and creatures (deer, wolves, foxes, bobcats, among others) that are native to the region. This material is interspersed with "irrelevancies" such as his story about the marine's death in the bunk next to his on Saipan, stories about bootleggers and lawmen, a story about an Arab father with three retarded children, and the fictional story of the O. F., which serves generally as the break between the first part's concern with natural creatures and the second half's consideration of farming, building fences, setting stones, and other aspects of "the war with Mother N."

Like *Goodbye to a River, Hard Scrabble* generally received good reviews in such publications as the *New York Times Book Review, Atlantic Monthly, New Yorker,* and *Sewanee Review.* Edward Hoagland, reviewing for the *New York Times Book Review,* concluded that the "exceptional staying power is a tone that suits the book." While the greatest criticism has been that it lacks the structure of the first book and Hoagland called it a "homemade book—clumsy once in a while in the way it's put together or rhetorically empurpled," he further described it as "imperfect like a handmade thing, a prize." Timothy Dow Adams in a later analysis in the *Dictionary of Literary Biography Yearbook* noted:

> For some readers the disjointed structure of *Hard Scrabble,* the agricultural details, and the author's occasional crotchetiness on some topics might be irritating at times, more

> jarring in the relative civilization of the author's farm than similar eccentricities were out on the river in his first book. But for scope and detail, for the harsh juxtaposition of nature at its worst with a sweet afternoon rain in early autumn, *Hard Scrabble* is nearly equal to *Goodbye to a River* in its power to make the reader stop reading and consider moving to the countryside. (236)

Like Graves' first book, *Hard Scrabble* won the Texas Institute of Letters Carr P. Collins Award for nonfiction for 1974.

Graves' third book, *From a Limestone Ledge: Some Essays and Other Ruminations about Country Life in Texas* is clearly a collection of essays, all initially published in *Texas Monthly* between 1977 and 1980 in a regular column, whose background Cory Lock traces in the present collection. In the preface, Graves calls many of them "footnotes" to *Hard Scrabble,* noting that they "are expansions or variations on themes found there" (xiii). Indeed, this third volume returns to several of Graves' concerns and amplifies ideas introduced in the earlier books. *From a Limestone Ledge* is divided into three parts. The first part, "Coping," covers various topics related to working the place, with essays on fences, preparing meat, growing grapes and making wine, collecting trash, and sensing the spirits surrounding the accumulating things. The second part, "Creatures," as its title indicates, considers the rancher-farmer's domesticated natural creatures—cows, goats, bees, dogs, and chickens. Part 3, "Ponderings, People, and Other Oddments," is something of a miscellany, with essays on noticing, the weather, treasure hunting, snuff, chewing tobacco, country ownership, and a farm auction.

From a Limestone Ledge lacks the unity and metaphysical analysis of Graves' other two books, primarily because it was written with space and time restrictions for a specific audience, as Graves explained candidly to Patrick Bennett in a 1979 interview: "You do edit yourself to some extent when you're writing for any publication; you know what their slant is, what their readership is largely like. Those pieces, even though they're fairly honest, don't for the most part have a lot of depth to them" ("John Graves," 68). There is, however, the same persona, the cosmopolitan wanderer who has chosen to settle in a hardscrabble world where he observes the details of that world with clarity. In "Noticing," for example, Graves begins by recalling the time he lived in New York City and observed the trivial events in the rooms of a department store across from his apartment. He then contrasts the level of observation in the city with that required in the country, what he calls the "noticingness" of rural life:

> It comes from having a personal stake in the landscape that envelops you, in the various beasts and fowls and crops and objects it contains whose ownership you claim, and in the activities of many wild things that own themselves. To take stock of all this daily, to exercise surveillance, is about as much a requisite for survival as was my Fifteenth Street indifference—survival for your chattels alive or inert and therefore for you as a countryman. (155)

This quality of noticingness typifies the essays in *From a Limestone Ledge,* and Graves becomes a kind of country Boswell to the valuable and possibly soon-to-disappear country life that is his subject.

Graves reinforces the elegiac quality of the book with the last essay, "A Loser," which tells of Graves' attending a foreclosure auction of a 125-acre farm in another county, drawn there by an advertisement for a grain combine. Graves captures the sights and sounds of the auction and the auctioneer's snappy, garbled patter: "'Urba durba dibba rubba hurty-fie,' said the auctioneer in abandonment of the subject. 'Hurty-fie hurty-fie hurty-fie, who say fitty: Fitty, fitty, fitty, fitty, durba dubba ibba dibby who say forty-fie? Forty-fie, forty-fie, come on, folks . . .'" (226). Ultimately, Graves makes this specific, pale, "pinched waxy" man losing his farm a representative figure: "The Loser had made us view the fragility of all we had been working toward, had opened our ears to the hollow low-pitched mirth of the land against mere human effort" (228). This is one of Graves' continuing themes: those who work with the earth possess and understand its value; the more we lose this ability, the more diminished our humanity. But again Graves achieves his purpose in a subtle, understated way by allowing the narrative and the details to carry the point.

What makes Graves a memorable writer is this subtlety and his distinctive style, an amalgamation of fiction, folklore, philosophy, history, nature, personal experience, anecdotes, and allusion presented with repeated use of sentence fragments, ellipses, dashes, parenthetical remarks, and dialogue. Graves achieves a balance of high and low, moving from a quotation by Shakespeare or Veblen to regional dialect and sounds such as the auctioneer's. He is also fond of shifting from the formal third person "one" to the informal second person, with the "you" referring both to the narrator and the audience. His style, as the following quotation from *Goodbye to a River* demonstrates, reflects his theme of assimilation:

> Neither a land nor a people ever starts over clean. Country is compact of all its past disasters and strokes of luck—of flood and drouth, of the caprices of glaciers and sea winds, of misuse and disuse and greed and ignorance and wisdom—and though you may doze away the cedar and coax back bluestem and mesquite grass and side-oats grama, you're not going to manhandle it into anything entirely new. It's limited by what it has been, by what's happened to it. And a people, until that time when it's uprooted and scattered and so mixed with other peoples that it has in fact perished, is much the same in this as land. It inherits. (237)

One of the major aspects of Graves' style grows from his ability to merge personal experience and fiction. The persona he creates in his four major books is ostensibly the writer himself. But Graves makes it clear in a note at the beginning of *Goodbye to a River* that although it is a work of nonfiction, "it has some fictionalizing in it," including the dramatic presentation of historical events and the transposition of places and incidents. He also states that some "of the characters, including at times the one I call myself, are composite," but he concludes that "even those parts are true in a fictional sense. As true as I could make them." This fictionalizing reflects Graves' early academic training, having written a master's thesis on Faulkner and published a first story in the *New Yorker.* He told Patrick Bennett that having his first story accepted by a major magazine was "far too auspicious a beginning" and that he "couldn't duplicate it" ("John Graves," 67). Still, he has worked hard at fiction over the years, with two unpublished novels, one finished, one unfinished, and he has used his talent as a fiction writer to create his persona and to merge fictional elements, such as the story of the O. F. in *Hard Scrabble,* into his books.

The subject matter of his published stories is as varied as Graves' wanderings. "Quarry" concerns New York apartment dwellers who capture a mouse, keep it overnight debating whether to kill it or set it free, and release it only to see it fall from the fire escape and die. Several stories are set in Mexico. "The Aztec Dog," selected for *Prize Stories 1992: The O. Henry Awards,* examines a Mexican aristocrat and a feckless American who spar over the old man's dog. "The Green Fly" concerns a young American completing a PhD in English literature who goes to Mexico to fish and relax and ends up in a complicated relationship with an old doctor. "The Off-Season" focuses on two veterans who visit Acapulco after the war to escape from the complications of life, only to find a different reality when two women arrive.

The passing western frontier is the subject of two stories. "The Dreamer" involves a former hunter, trapper, and mountain man who had married and then lost a Ute wife. After he returns to civilization, he is often lost in "dreams," times of despondence during which he recalls his life experiences. The end of the frontier is the subject of what is probably Graves' best story, "The Last Running," called by former *Texas Monthly* editor William Broyles "the best short story in the English language." Gordon Lish describes it as "one of the great stories in American writing." A. C. Greene says it is "a classic . . . American short story"; William Kittredge calls it "the great father of stories written about the American West." And in a 1990 review of a reprint of the story, Rick Bass asserts that it should be "required reading" because the "story and the emotions are as real and honest and important as the land across which they drift: the land having been developed, and the emotions fading too."

Based on an anecdote originally told in *Goodbye to a River* about Comanches coming to beg a buffalo from rancher Charles Goodnight long after those Indians had been confined to a reservation in Oklahoma, the story fictionalizes the events. Goodnight is transformed into Tom Bird, an aging rancher who in 1923 lovingly keeps fourteen buffalo on his caprock ranch. A ragtag group of Comanches from the Oklahoma reservation, led by a crippled chief named Starlight, come to get a buffalo so that they can perform a ritualistic buffalo hunt one last time. The old rancher initially refuses, but Starlight, who had once fought against Bird after a horse-stealing raid, persists and eventually gets Bird to give them not just a buffalo but the prize bull, Shakespeare. The group then performs the ritualistic last running, kills the buffalo, and leaves.

Many of these stories and occasional pieces are collected in *A*

John Graves Reader, published by the University of Texas Press in 1996 as the first book in the Southwestern Writers Collection Series. The *Reader* includes selections from Graves' books, as well as "Self-Portrait, with Birds," a long, autobiographical piece that focuses on Graves' growing experiences as a birder; character studies of friends and a former teacher; a previously unpublished story, "A Valley"; and most importantly, selections from Graves' unpublished novel *A Speckled Horse.*

In 1999, *Texas Parks and Wildlife* magazine began publishing Graves' discussions of Texas rivers, in which he wrote about the Canadian, the Pecos, and the Llano rivers. Then, in 2002, those pieces were published in *Texas Rivers* along with essays about the Lower Neches, the Brazos Clear Fork, and the Upper Sabinal, accompanied by photographs by famed Texas photographer Wyman Meinzer. In a prefatory note, Graves remarks that the book does not try to cover all of Texas' rivers, but the ones included have some similarities:

> The main things that these rivers—some of them just sections of rivers—have in common is that they all flow within Texas, and that the country through which each one passes is typical of a distinctive part of the state. Those in the wide and varied region we call West Texas do share some historical memories from the eras of Indian warfare, northward trail drives, and so on, but the lands they drain, like the tone of their people's lives in the past and now, differ significantly, and in pictures and words we have tried to define some of those differences.
>
> All the rivers too have suffered to some extent, often greatly, from modern mankind's manipulation and exploitation of their waters and their basins, and we have tried also to be honest about those matters. (6)

These essays demonstrate Graves' distinctive combination of history, geography, and folklore, but he has a less personal connection with these rivers that he does with the Brazos.

Graves and Meinzer teamed up again in 2003 for *Texas Hill Country,* another coffee-table book with Meinzer's photographs of the "old land" and the "rumpled terrain" of the Hill Country. Graves' essay emphasizes the effect of change on this now gloried area of the state:

> At New Braunfels where long ago I used to stop and fish, the lovely little Comal below the springs is now overwhelmed by a huge water park with rides given coyly faux-German names like Blastenhoff and Surfenburg, and in season the river's daily hordes of innertubers drifting downstream make happy noise and adorn the shores and streambottom with emptied beer and soft-drink cans and various forms of paper and plastic. . . . The peaceful era in these places has faded away, and many natives, not having known much prosperity before, relish the change. Others don't, nor does an aging outsider like me, who preferred the towns as they used to be. (60)

Over the years Graves has lamented the time wasted on trying to produce a major work of fiction, a subject that becomes especially clear in Graves' memoir, where he suggests that he should have produced more but was too often distracted. The memoir clarifies the record and demonstrates how Graves' life is all of a piece, with a full commitment to the literary life. Taken from the journals he kept mainly after his graduation from Rice in 1942, dealing with his marine experiences in World War II when he lost his sight in one eye, graduate work at Columbia, and travels to Mexico, Spain, and the Canary Islands before returning to Texas at the end of the 1950s, the book details Graves' apprenticeship as a writer.

Graves splits the material into two types: the raw journal entries as recorded and his contemporary comments by the then eighty-three-year-old "Old John," who often corrects, chides, or compliments the observations and activities of "Young John." To those who followed Graves' career, *Myself and Strangers* provides the backdrop for his life's work.

There is a confessional quality to the memoir, answering questions about many of the ideas and issues that Graves alluded to in the previously published works, such as the details about his World War II experience, his failed first marriage, and his ill-fated attempts as a novelist. For those who have been following Graves' work over the years, reading the memoir feels like sneaking into someone's study and furtively reading private papers. There is a rush to learn the details about events that have been only faint subtexts in the major works. For example, the beginning of *Goodbye to a River* indicates that the John Graves who is going down the river seems to have returned home from some sadness akin to Ishmael's "damp, drizzly November" of his soul in *Moby Dick* that sent him on a water trip. Graves only suggests that he has been a traveler and has now returned and that those travels included some war experiences that seem painful for the traveler to recall. In *Myself and Strangers,* Graves makes that background clear, spelling out the war experience:

> The beaches [on Saipan] had been rough for just about everybody, but I lost only two men while engaged in that later surveying work, neither of them badly wounded, then received my own comeuppance at battalion headquarters one misty early morning, when thirty or forty disoriented Japanese, trying I think to get back to their main force, barged in on us over the top of a little hill and a brisk firefight ensued. They had the advantage of surprise, but we had a machine gun and more people and after a time the hill was quiet. I joined a group going up to check on things, but when we got among the bodies one turned out to be not a body but a live Jap playing dead, who—a friend told me later—rolled a grenade out in front of me which exploded.
>
> The permanent damage turned out to be only the blinding of my left eye, but that was the end of my career as a combatant. (7–8)

We also learn about Graves' first marriage, something that, as far as I know, Graves had never written about directly before. If you read someone's private journals, there's often an uncomfortable feeling that you've intruded into personal space, a trespasser beyond accepted boundaries. So it is sometimes in this memoir, even though the subject has decided to make these private entries public. That's especially true in the parts that deal with several of the romantic relationships Graves had over those wandering years after the first marriage and the successful, longtime second one. Young John was often on the prowl, and he tells of relationships, some brief, others long-term, with Spanish women caught in an older system with their own failing marriages that meant they were condemned to the solitary life unless a wandering American might join them in furtive encounters.

But the heart of this memoir is Graves' emphasis on the literary life. It's clear that he dedicated himself to writing and especially to writing "the book." Over and over Young John laments that the only way he can cement his life as a real writer is by completing the book. And for much of the time, he follows the trails of one of his literary mentors, Ernest Hemingway. Graves travels to and around Spain, goes to the running of the bulls in Pamplona, and even sees the great man, Prince Ernest, who was back in Spain for the first time since the Civil War. Young John sees Papa in a sidewalk café but decides not go over and introduce himself: "I had not yet proved myself as a writer, a real one, and until I managed that I didn't feel I had a right to impose myself on established authors, however much I might admire their work" (67–68).

He continues to follow Hemingway's lead, buying a sailboat and heading out to fish. But mainly he reads and reads. And throughout the book we learn of Young John's opinions about his reading. After reading James Michener's *Tales of the South Pacific,* he writes: "Michener to me at present looks like nothing at all—can't write, can't tell a story or even the truth, can't deal with complexity in characters, can only recognize good material and milk it" (174). And on Thomas Wolfe's *Of Time and the River,* he concludes: "There is much acute observation but it gets lost in the shouting. There is real poetry, but the fatigue induced by the rhetoric that precedes it keeps you from rising to it . . ." (211; Graves' ellipsis). His reading leads him to Gertrude Stein, and in *The Making of Americans,* Stein writes: "I write for myself and strangers." That's where Graves takes his title.

This then is the literary apprenticeship, the long, intense journey to becoming a writer. There's a large irony here, since John Graves' reputation as a writer is built upon his connection to his home country, particularly to his own part of Texas along the Brazos near Glen Rose. He got there by following the old mythic pattern of Odysseus and the Prodigal Son who can know home only after escaping from it and viewing the wide world. Graves' long journey led him, unlike Wolfe, to conclude that he could go home again.

In his memoir, as he does through all of his writing, Graves demonstrates how a writer with a clear sense of purpose, a respect for the bounty of the natural world, an understanding of the depth of simplicity, and a strong grip on language can step forth and move people in ways that last. It is the work of a masterful writer.

One final irony remains about John Graves. Near Hard Scrabble and not far from a small hill called Comanche Peak, a nuclear power plant named for the hill began being constructed shortly after Graves finished *Hard Scrabble.* A troubled nuclear plant in the shadow of a historied place seems a fittingly complex image for a writer who has attempted to dramatize his own awareness of the world's multilayered and paradoxical realities.

Note

1. This introduction updates and revises my entry on John Graves in *American Nature Writers,* edited by John Elder (Scribner's, 1996).

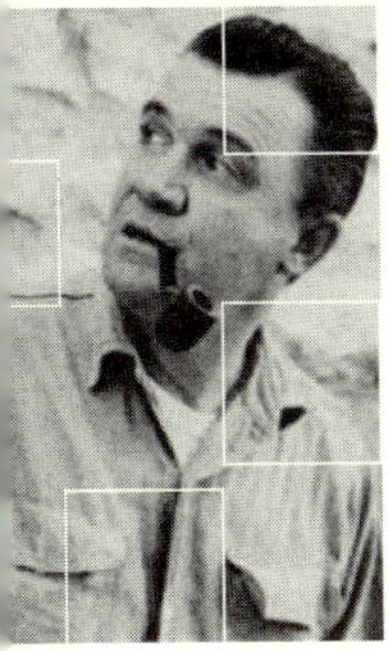

PART ONE

Talking with John Graves

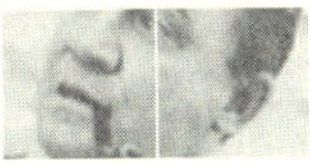

The Writer John Graves Symposium

SAM HYNES, DAVE HICKEY, JOHN GRAVES, AND MARK BUSBY

EDITORS' NOTE: The following is a transcription of a Saturday morning session of the symposium held at Texas State University–San Marcos on September 6–7, 2002. Coeditor Mark Busby served as moderator of the session, which included John Graves' classmate at Columbia, the distinguished Princeton professor Samuel Hynes; Graves' student at Texas Christian University, the always provocative polymath and MacArthur "genius award" winner Dave Hickey; and John Graves as respondent. After introducing the participants, Busby directed his first question to Sam Hynes.

MARK BUSBY: When did you first meet John, and what has been your relationship?

SAM HYNES: Well, you brought up the subject of embarrassment. You've embarrassed us [with the introductions], but John, as every one knows who knows him, is the world's most reticent man, so we're not here, I think, to tell the truth about John. We're here to try not to embarrass him. If it weren't for that, I could start out with my story about the day I passed my doctoral orals at Columbia, and John and I got drunk with the only twelve-fingered Phi Beta Kappa from the state of Maine. Or the time when he was living with my family down in a cottage on the south coast of Devon, while we were off at the pub, and my one-and-a-half-year-old daughter climbed up on his parked motorcycle and pulled it over on herself and broke her leg. Well, after we had gotten her to Plymouth Hospital and got the leg in plaster, we consoled ourselves for this accident by getting drunk with the vicar and in the end had to carry him home. There's a certain amount of drinking in those stories, but we were younger then. Or I could tell you the story about how John once dived off a pier in Mobile Bay, not noticing that the tide was out, and buried himself headfirst in the sand like a piling and how I had to pull him out and take him to the naval hospital in Pensacola to get his neck unknotted. Or I could even do my imitation of John singing "Further Along" and accompanying himself on the ukulele. How many of you knew that John plays the ukulele? There you are; you've learned something today. So if I can't tell those stories, I thought I might talk a little bit about what it was like to be us and the place we were in when we first met. That was 1947; John thinks 1946.

JOHN GRAVES: No, I don't anymore. I went to Columbia in 1946 right after the war; Sam was finishing up at Minnesota and didn't show up till '47.

SAM HYNES: So it is really only fifty-five years. We were both ex-marines a couple of years back from the Pacific Islands, we both majored in English literature and wanted something to do with writing, we were both provincials or hicks, and we had come to the greatest city on earth to get what we wanted out of it. New York in 1947 was a wonderful place. Talleyrand said somewhere no one who wasn't alive before 1789 can know the sweetness of life. Well, no one who wasn't in New York in 1947 and twenty years old can possibly know the sweetness of life. I'm sorry, but that's the way it is; it was great. *A Streetcar Named Desire* had just opened with Marlon Brando and Jessica Tandy. *The Member of the Wedding* was starting a long run; Judith Anderson had just opened in *Medea.* I remember that particularly because my wife was from Alabama and invited her mother to come up to visit us. We thought *Medea* would be a nice play for her to see. We sat there in the theater as we came to the climactic moment when this voice rang out through the theater, "Ma, she's not gonna kill those little babies, is she?" Well, it was like that. Enzio Penza—I saw Enzio Penza sing his last Don Giovanni at the Met, the one at Lincoln Center, the *real* Met, the one at Broadway and Thirty-ninth. You could stand at the back for a dollar. I was standing there when Penza came bounding on the stage in his tights, and a voice, a sort of male voice, behind me said, "Look at those legs." Well, that was all part of it, and those great buildings—the Empire State, the beautiful Chrysler Building, Penn Station, the real Penn Station. The most beautiful Greek Revival building Americans have ever built, so, of course, doomed to be pulled down and replaced by that place where they play basketball. It was great, and there we were gawking at it. We had just come from the war; the war was very much a part of the atmosphere. We were done with the war; we had won it. America was like a place with a huge high-pressure area over it. The weather was great everywhere. Everyone was optimistic. We knew what we could do. We knew what we wanted. We knew we could do what we wanted. That, for most of us, was not unreasonable, I suppose.

I knew I was going to get a PhD, get tenure somewhere, have leather patches on my elbows, smoke a pipe, and write book reviews for the *TLS.* That didn't seem impossible, and indeed it wasn't impossible. Old twelve-fingers thought that he would become an editor and write stories for the *Saturday Evening Post,* and he did. We felt that John's aspirations were different from ours. We were just going to succeed. It's not too hard to succeed. You just keep your standards low. John was going to be an artist, was an artist; he knew that. I talked to a friend of ours from those days the other day on the phone, and he said, "Yes, I remember I'd meet John on the campus and I'd say, 'How's it going, John?' And he'd say, 'Bad Graves' or, occasionally, 'Good Graves.'" What he meant was that day he had written badly or well, but notice that the measure was Graves. It wasn't just good writing; it was good Graves. He was going to be the writer of whom there is only one and ever will be one, the one, original John Graves.

So when I went off to get my first job and old twelve-fingers got his first job at the *New Yorker* for a while, John set out to Spain to do all of the things that Hemingway did. He went fly-fishing in the Pyrenees; he watched bullfights—and knows quite a lot about bullfights actually—and wrote and wrote and wrote and became the one, original John Graves. So we knew it was going to be tougher to be him than to be us, but in the end he was going to be like the pilot who has shot down five enemy airplanes. He was going to be the ace. We were going to be writers too, but we weren't going to be aces, and that was OK.

One other thing—then I'll stop. About that time—it was the time of the GI Bill. Now, the GI Bill was the best thing to happen to the United States in the twentieth century. It came after the only democratic war we had ever fought (except the war against ourselves) when everybody went, and after everyone had gone, everyone who wanted to could go to college. It only lasted that one war; then we went back to letting the poor fight our wars while the middle classes and upper classes went to college. That was kind of a deep wound for democracy, I think, and it was part of the optimism you see of that time that anybody who wanted to go to college, most of them for the first time in their families, could go to college, and you would see them on the campus. They'd wear parts of old uniforms. They'd sometimes be leading a child. They always went to their classes, but they never did anything else. They didn't give a damn whether the football team won or lost. They didn't drink beer with the students in the local slop shop—they already knew how to drink; they didn't join fraternities to be paddled by eighteen-year-olds, but they would take any course that they had to take. It didn't matter if it was interesting or if it made any sense or not. If you had to take the course, you took it in order that you could graduate and get the hell out of there and do what you wanted to do with your life. It was a golden time.

Another thing about it that was wonderful, I think, was the books. Fourth Avenue, for example, in New York was all secondhand bookshops. I think there is one left. Some of them covered acres. You could find anything there for a quarter or fifty cents, some book you had heard of or some book that your professor had recommended. I went down there, and for fifty cents I got a remainder copy of *Let Us Now Praise Famous Men,* because Lionel Trilling said it was a great book. And it is a great book. Another time I got a copy of *Parade's End.* Later I ran into John, who at that time was living on a mountaintop in New Mexico, I believe—I forgot why you were on the mountaintop. But he was, and I lent him *Parade's End,* and he lent it to a friend who drove back down the mountain and crashed his car and was killed. The car burned, and *Parade's End* burned too. Well, that I think is enough about the young John Graves to begin on, don't you?

DAVE HICKEY: I'd like to do one of those flashback things starting right after I took John's course in creative writing at TCU [Texas Christian University] in the early sixties. I learned a great deal about writing from John, and I learned even more by reading his writing. Also, for better or worse, I also took from John the inference, which was never really offered, that one should go out and have adventures. I have always been happy to take this inference.

After leaving TCU, I came down here to Austin to enroll as a graduate student for the length of my draft eligibility and had numerous Austin adventures. I spent four days in the SDS [Students for a Democratic Society] until I read the Port Huron Statement. My friends and I began publishing Zap Comics down here. We worked for all the local magazines and published a wonderful Kennedy assassination issue in the *Texas Ranger.* The headline said, "Who Killed What's His Name?" Then I turned twenty-six, and I realized that I wasn't cut out for academic life. I walked off the campus, opened an art gallery down at Twelfth and Nueces in Austin, and began showing contemporary art. I liked hanging out with artists better than writers, for some reason, so I had all my painter friends, and I ran an art gallery called A Clean, Well-Lighted Place, after the Hemingway short story that ends with a deconstruction of the Lord's Prayer: "Our *nada* who art in *nada, nada* be thy name," et cetera. At the time, we were deeply into "nada."

So I had a really great time running an art gallery and eventually took a job running an art gallery in New York. I did that until the New York art world got depressing. I quit dealing art and edited an art magazine. Then I quit the art world entirely, became a slick-magazine writer, and started going to Nashville on weekends just to hang out with Kinky Friedman, Billy Joe Shaver, and Waylon Jennings. I wrote about rock and roll for the *Voice* and *Rolling Stone* and came away with lots of flashy memories: Lou Reed's "Rock 'n' Roll Animal" tour, Lynyrd Skynyrd's "Give Me Back My Bullets" tour, Aerosmith's "Rocks" tour. I am still embarrassed about things I did on that little adventure. Eventually I detonated my marriage and moved to Nashville, where I took up with a rock-and-roll girl singer. We had a band, played the road, and wrote songs together. I worked in the daytime with Waylon Jennings and Tompall Glaser.

Anyway, for fifteen years I lived almost exclusively on cocaine and cheeseburgers; then I got up one morning and thought I was tired. I went to the doctor in search of amphetamines. He told me that I wanted in a doctor what Mickey Cohen wanted in a lawyer, and he diagnosed walking pneumonia. He said that I should take these antibiotics and lay down for six months, and since I didn't have a place to lay down in Nashville, I came home to lay around my mom's house in Fort Worth. For six months I watched *I Dream of Jeannie.* I would be stretched out in bed and my mind would say, "Dave, get out of bed and do something." My body said, "Watch *I Dream of Jeannie.*"

Eventually, I sort of came around and began to teach some courses at TCU. I began meeting some young artists, and suddenly I understood how John must have felt when I met him at TCU. He had, at that point, just returned from a fatally analogous series of adventures and was similarly guarded about his prospects and the world. But in the class I took, he gave us what he had, which was a lot, and rather happily, I suspect, sent us out on the adventure from which he had just returned. When I enrolled in John's class fifteen years earlier, I had just completed three and a half years in engineering school at SMU [Southern Methodist University], because the engineering school was across the street from the Kappa Sig house, and it seemed so convenient. Eventually I was about to become an engineer, so I quit, came to TCU, and became an English major because I wanted to be a writer. I did not want to be an engineer, and I didn't want to be a professor, so I thought I would be a writer. I wrote really terrible things for John, and he found some value in them. He encouraged me and was genuinely supportive, which surprised me because I was already a critic, so I knew that what I wrote was not swell. I can still remember being impressed that John would take these terrible things that I wrote and write careful observations about the subjunctive mood in red ink in the margin, along with a mild critique of my bourgeois romanticism and a few "perhaps you should's."

Today, having had a few writing students myself, I realize that one sentence, three or four words, can jump off a page of crap and tell you that someone can be a writer. At the time, I just loved being taken seriously. I hadn't the faintest idea what I was doing, but John gave me the impression that I could be a writer and that I might be pretty good. And, of course, after you are pretty good, you don't need to be given this impression. So I took that from John, and although he didn't say it, I also took from him a sense that writing was really hard work. You wrote it, and you rewrote it and wrote forever. He never said this, but it was obvious in his manner of address—and, obvious too, in those long, red ink notes on the margins of my pages. John wrote more in the margins of my pages than I had ever written in my life, and I learned from that too, from the careful attention.

Anyway, when I came back to Fort Worth after the rock-and-roll wars, it really helped me to recognize that I was in a position roughly analogous to John's in the year that I met him. It saved me from behaving like a bitter, cynical asshole around the kids I met, because they deserved better. They deserved to meet at least one practicing adult who cared and wasn't a loser, so I tried to be that person. This helped me realize that I didn't regret anything, even the pneumonia and bad romance.

Today I've been a teacher long enough to know that students never get from you what you're teaching them. They just don't. You tell them something. A week later they come back and say, "Wow, I did just what you said," and show you some incredible piece of weirdness. So with that in mind, I think what I really got from John—and it was a wonderful gift—was a real respect and understanding for writing about parts of the world that stay around to critique what you have written about them. John writes about the natural world, and I write about art. Nothing could be more different. Each of us probably hates what the other loves, but the fact remains that the discipline of writing about things that are not going to go away, that you cannot lie about, whose color you cannot change, whose shape you cannot change, seemed to me an inspiring discipline.

By way of commenting on this, I was reading the novel excerpt at the end of *A John Graves Reader,* and there's a lovely little scene at the filling station after the main character's friend has been killed, and a dog is hit and crippled by a car. I mentioned this scene to John the other day, and he said that it came directly from life. It occurred to me, then, that this scene was a pretty good reason not to write fiction anymore. There came a point in the American postwar world at which the whole idea of fiction creating a plausible universe was overthrown by the sheer implausibility of American life. To write fiction was really to delimit the weirdness of what was going on. I have never found any reason to doubt that, so basically what I got from John was a respect for writing about the hard stuff of the world. People are assholes, ideas are smoke, objects are irrevocably there, so let's address them with respect. That has been my ongoing endeavor, and I owe John more than that. Thank you.

MARK BUSBY: And now I would like to ask John what he remembers about these two guys.

JOHN GRAVES: In the old phrase, these are hard acts to follow. I'll pick on some details and maybe amplify a little bit. Sam made several references to old twelve-fingers. This was a classmate of ours in Columbia. Sam, who was pretty good at nicknames and rather cruel with nicknames, used to call me Cyclops because I'm blind in the left eye. Anyways, there was this fellow he called the old polydactyl. He was a nice sort of innocent fellow; he didn't still have the six fingers [Sam

Hynes (aside): I always thought he had them in a jar], because he had them removed at birth. But there was a scar on each hand where the little finger had been taken off. He married while we were still in Columbia, I believe to a tire heiress from Akron. Well, they immediately had a child, and Sam and I went down to see it with the father. [Sam Hynes (aside): We went to count the fingers.] We were trying to take our eyes off of the child's hands because we didn't want to cause any trouble. Anyway, that's the story about old twelve-fingers.

New York was a wonderful place at that time, but it has never been my kind of town except for that period at Columbia and then when I went back and lived there for another year in 1952 or 1951, I guess. It was a gentler place where there was much going on. There was much less activity and animosity than there is now; you could walk the streets at three o'clock in the morning and feel no apprehension at all. I mean in that period of 1950 or '51. I had a grubby little apartment down on Fifteenth Street, and I was writing like crazy, mostly bad stuff. At about three o'clock in the morning, things would be running through my head, some different passage in writing that I couldn't get on top of; and I would get up and walk all over Lower Manhattan, and it was fine. The only people you met were the occasional foot policemen, and they were very genial, asking where was I wandering off to.

MARK BUSBY: Do you remember when you first met Sam?

JOHN GRAVES: Well, obviously I don't remember very well because it came up between us yesterday, and I said we met in 1946, which is when I went to Columbia. He said he didn't come until 1947, when we were in several classes together. There is an "I don't care how liberated you think you are" from anybody who has ever been in the Marine Corps. Way down in there is a marine chauvinist. They think that other ex-marines grant them a considerable tolerance they won't grant other people. I don't want to get too far off on that, because I'm not really that much of a chauvinist, but that was part of it. We also shared classes, and they were good classes at that time. We had lecturers like Lionel Trilling, Mark Van Doren, Bill Tindall, Joseph Wood Krutch, Marjorie Nicholson—all first-rate in their field. The classes were huge because those were the GI days, and all of them were flocking in. They were a lot better than the nonmilitary undergraduates, I remember, because they were there with a purpose, you know. As Sam said, they did their work, and they moved along.

The best contacts we had were with the faculty, but there were huge lectures so you didn't get to know the professors very well. But we were all part of—what do you call them?—study groups, proseminars, under one or another senior professor. The senior professor I remember, Sam, was Tindall, who was the main British literature man there. I used to go sit in on Sam's seminar and the one that I was in, to make sure I didn't miss anything.

SAM HYNES: There was Martha Foley too; we should mention Martha Foley.

JOHN GRAVES: I was in Martha Foley's writing class. In fact, what teaching I did after that—when I was senior enough to have a writing class and not just teach freshmen—I modeled it on Martha's. She didn't really teach much. She just talked, and we had to turn in one thousand words a week. It didn't matter what it was like, fiction or nonfiction. You could do poetry if you wanted, and it would go anonymously into a folder in the library, and everyone had to read them before the next session. The sessions were three-hour seminar classes once a week, and sometimes it would get all heated up in disagreement, and sometimes you would know who wrote it. A lot of antipathies in those classes, but it was highly stimulating. Afterwards when I taught a writing class—mainly at TCU, and I think David was in the first or second one that I taught—that's what we did, and it worked.

MARK BUSBY: Do you remember Dave as a student?

JOHN GRAVES: I remember he was one of the best writers I ever had in one of those classes, in spite of what he says about himself. Yeah, I remember David well; I remember most of those kids well. They were some good people. They're scattered all over the world now, doing different things. Some of them are academics, some of them are . . . Do you remember Maryanow? He was a colonel in the infantry, artillery or something. [Dave Hickey (aside): He is now at Georgia State, poor devil.] I think that my relationship with David, from the start—you know how you meet somebody and you recognize kinship? It was that way with us.

David said something that I want to disagree with or agree with, but I can't remember what it was.

DAVE HICKEY: You were probably going to take issue with the fact that you messed up your life when you came back to Fort Worth.

JOHN GRAVES: Yes, actually I could take exception to that. I thought I had messed it up. I had just written that novel—one of the fragments that you referred to a while ago; I had decided it was a failure. It hadn't done what I wanted it to do, and I was down about that. I had been living in New York and Spain and various places for several years before that. I hadn't been near Texas. Came back to revise that novel, which I did in Mexico, then came back. My father got bad cancer, and I stuck around to see if I could help him and my mother. Then all of a sudden I was back into old youthful interests. You know, the Comanches and ranchers, natural history, and all those things. And it became a homecoming rather than a trap, which I thought it would be.

SAM HYNES: There is a point right there that we might just touch on. I wonder how many novelists you know who can finish their first novel and just decide it's not good enough and put it aside? Not many, I would think. When we were graduate students together, we all knew John was a writer in that special sense that you use the word "writer," and then he went and proved it by just publishing a story in the *New Yorker*. You know, that's like dying and going to heaven when you're twenty-two or twenty-three years old.

JOHN GRAVES: It wasn't much of story though.

SAM HYNES: Well, listen to him. There you go; that's a guy with a standard that's very hard to live with. I don't think, well, you probably all still read the *New Yorker*, but in those days when Harold Ross was still editing it, Thurber was still putting cartoons in it, and John O'Hara was writing for it. There was a new guy who wrote short stories about a family called Glass. We would run to the newsstand on the corner the week that there was a story by this guy to make sure we got a copy before they sold out. Salinger, do you remember Salinger? No one had ever seen him, of course, and still haven't, but he was nevertheless a presence.

The *New Yorker* itself was a presence. It was a place, first of all, where you could learn to write in a certain way. You could learn to keep the tone of your voice down; you could learn to write plain sentences. But more than that, it was a guidebook to yokels like us on how to pretend you belonged in a place you didn't belong, New York in 1947. You could learn about and read about art. What's that man's name that used to review in it? [Harold] Rosenberg? Yeah, you could read about the latest Jackson Pollock and stuff. You could learn how to look at movies. We had been looking at movies all of our lives, but we didn't know how to look at movies. If you could find that out, you could also learn how to dress like a New Yorker, like a Yalie. All those thin columns of ads from Brooks Brothers that went down the outside columns of the pages. They were thin like the lapels on Brooks Brothers suits, and their neckties, and if you would dress yourself up like that, then, until you opened your mouth, people would think you were important. So it wasn't snobbishness, I think—at least in my case. I think none of us thinks we are snobs. I don't think it was snobbishness; it was seeing if I could disguise myself as an East Coast person who belonged on Madison Avenue. And almost succeeded. I think John wrote this story. Look in *A John Graves Reader.* Is "The Quarry" in there? It's not. Like the novel, it's gone down the memory hole. Well, I stand in awe of John's standards. OK, that's the end of that one.

JOHN GRAVES: David is one of the major beaux artists in the world today as far as I am concerned, one that I remember particularly. Was it at *Art in America* that you were working for at one time under a man named Reese Bailey?

DAVE HICKEY: I ran a gallery for Reese Palley and then left there to go to *Art in America.*

JOHN GRAVES: He got into big trouble and crashed somehow, didn't he?

DAVE HICKEY: Eventually, yes.

JOHN GRAVES: Well, David by that time was important enough that they interviewed him about this little business. He had quit Palley—you call him Palley? OK, he had quit Palley not long before that and said that he was like a ship leaving a sinking rat.

MARK BUSBY: Sam, I know that you and John have corresponded over the years and that that correspondence is here in the Writers Collection, sealed until your deaths. Could you describe how you kept the relationship between traveling and being in different places over the years?

SAM HYNES: I don't think there was anything complicated about it. We were friends, and we weren't living in the same place. We wanted to keep in touch and have. You will find in that file [in the Southwestern Writers Collection] that you're all eagerly waiting to open—what a disappointment; I'm glad we won't be here—well, you'll find me writing to John and saying, "I've got to write this book about William Golding. What do you think?" And John writes a wonderful long letter about ideas I never had about William Golding. I steal them all and put them in the book, and we go on writing, and there we are. It was just a friendship that was too good to let go of. How is that?

JOHN GRAVES: I think both Sam and I have a considerable capacity for friendship. In other words, we've had—I've certainly been lucky in having a number of good friends—the kind of friends that you really have kinship with. This doesn't mean you don't disagree from time to time, sometimes violently, but you have somebody who speaks your language. There are not too many of those. Sam was one, and I was that way for him, I think. So you just keep it up. Both of us are writers anyhow; to express ourselves in writing is perfectly natural. We have not, except on occasion, been living very close to each other, so we just kept writing. I don't know what's in those letters.

SAM HYNES: That is the thing about this man's standards. He wrote a wonderful journal of his years in Spain. That was fifty years ago, and it is not good enough to publish yet. [*Myself and Strangers* was published in 2004.] Jesus, I have seen drafts of that, and we have talked about other projects, but who will consult me about how to write about the Brazos River? My river is the Upper Mississippi, so I don't have much to contribute to the Texas side of John, though I enjoy it.

MARK BUSBY [to Sam]: You've written about your war experiences and published a collection about war. Did you talk to John about writing about his experiences for your collection?

SAM HYNES: I've talked to him about it. We just got in a book the other day from one of your Marine Corps buddies, didn't we, John? Who had sort of done it for John. He was in the same battalion, I think.

JOHN GRAVES: We went through our artillery training together and ended up in the same division. He was in another battalion.

MARK BUSBY: And the book is published?

JOHN GRAVES: It is being self-published. It's not literature, but it was fascinating to me because of the people he mentions and the events. I last ran into that fellow personally—we corresponded a little over the years—on the beach at Saipan. He'd just lost a bunch of his people to a shell burst, and he was mad. He was coming along the beach with a great artillery aiming circle over his shoulder, which is used to survey a gun position. I was coming the other way looking for my battalion. You know, those landings were really confusing.

MARK BUSBY: Why don't you write about that?

JOHN GRAVES: Oh, there wasn't enough of it. It didn't last long enough, but I ran into Paul and he was glowering. I said, "Paul, you better be careful up there. There's direct machine-gun firing on the beach." He said, "Fuck the machine guns." Well, that is the marine word and the Australian word.

MARK BUSBY: Let me ask you about your relationship with Dave over the years and as your student? Did you follow his career?

JOHN GRAVES: Well, I did follow his career, but we did not see much of each other for many years up through the time he and Mary Jane moved to New York.

DAVE HICKEY: I was just thinking what John was saying. I recognize that there is a certain kind of Texas friendship you can have, which is basically a hedge against intimacy in which the principal thing with someone is you don't have to say anything. I didn't realize this until I became friends with Mary Jane's father, who was an ex-rancher and contractor in Lubbock. Elliot and I had a lot of the same relationship John and I have. I one day realized it was all based on the idea that we never had face-to-face conversation. We would stand there and talk, looking at a horse, a cow, or, ideally for Elliot, looking at a road maintainer, but as long as there was some correlative in the world, we could sustain that. I think John has that ability too. We spent a lot of time looking at John's property.

JOHN GRAVES: Mainly for us, the kinds of things that attract us and interest us are quite different. One time in my early tenure at that rocky, country place of Somervell County—I did a lot of work on that place—I had a waterline ditch dug from the pump house down to the site of the house that I was getting ready to build. David came out. It was a hot summer day. Of course I was working too, but I put him to work on assembling pipe in that ditch on this 110-degree day. I don't think he ever came near that place again.

MARK BUSBY: Do you remember hearing that Dave had been selected for the MacArthur Award? Did you read about it, or did he call you?

JOHN GRAVES: He wouldn't call; I don't remember how I learned it. I think it was published somewhere.

DAVE HICKEY: Well, I didn't actually feel like I could call John until I had written a really great book. So far, I've written about twenty really good paragraphs.

MARK BUSBY: I think we'll have some questions from the audience now.

QUESTION FROM JANE GRAVES IN THE AUDIENCE: I would like to ask David a question. I remember you when you were a student of John's. Now, in your heart, what do you consider home? Is it Fort Worth?

DAVE HICKEY: No. I grew up in Texas, but I spent most of my youth in California, in Santa Monica and the Pacific Palisades, from about the time I was in the sixth grade until about a year into high school, so I am probably in my heart a beach boy. I used to say I got my accent from Texas and my morals from Southern California. So I like the beach, and I like Las Vegas too. I like Texas as a writer because it's so much about the invisible experience. I mean, all of that space is out there to be filled with language, and I know that whole oral tradition that I grew up with around my grandparents and around Texas, and around Texas music, which is an incredibly important part of it, but I discovered early on that I am just too edgy for this place. In Texas we really love creative people, we really love scholarly people, but we really don't like critical people. It's just a fact. There are almost no critics in Texas, and those who have been here have been run out. I see them in New York and Los Angeles all of the time. I really love to come back here. I like the wide roads and yellow bar ditches and wire gates, but there's still the fact that no one in Vegas has ever asked me to dig a ditch, so I have a very peculiar relationship with Texas.

QUESTION FROM BILL WITTLIFF IN THE AUDIENCE: John, was there a specific moment in your writing career when—in a sentence or paragraph or piece of writing—when you recognized that you had crossed the line and were in fact a writer, where you went from hoping to knowing?

JOHN GRAVES: I can't pick out a moment. It was back during the period covered by that memoir we've been talking about, which both you and Sam have read and criticized. Some point in there, probably after I was living in Spain. In the middle-fifties, language would occasionally not always come out on tiptoe and start writing itself. That had always been the finest feeling about writing to me. It's not constant; it's never constant. Yeah, that happened somewhere in there, but I couldn't put my finger on a time.

QUESTION FROM THE AUDIENCE: Was Sam reading those pieces?

JOHN GRAVES: No, I don't believe so. I wasn't showing my stuff to much of anybody at that time. We talked about writing some, but I don't think so. I've always been kind of a lone wolf on writing.

QUESTION FROM THE AUDIENCE: When did you first realize that you wanted to be a writer?

JOHN GRAVES: Well, I had a wonderful teacher at Rice about whom I have written in a couple of places, George Williams. He was an English professor but rather a maverick. He would refuse to go on and take the PhD. He was of the few MAs teaching at Rice at that time, but he had a wonderful class in poetry, and he taught a good writing class. I sort of was one of his better students, let's put it that way, but I didn't have writing as a particular ambition at that time. The war was coming up. It was there, you know; nobody was looking too much beyond that. I guess I was at Columbia studying under Martha Foley. Even though my main studies were in English literature so that I could teach and make a living if I had to. I believe I began to think of myself as at least a potential writer.

QUESTION FROM THE AUDIENCE: When you were growing up in Fort Worth, did you do a lot of reading?

JOHN GRAVES: I have always read a lot, yeah.

QUESTION FROM THE AUDIENCE: I understand your connection with Martha Foley, and she seems to have a connection with the 1930s and the early period of literature. She had an enormous influence in the 1930s on the best short stories.

JOHN GRAVES: She was the editor of *The Best American Short Stories* of each year for many years. But she was quite a contrast to the literary style emerging after the war. People like Lionel Trilling, it seems, were much more like her than, say, the other professors at Columbia.

QUESTION FROM THE AUDIENCE: Does it make sense that I am asking that it seems you were drawn more to Martha Foley and what she represented than, say, Lionel Trilling?

JOHN GRAVES: Well, yeah, that is consistent with what I said a moment ago. That it was at Columbia that I began to have genuine aspirations as a writer, and yes, I probably did consider it more important at that time. She was quite an old gal; she didn't make a lot of sense. She was extremely feminine in a kind of excitable way, smart as she could be, very smart, and wonderful taste in language, but she had all kinds of hang-ups with her former husband, Whit Burnett. You know, he ended up with *Story* magazine, which they had started on the island of Mallorca back in the early thirties under the Spanish Republic. I think that's why when I went to Spain, I first went to

Mallorca. Because I had heard so many of her tales about it. She had liked the island a lot, but she and Whit broke up. Well, he bailed out with another lady, I think. Martha ended up in New York running that annual thing and teaching at Columbia.

DAVE HICKEY: One of the things that John did do for me—when you talk about Columbia—is that after I left TCU, I used to go to New York in the summers. I took a summer writing program from this person named Lish, this famous writing teacher, and the perfect felicity.

JOHN GRAVES: Lish, Gordon Lish. I knew Gordon well.

DAVE HICKEY: Lish. That's right, that was the class that I took, and it was absolutely not about standards and all about careers. We sat and talked about all the things that you would do for the *Atlantic* or the *New Yorker* and things like that. I was shocked.

QUESTION FROM THE AUDIENCE: John, you write very lovingly about Hard Scrabble and the county in which it exists. How long do you think before we don't have any Hard Scrabble places anymore because of the tremendous development of the city?

JOHN GRAVES: Well, I keep hoping for a major depression, and it will slow it all down there. It hasn't happened yet. The thing that ruins little places, one, is the drainage of the population to the cities, where the jobs are, and another one is proximity of the cities, which makes them better communities, and so on. We are not quite that bad yet, but Granbury just north of us is. It's just a suburb of Fort Worth. This process is a huge subject, you know. It can take several seminars to scratch the surface of it.

The fact that I have written so lovingly about that place is it brings out one of the advantages of being a writer, particularly if you're like me—a chronic waster of time on all kinds of personal passions and interests. That particular set of passions led me to build a house down there, run cows and goats, build fences, and all that kind of thing. A nonliterary person on that scale—which was pretty much uneconomic—I mean, we couldn't have made it living there. But if you happen to be a writer, you can write about it and therefore justify wasting all of that time.

QUESTION FROM THE AUDIENCE: Since we are talking about that, John, maybe Sam can tell us, has he always had this variety of interests? He says he just writes about these things, but we know that he learns how to run a vineyard; he learns how to do his beehives. I mean he really focuses and concentrates on all of these things that he says he just writes about. The writing comes from really knowing about it. Was he always that way?

SAM HYNES: Awesomely. I can describe the range of John's interests. He knows everything about the parts of the world that I don't know anything about, starting with riding a motorcycle to fly-fishing, sailing—I know a little bit about sailing, but you wouldn't go out with me, I don't think—cows, goats, a ranch. As Dave says, it's the world of objects.

DAVE HICKEY: And cross-dressing.

SAM HYNES: Well, it's the world where cross-dressing is wearing one of those caps. Farmers used to wear a special kind of hat that looked sort of like a baseball cap, but it went up like this and had stripes. It looked like it was made out of mattress ticking.

JOHN GRAVES: It was a railroad engineer's cap.

SAM HYNES: That's sort of a symbol of John, I think. I wasn't kidding when I said "awesome." There is a kind of awe in hanging around a guy who knows the actual physical world as though that was where he lived. People like Dave and me live in this world of words, which you can take with you where you go. It doesn't go straight down into anything solid. So John is a national treasure for people like us. And we're trying to preserve it.

JOHN GRAVES: Well, lots of luck.

MARK BUSBY: This leads me to a question for all three of you. I want to quote something that Dave has said in an interview, because it relates to what Sam just said. In an interview, Dave was asked something about how he made a living as a critic, and his answer was, "I am really a writer. I am a writer. My whole idea in life is to be able to make a living doing what I like to do. I like to write, and I like to write about hard things in the world. I don't usually like to make things up, although I do occasionally. It's fine to make things up at times, because it is so hard to write about things in the world. I'm a pretty good writer. I mean, some days I write better and others worse, but I have skills and my view of the world is solid enough that regardless of the topic you give me, I will say some version of the same thing."

And it seems to me that a number of people have said to me, when they talk about this panel, that Dave Hickey and John Graves, as Dave mentioned a few minutes ago, seem like they are in different worlds, people who have different views of the world, different experiences, and yet this quote almost could be, I think, a quote from

John Graves about writing about the world and sometimes making things up.

But my question sort of has to do with writing about the real world or making things up. Sam, you've written a lot about creative writers, about fiction writers like Hardy and so forth, and I wanted to ask all three of you something about what you think about this notion you mentioned earlier that the real world now seems to be unusual. That it is harder to write fiction. You started out writing fiction, John started out writing fiction, and you both tend to write more about the real world now. I was wondering if you would say something about that?

DAVE HICKEY: Well, I just not long ago wrote a little book of short stories that was about the art world. It was based on the zodiac, and I just wrote one a day. It was so great to make up what color people's hair was, so exciting to say, "It's going to rain." I was so proud of just making things up that I was actually embarrassed by the time that I finished it. I spend my time, especially when you're writing about works of art, trying to be relatively precise about what I'm describing. At the same time, I think writing about the world—for me and also, I suspect, for John, from what I've just been reading in the *Reader*—became an absolute liberation from influence. I mean, I really feel like if I am reading my fiction or John's fiction, I can feel in the machinery of the fiction the history of the influence of American literature. The minute that it's nonfiction, that influence is no longer palpable. One of the most interesting things is just a couple days ago I sat down and read the novel section at the end of the *Reader*. It's the first time that I've ever sort of consciously thought, "What are the real influences here?" The presumption has always been that John does post-Hemingway things—that he was primarily influenced by Hemingway in some way. I kept sort of looking at the prose. I decided that it's not really Hemingway-style writing. It's as if Fitzgerald were writing Hemingway. The sentences were longer. They're more recursive; they end with a lift or a drop, which Hemingway never does. They lift up on sort of a conversational level. John would consider it a defect that you could even think this about his prose, I'm sure, that you could say, "Oh, there's other stuff in here," and I understand that. But the truth is, the minute that it starts being nonfiction, it's really John's.

One of the peculiarities of nonfiction, having written a lot of it, is that it's less self-effacing than you think. It's like photography because when you're taking a picture of something, all that's in that photograph is your decision, your choice, since everything in the photograph is just the stuff of the world. And so nonfiction tends to allow one to theatricalize one's prejudices and under the guise of self-effacement. I find this appealing, and I know that John certainly does, but it also liberates you.

JOHN GRAVES: This difference between fiction and nonfiction, because I ended up doing nonfiction in keeping, I suppose, with our generational interest in fiction. That's the main thing I tried to do for a long time. I finally decided that I wasn't suited for long fiction. I did write some pretty decent short stories, not very many of them. But I am grateful for that long effort to write fiction, because of the freedom it brought to my nonfiction when I got to it. I have been frank in most of my work. Well, there's a little, I don't know what you would call it, that little pre-note in *Goodbye to a River,* which says, "some of these things aren't true, but they're true in a fictional sense." I can't quote the thing exactly, but I have tried to preserve that freedom ever since. Write about reality, but shape it to give it a meaning that I see in it. I think that the experience in trying to write fiction for so many years helped me in that, if indeed I got away with it at all.

MARK BUSBY: Sam, do you want to comment on fiction versus nonfiction?

SAM HYNES: I was thinking, as Dave was speaking, about the third book of *Gulliver's Travels,* in which there is a character of one of the projectors who is trying to replace words with things altogether. He carries a great sack of things on his back and pulls one out and offers it. Where you might say bread, he offers you a loaf of bread. This idea doesn't catch on, but it would be ideal. Well, you would have an unusual vocabulary based on weight, but I think John is a little bit like the projector with the sack on his back. What he is doing when he is writing about the world is bringing pieces of it out of this sack and offering them to us. So we're getting closer to thingness than language usually gets, and we all respond to that. We don't maybe say at the end, "Thank you, John Graves; you got us closer to reality," but that's what we feel when we close the book with a feeling of satisfaction.

DAVE HICKEY: I think that's close, Sam, pulling objects out of a sack, like a kid pulling a frog out of his pocket. It's those things, the thingness of language that distinguishes writing from typing, the euphony of words, the way that they sound and are sounded in certain situations.

JOHN GRAVES: Not long ago this nice little girl showed up. She had called ahead of time. She showed up to interview me for a radio program of some sort. I don't remember much about it, but she had read some of my stuff. She was intelligent as she could be, but she kept pushing for me to have a cause. I think this was one of the journalism schools. I don't know, but you're supposed to be for and against in writing as a writer. I tried to explain to her that the language itself is a point. We've got such a beautiful, flexible language, and you can do so many things with it. You can write a sentence and you know no one ever wrote one like it before. That in itself is an objective. You don't have to have a cause. You have to have a subject perhaps, but there are a lot of subjects around. But the beauty of words and the correct use of them have always just fascinated me almost completely at times. Back in the twenties when they had so many movements going, particularly in literature and painting both, was it dada that just made sounds? I could have been a dada if they were good sounds, you know.

SAM HYNES: The trouble with dada is it's fun to do, but it's hell to listen to.

MARK BUSBY: This leads me to a question. You're talking about the notion of the relationship between writers and persuasive purposes. Now, this is September the 7th, 2002, and we're about to have a number of remembrances and observations about 9/11, and I wonder if you have any comments or whether you think writers should?

JOHN GRAVES: It depends on what kind of writer you are. For me it . . . I mean, I'm aware of the meaning of the whole thing, but I am not the one to talk about it.

DAVE HICKEY: I was amazed, and I'm sure John Graves was even more so. A lot of my students were very shocked and unnerved about the whole thing. I wasn't. My whole high school class came back from Vietnam as ground chuck. And things are totally different after 9/11? I don't quite grasp it myself. It seems like I turned the radio down for a few days, then turned it back up.

MARK BUSBY: Do you have any observations on it?

SAM HYNES: It's so complicated. I've been reading a book about Berlin in the first days of the Nazi takeover of the German government. And one thing they did in those days—Hitler had stolen the government, as you know, stolen the chancellorship, stolen the law, and made it all Nazi. And one thing they did in those days, they had lots of parades. Bands marched. Swastikas everywhere. Every time

Hitler would open his mouth, they'd declare a celebration and all meet in the Whatzit Platz and, you know, salute each other, and the band would play. I mistrust celebration, and that, in a way, is what we're doing already about September 11. The *New York Times* has had front-page stuff about it for already about a week. And it goes on and on and on. It's hard to say to American people like you that it isn't that important. It isn't as important as whether we invade Iraq or not. Terrible things will happen if that's done. It's unfortunate. It's partly our tendency to call everything in which people die a tragedy. September 11 wasn't a tragedy. Those people weren't martyrs. They weren't, except for the firemen and policemen. They weren't even heroes. They were just victims. They were like the Jews in the death camps, and the homosexuals and the socialists and all those other people that were in the Nazi concentration camps. They were pure victims. And that's sad, but it's not tragic. But what we're about to do might very well be tragic. And I hope we don't do it.

MARK BUSBY: Well, we're coming to the end of our announced time. We got started a little late, but there are more sessions that are going to go on this afternoon. And there will be book signings and books available. But before we end, Sam has a closing quote that he thought was appropriate. So I'm going to turn to Sam.

SAM HYNES: I'm breaking John's confidence by reading you two sentences from his journal from 1954, which are probably not quite right yet. It's 1954, and he's been in Spain for two or three years. He's come to the end of it. He's dissatisfied with himself and with his writing, but, well, listen to this. He is going to leave Spain. "I will go to the Canaries," he says, "and will write some kind of book. Also, I'll live to be a hundred, very wealthy, and wise, and famous." Now there is a certain ironic note there.

JOHN GRAVES: It's totally ironic.

SAM HYNES: But there's no doubt in it, I think. It is not a doubt about his vocation. He will go to the Canaries, and he did. He will write some kind of book, many kinds of books, including a journal, which is still not good enough to publish. He will also live to be a hundred, more or less. Whether he is wealthy or not? Well, I could ask Jane about that, but I won't. As for the rest of it, the famous—obviously he's famous or we wouldn't be here, would we? And though it will embarrass him, we're also here to celebrate his wisdom.

MARK BUSBY: Thank you very much. Thank you all for coming.

An Interview with John Graves

DAVE HAMRICK

INTERVIEWER'S NOTE: John Graves is a quiet, somewhat reclusive man who would prefer not to talk about himself. To learn about Graves the man, I suspect he would recommend that one read his four major Knopf works, which to a large degree are autobiographical. Nevertheless, John generously consented to do the interview for this publication. The broad-stroke, general nature of the questions put forth was intentional on my part and a deliberate attempt to complement the critical pieces included in this volume. Graves and I agreed that I would submit a set of questions to him in writing, that he would respond to those questions in writing, and that we would not go back and revise or modify the interview after he had completed his responses. The format dictated a certain kind of lengthy, multiple-part question, and while this type of exchange allows for more thoughtful, expansive answers in some instances, it admittedly loses some of the conversational spontaneity and multidirectional flow of a taped or recorded interview format.

Myself and Strangers

DID THE IDEA OF WRITING the memoir emerge in the recent past, or was this a book you had always planned to write?

This depends on what is meant by "recent." No, I had not always intended to write it. As noted in the book, I dug out the old journal in the early 1990s with the idea of reading it and then consigning it to the flames. So the book idea certainly didn't exist back then. However, I got interested enough to do away with much of the journal's dross and to preserve its gist in a typescript, a copy of which I sent to my old, close friend Sam Hynes of Princeton University in about 1994. He was enthusiastic and said it would make a book. I replied that it wouldn't, or at least not a book I wanted to write, but the idea must have lodged itself within my mind.

After that I tinkered with the journal from time to time in between other pieces of work, adding present-day observations and sending Sam an occasional draft. At some point in the late nineties we evolved the concept of "Old John" and "Young John" and the book idea began to make more sense. But the earliest draft of the memoir itself in my records is dated December 2002, so it didn't really get to steaming for nearly a decade after I started fooling with the material.

THE MEMOIR CLEARLY RECORDS that you were working very hard, really struggling, to become a writer—setting very high personal standards. As you look back on the "apprenticeship," particularly the years in Europe, was this a good period of your life, time well spent? Essential to do what you felt you needed to do? Was it important that you leave the U.S. to accomplish your goals?

It was a special and rather wonderful time for me, despite the ups and downs and many worries and doubts the book expresses. Whether it needed to last as long as it did, counting the Mexican, New Mexican, and New York stays, is not a question I'll try to answer. But the end effect was that all that time in places far from my youthful environs enabled me to see those environs much more clearly than I had been able to see them before.

YOUR WORK HAS ALWAYS BEEN very personal and autobiographical. It seems to me that, in one sense, *Myself and Strangers* completes the arc of your writing career—the memoir is the beginning, *Goodbye to a River* the transitional book, and *Hard Scrabble* the last book in that sequence. Do you view these three Knopf titles as a trilogy?

I guess that in view of the small number of real books I've published in a lifetime that's getting pretty long, I'd damned sure better consider those three a trilogy, or make it a tetralogy if you throw in *From a Limestone Ledge.*

THE JOHN GRAVES that emerges from *Myself and Strangers* is a very different fellow from the Texan known as "the sage of Glen Rose." You state in the preface that you wrote the memoir to not lose "an image of what I was once like." Why is it important to you now that your readers know "Young John"?

Oh yes he was quite different in certain ways, though not in others. I guess I finally decided to show him as he was back then in order to fill out the story, in the hope that my work (and one always has such hope, however uncertain it may be) will outlast my corporeal self by a few years.

YOU ALWAYS SEEM to totally immerse yourself in the subject you are writing about. While you were traveling and living in Europe in the 1950s, were you consciously seeking material or collecting "research" for the apprenticeship novel? Is that unpublished novel, "A Speckled Horse," largely an autobiographical novel?

"A Speckled Horse" was largely autobiographical, yes, though not in all its details. Its story included many people and events from my own life, but also many from the lives of other people I'd known. And some that I made up.

THE MEMOIR has several pages about your World War II service in the Pacific. That war shaped or, in your words, "loomed behind" your generation. You have written sparingly of this period. Did that experience shape your writing in any way? I ask that question because Bill Broyles once wrote that your war experience, like Ernest Hemingway's, lies "back in the deep water" of *Goodbye to a River* and compared "Big Two-Hearted River" to *Goodbye.* Do you agree with that analysis?

I'm sure WWII must have shaped my writing to some extent, as it shaped me. But I had an incomplete feeling about the brevity of my war experiences, as the memoir notes. War is by nature intense and always leaves its marks, though individuals like me are not always certain what the marks consist of. One main thing it did, I believe, was to leave me determined to go my own way afterward, insofar as I could find it.

Yes, I think Broyles is right to a considerable degree. I particularly like that "deep water" insight, which jibes with my feeling about the uncertainty of war's meaning to individuals. Most veterans who have really seen action seem to fluctuate, looking back, between nostalgia for the esprit and self-sacrifice and comradeship that are genuinely present in effective fighting units, and the horror of events that surround and sometimes overwhelm those units and their men.

Sam Hynes, who was a marine pilot in "our" war, has written most perceptively about these things. His *The Soldiers' Tale* (1997) is a study of the published recollections of actual participants, not theorizers, in WWI, WWII, and Vietnam.

SPEAKING OF HEMINGWAY, in the book you mention seeing him sitting at a café in Spain. Can you describe the pull and influence he had on you and your generation? Do you have favorite Hemingway pieces? Do you consider him to be one of the most important American writers of our time?

Hemingway was just *there* for my generation, inescapable. We—at least I and many others like me—devoured his books, mourning with the hero of *A Farewell to Arms* beside his lover's deathbed, hoping to run with the bulls at Pamplona, cheering on Spanish guerrillas in the Guadarrama Mountains. Even at this late date, when I have long since digested a few unsavory facts about his life and ways, his main work retains its magic for me. I like best some of the short stories like "The Snows of Kilimanjaro" and nearly all of the longer fiction. Yes, I think his work will stand as some of the best of his era, which coincided more closely with that of my parents than my own.

WILLIAM FAULKNER was also an early influence. He was the subject of your MA thesis at Columbia. What aspect of his work did you admire the most?

I don't remember reading any Faulkner before the war except a few short stories of the sort he published in slick magazines like the *Saturday Evening Post.* But I went at him full blast afterward, in graduate school at Columbia. That was before he got the Nobel Prize, and you could buy first editions of most of his books on Fourth Avenue for a dollar or two or three. He was the first writer I had encountered who had gotten down the genuine feel of the South, which was an integral part of my own background. (Later I discovered others, especially Carolyn Gordon of the Fugitive group.) His distinctive use of language at its best is magnificent, even if it sometimes gets out of hand and goes florid. My favorite among his books is *Absalom, Absalom!*

Oddly, I don't reread as much Faulkner as I do the work of some of his contemporaries, but he is always with me.

CAN YOU MENTION other writers who mattered to you during these formative years?

Joyce, Hemingway, Faulkner, Ford, O. Henry, Tolstoy, Shakespeare, the King James, Mark Twain . . . To these I could add many others, especially poets like the Elizabethans and post-Elizabethans, Milton, the Romantics, and Yeats, always blessedly gifted Yeats.

YOUNG JOHN SEEMED to have a preference for Spain, Mallorca (and before that, Mexico) rather than Paris, which was the residence of choice for many American expatriates. Can you articulate your affinity for these particular places?

This preference is I guess in part linguistic. Beginning as a kid, I learned Spanish from wetback laborers, high school and college classes, and occasional visits to Mexico, finishing up in Spain where I became rather fluent. And I seem always to have been drawn toward Hispanic cultures, including that of our South Texas region, in part perhaps because of reading Dobie when young but also because my paternal grandmother's people were ranchers in that region.

WOMEN. You write about the pursuit (and conquest) of women during this bachelor period in some detail and in a very personal way. Any hesitation to include these sections?

The amorous links with various women were a contributing part of my reluctance about publishing the old journal's material, for I have never been a kiss-and-tell type. They were an integral part of my life back then, however, Young John being an unmarried male in his thirties with a normal libido. And at least two of them meant a lot to me in much more than sexual terms. Certain considerations finally persuaded me to leave them in the book: (1) As noted above, the picture would be incomplete without these ladies, (2) So much time has intervened that many of the memoir's characters, including women, are dead or getting as ancient as Old John himself, and (3) It was possible in the memoir to alter not only names but sometimes circumstances as well. Ever since *Goodbye* I have been frank about my belief that I have a right to fictionalize nonfiction when I need to, and there is certainly some of that in *Myself and Strangers.*

Rivers

I WANT TO MOVE to the subject of your relationship to rivers. In 1966, Stewart Udall, secretary of the Department of the Interior for LBJ, wrote that you were "one of the finest river historians of our country." *Goodbye* had been out for six years, and the Potomac River piece for Udall was finished. Since that time you have written about the Rio Grande and the Concho, Canadian, Lower Neches, Pecos, Brazos Clear Fork, and Upper Sabinal rivers. In a broad sense, can you talk about your attraction to rivers?

The main Potomac piece I did for Udall, called *The Nation's River,* was not finished and published until 1968.

In Texas, if you care at all about the natural world, you just about have to love running water, since most of the state does not have the copious flows that characterize the East Coast and European regions where our culture mainly evolved. Hence it has a magical pull for Texans, or at least it has had for this one since early youth.

Along with this appreciation goes a resentment of the abuses that have been and are still being imposed upon the rivers. I am not much of a polemicist in general, but I can't help being one in this field. And the whole of Udall's multi-agency Potomac campaign was polemical, its aim being "to clean up the Potomac and make it a model for the nation." The immediate results of this effort were not widespread, in large part because Vietnam was eating up the money and also because Lyndon Johnson decided not to run for reelection in 1968, again because of Vietnam. But later many of our recommendations began to be implemented on the Potomac and elsewhere, and all in all those were a good three years, with like-minded, knowledgeable people all around me and a strong belief in what we were trying to do.

WHEN *Goodbye to a River* was published in 1960, a number of reviewers immediately compared the book to the work of Dobie, Webb, and Bedichek and identified you as the writer best suited to carry on the tradition of the "Old Guard." Looking back now after forty-five years, do you agree or disagree with those critical assessments of *Goodbye*? Each one of you wrote about the importance of human contact with natural things. As the culture becomes more disconnected from the environment, do you think the work of the "Old Guard" will continue to be read? Has it lost any significance? You also wrote in *Goodbye* that man had lost the "organic kinship to nature" that earlier generations possessed. Do you think we have lost that connection forever?

I have always felt a bit edgy about being lumped with other writers, but there is some validity in this comparison. All four of us were Texans, and we all cared about the natural world and the historical background of our region. But all of us were individuals too, varying greatly in our views.

Whether the writing of the "Old Three," as I think of them, will continue to be appreciated in the future (and whether my own work will be, for that matter) is not something that I or anyone else can answer at this point. Texans are so increasingly urban in their focus, so much more like all other Americans, that it is possible to doubt that writers primarily concerned with Southwestern natural and rural and historical matters will retain their appeal much longer.

On the other hand plenty of Texans, including many in the cities, do still feel the pull of the countryside and its history and its people's former ways, and this may serve as a counter-force against such urbanized homogenization. I for one hope so.

Of the Old Three, I think Webb runs the most danger of being ignored by future readers. He had some keen and original insights as a historian and carried our awareness of the West and its ways into areas unexplored before. But others afterward carried those insights further, altering and expanding them, and Webb's use of prose was not eloquent enough to ensure the survival of his books except among devoted scholars, where his name will endure.

Bedichek was the most accomplished stylist and naturalist of the trio, but he got a late start and wrote very little, and some of it is quite quirky. I will reread him for the rest of my life, but how many others will? Maybe a lot.

Dobie has had to take more posthumous whacks from critics than the other two combined. Yet his best work survives, and I think it will keep on doing so, because of the people-oriented warmth and often humor of his depiction of the ways of that older Texas that had shaped him.

As for the link between man and nature, I don't believe it can be truly destroyed, because it is genetic, innate. I am a pessimist in this as well as other ways, however, and I doubt that the attachment will ever again be as instinctively strong as it used to be. That, I think, is a great loss.

J. FRANK DOBIE was an early supporter of *Goodbye,* and you developed a great friendship with him that lasted until his death. Can you describe in some detail what Dobie the man was like and talk about your friendship?

I am going to skimp my answer to this question, chiefly because I have written about the friendship with Dobie elsewhere, notably in the footnotes of *John Graves and the Making of "Goodbye to a River,"* a compendium of correspondence from the period just before and after the publication of that book.

He and I cottoned to each other, and our relationship in the few years between our meeting and his death was warm. With me and with certain other friends he was open-minded and discursive on just about all subjects. But he had another self that hated arbitrary authority and anything he saw as injustice, and he could stir up public trouble when he felt like it. This endeared him to the Austin liberal set and identified him with that set among extreme conservatives.

He believed in inconsistency, however, and once told me he was going to have a mesquite-wood plaque engraved with a quote from Emerson: "I shall carve upon the lintels of my doorway, Whim!" One evening while Jane and I and another couple were having dinner with him and Mrs. Dobie at a Mexican restaurant in East Austin, the proprietor wheeled in a TV set and set it up beside our table. On the screen was J. Frank Dobie himself, fulminating against the city for not granting a raise to local firemen.

Dobie viewed his other self for maybe thirty seconds, then shook his head and returned to his enchiladas. "You know," he said, "I believed that stuff yesterday."

THE PUBLICATION of *Goodbye* also provoked an irresistible temptation for critics to compare you to Thoreau—in fact, you were called the Texas Thoreau. Just as often you have rejected the comparison, and if I recall, Dobie agreed with you. The parallels are remarkable: river trips and firsthand written accounts of those experiences, houses built with your own hands, the affinity for solitude, a rejection (or sideways glance) at contemporary society's values and beliefs, a somewhat misanthropic worldview. What about Graves and Thoreau? Another chance.

Well, yes, there are a number of similarities between "Saint Henry," as I call him in *Goodbye,* and my own rustic self. But I don't think they outweigh the big differences in our temperaments and our writing. The principal one of these differences involves *purity.* I have always admired purity in others, at least when it fosters adherence to principles I agree with. I admire it in Thoreau. But I most often distrust its symptoms in myself, because it constitutes a barrier between me and the whole messy, sinful, sensual, fallible, unpredictable ruck of humanity of which I rather gladly know myself to be a part.

This could turn into an essay, but won't . . .

AS YOU PADDLED DOWN the Brazos, you were writing the chronological history of the river. You point out society's lack of a cultivated awareness of the past and its unquestioning acceptance of change. Is this another reason the natural world is in trouble? You are a self-proclaimed pessimist, yes?

Yes, it's a reason for the natural world's troubles, and yes, I am a pessimist. Inconsistently, though (see the passage on Dobie above), I am delighted to be here and to have been here since a time when change was much less drastic and ugly. I exult in what is still here, in friends and other decent people, and for that matter in waking up each morning.

I THINK *Goodbye* anticipated and is a fine very early example of American "nature writing." You wrote thoughtfully about treading lightly on the land; population growth; the importance of "knowing" wild places; birds, native plants, and ecology. Your work has been included in several major anthologies. Do you consider yourself a nature writer? Do you read the genre, and if so, do you enjoy any particular writers?

I don't really think of myself as a "nature writer," but as a writer who tries to put words together as well as he can, regardless of the material involved. The natural world has certainly been important to me as a personal interest and as subject matter. But so have other things such as history and its people, country work, domestic animals, etc.

I have read a good bit of real nature-writing. Much of it is over-exclamatory or sentimental, but some is excellent. I can't make a full list right off the bat, but among the writers I have liked are (yes) Thoreau, Aldo Leopold, Barry Lopez, Farley Mowat, Rachel Carson, and Wendell Berry, the Kentucky poet.

YOU WRITE ABOUT your father in several different books and essays, and it was his illness that brought you back to Texas. Did he read any version of *Goodbye,* and what did he think of it?

My father had a horrendous if successful cancer operation in 1957, and lived until 1962, when he died of a heart attack. So he was alive when *Goodbye* was published and did read and like it. He was increasingly feeble in those years, however, and I don't remember any discussions with him about the book, except that he was proud that it had been well received.

Hard Scrabble

WHEN DID YOU purchase Hard Scrabble and did you really buy it with the advance money you received for *Goodbye*? What did you like about this particular piece of land? Can you give us the background?

I bought the first part of this place in 1960. Land was still quite cheap in these cedar hills back then and my unspectacular *Goodbye* advance not only covered the purchase price but I had about half of it left over. I had been coming down to hunt and fish and camp in this area since just after WWII, when a prosperous friend of mine was building up a ranch by buying small deserted homestead tracts like this one. My tract adjoined his holdings.

The area is not hard to like, being much like the Hill Country west of Austin, with creeks, steep limestone hills cloaked in cedar and oak, and a few little bottomland fields. It is hell to make a living from, though, which is why so many homesteads remained unoccupied after the armed services and aircraft-factory jobs had drained away their old-time occupants.

WAS THE MOVE to the country—a dramatic change, it would seem—in part a conscious, intentional desire to return to a kind of preindustrial, subsistence living (a return to the "old ways") not unlike what you rediscovered in the historical reading and research for *Goodbye*?

The move to Hard Scrabble wasn't all that sudden. Since our marriage in late 1958, Jane and I, along with our infant daughters as they came into existence, had been living in a rented farmhouse beside a creek a few miles west of Fort Worth, where we ran some cows. I was teaching part-time at TCU, but had begun to construct things on our Somervell County place as time permitted, first a well house and a cottage, both built of native limestone. When the daughters reached school age they began their studies in the city and I continued to flit back and forth between the rented Mary's Creek place and Hard Scrabble until 1965, when I began my three-year stint with Udall in Washington, coming home often.

I don't recall actual dates, but it must have been 1969 or 1970 before we were living as a family in Hard Scrabble's little limestone cabin, with a frame bedroom added on for the kids. Then a few years later we started leading another split existence, when the daughters started high school in Fort Worth, Jane went back to her designer work at Neiman Marcus, and we took an apartment for them in the city, while I was still down in the country much of the time, building things and writing and tending livestock. After that period, it was not till the girls were in college and Jane retired that she and I began living down here together, full time.

Nor do I remember having noble thoughts about returning to the old ways and all that, though I suppose this motive was at work underneath. I was just doing the things I wanted to do at that point in my life.

WAS THE TRANSITION from city living to the farm difficult? You were married to Jane and had two young daughters. Did the women revolt? Did you want the girls to grow up having that direct relationship to the natural world?

No revolts. Jane, a New York City native, adjusted smoothly to a rustic existence and still gets along with local people as well as I do, often better. The girls had access to two worlds, city and country, and though they now both live in distant, more sophisticated places with husbands and offspring, they look back with nostalgic pleasure on the time spent at Hard Scrabble among animals and chores and natural forces, and thank me for it.

IN RETROSPECT, does the move to Hard Scrabble seem now to be a logical progression in your personal evolution and evolution as a writer? Did you find the subject, or did the subject find you?

I guess, in view of the observations above, that the subject matter really found me.

HOW LONG DID IT take you to complete *Hard Scrabble* from start to finish? When you began to write the book, what did you want the book to say? What were some of the country "diversions" that appealed most to you?

I don't recall how long it took me to write the book, probably the better part of a year, with country activity interrupting the process along the way. More than my other books, it more or less wrote itself, coming up with the tales and events it chronicled. My job, as I saw it, was to let it tell these tales and have its say, whatever that turned out to be, in the best language I could muster. I know this sounds a bit esoteric, but for me it has been pretty much what happens when writing really starts to roll.

Country diversions? Unless you call carpentry, stonemasonry, fence-building, and other labors "diversions"—and I did enjoy them all—my country pleasures have not been highly original: hunting, fishing, birding, looking under stones to see who was living there. And always reading, a necessity in my life whether done in town or up beyond the forks of the creek.

I GET THE SENSE that this is your favorite book. The one that's the most meaningful to you.

Yes, I guess it is my pet work, though I like *Goodbye* and *Blue [and Some Other Dogs]* and some of the other things just about as well. The thing is, you like different pieces of your own work for different reasons. For me, though, *Hard Scrabble* seems to hold together the best.

The Last Running

WE HAVE TO AT LEAST touch briefly on the short fiction. You have written several beautiful stories, including "The Last Running," which has been in print since 1974. It is different from most of the other short stories in setting and period. Are there any historical sources that the story is based on?

"L. R." was first published in the *Atlantic Monthly* in I think 1957, but you are right that in book form it dates back only to 1974. It was a by-product of my reading in regional history and natural history at that time, when I was just back from my apprenticeship wanderings and steeping myself once more in things Texan. I ran across a passage in some regional book whose name and author I can't now recall, which told of a time when some Indians, long after their defeat and consignment to reservations, showed up at Charles Goodnight's West Texas ranch and asked for a buffalo from the herd he had built up. With that as a starting point, the story started building itself in my mind, and I sat down and wrote it straight through in an afternoon and an entire night, although I'm sure I put in a lot of time later revising what I'd done.

I RECALL SEEING in one or two letters from your agent John Schaffner that the director Sam Peckinpah bought the film rights for "The Last Running." Was there serious talk about adapting the story for the big screen? Have you had other nibbles from Hollywood over the years? Have you attempted any screenwriting projects since the publication of *Goodbye*?

Yes, Peckinpah did buy an option on the story and renewed it once or twice, and he and I and my dear friend Bill Wittliff talked it over in Austin on one occasion. But Peckinpah was then on his terminal downswing and died in 1984, having let the option lapse.

I don't remember further Hollywood nibbles at the story itself, but at some point in the late eighties or early nineties Bill Wittliff, by then well established as a screenwriter, argued me into attempting a screenplay based on the story. I resisted the idea, as I usually do ideas from others, but Bill promised to advise me about procedures and technicalities and marketing, so I undertook the task.

About four drafts later we had it in good shape. It was expanded and altered from the story itself, but it held together, and Bill and his agent started peddling it. I don't have full recollection of the sequence of events after that. At one point Tommy Lee Jones was most interested and I met him with Bill in Austin, but for some reason that fell through. Finally a National Geographic films executive named Palmieri got enthusiastic about the script and paid good money for an option. Sam Shepard and Wes Studi agreed to be in it and things looked rosy. But then Palmieri died in his forties and that probability died with him. So by now I have for good reason started being quite philosophical about Hollywood.

Birds

BIRDS APPEAR FREQUENTLY in much of your best writing. Can you explain man's obsession with birds?

No, I can't really explain it. Many of them are beautiful, others sing nicely, and still others are very good to eat. They have been around a lot longer than *Homo sapiens,* and most species seem likely to survive him despite his poisons and his destruction of their habitats.

Primarily, I guess, their appeal derives from the fact that they are the most daily visible form of wildlife, and if I am right in believing that a need for response to nature is built into us humans, birds are nearly always there to respond to, even in cities.

The Writing Life

TALK ABOUT THE ACT OF WRITING, what the writing life means to you. When did you first know that you *had* to be a writer? Have you ever fallen out of love with writing? Writing is a solitary profession—as is paddling down the Brazos solo and living in the country on a working farm. You write beautifully about quiet, solitude, the need for being alone. A kind of melancholy is also present in those passages. Is this a necessary part of your writing life?

I have used this story on several public occasions, but it fits in here. When I was teaching a writing seminar at TCU many years ago, toward the end of a semester individual members of the class used to come around to my office when no one else was around. After beating about the bush for a spell, each would ask me what I thought his or her chances were of really becoming a writer.

Some few were clearly not cut out for writing and I could tell them that, as was only fair. A very few showed real promise and were told so. The potentiality of the rest remained something of a mystery at that point, and I worked out a little speech for these, valid enough I think: "If you *have* to write you're going to keep on writing, regardless of success or failure. If you don't have to write, you won't, and you're probably lucky."

I think I myself could have made a decent doctor or lawyer, or for that matter a first-rate academic. But as it turned out (the full realization probably came during a miserable spell of teaching freshman English at UT in the late 1940s), I was one of those people who *had* to write, which led to the years of euphoria and discontent chronicled in *Myself and Strangers.* When I finally came out on the other side, having found my own voice as a writer for better or worse, my life changed and became much more settled and meaningful, and has stayed that way ever since.

I don't think my own "writing life" has been necessarily typical. Writers are particularly individual people. Some start out good and remain so. Others, whether good or not, stay tormented all their days and tend toward alcoholism and messy living. Et cetera.

YOU HAVE DESCRIBED the form of *Hard Scrabble* as musical counterpoint (alternating nonfiction and fiction pieces) and the structure of *Goodbye* as numerous thematic strands (wildlife, history, people, etc.) twisting around the central core of the trip itself, making a neat cable (like a string of pearls). How do you approach form?

In graduate school at Columbia just after the war, I believed that form could be thought out and applied to writing by an author, and my thesis on Faulkner, a great experimenter with forms, was based on that assumption. As time went on, however, I learned that for me at least writing needed to find and shape its own form. That has happened with all of my better work. Maybe I did describe those two books in the way you quote, but those were afterthoughts.

YOU HAVE ALWAYS been a great stylist—a writer's writer. You once wrote that if you have any style at all it depended on rhythm and voice. Can you elaborate? Describe your style.

No, I can't really describe my style, any more than I can pin down the matter of form. Whatever personal style I have came with time, as I gradually "found my own voice" as noted above. I can tell you when something of mine sounds right, but I can't tell you just why. I know that much of my style derives from lifelong reading, but insofar as elements of it came from others' styles they did so by sinking down into the unconscious and when they came back up they were mine. I'm afraid this sounds a little precious, but I do think it is true. At times when I have more or less consciously and directly derived stylistic mannerisms from others' work, awkwardness has been a result, as in "A Speckled Horse," written at a time when I was much under the spell of Ford Madox Ford. What worked just fine for him didn't work very well for me because I hadn't digested it fully.

I KNOW YOU REALLY hoped that Knopf would publish *Myself and Strangers.* You have had a very rare relationship with them—one that has lasted a lifetime. Knopf has kept *Goodbye to a River* in print in hardcover since its publication in 1960. This is unheard of in the world of publishing today. You knew Alfred Knopf personally, had great editors, loyalty. Can you talk about this relationship and what it has meant to you? Talk about how the publishing industry has changed since you started writing.

A. A. Knopf, Inc., has always treated me fine and I am most thankful for this. Their friendship, for that was what it has amounted to, I find remarkable in view of the paucity of my literary output.

I was very fond of old Alfred with all his elitist, gourmet quirks, and was much impressed by his brilliant Blanche on one occasion when he brought her to Dallas. But my gratitude really flows toward the editors who have handled the four books of mine that Knopf has published, all of whom have been in tune with my own stylistic idiosyncrasies. First there was Harold Strauss, then head editor, who understood and approved when I flatly rejected a copy editor's pervasive changes of punctuation, relative pronouns, etc. in the manuscript of *Goodbye to a River*. He loved *Hard Scrabble* too, but died midway through its editing, which was then taken over by Ashbel Green. When *From a Limestone Ledge* came along, I gave Ash my little spiel about wanting my spellings and commas and such to remain as they were, whereupon he chose as copy editor a lady retired from Knopf and living in rural New Jersey. She was not only sympathetic but brilliant, and pointed out bloopers I had never thought of—for instance, the fact that I sometimes used British spellings and sometimes didn't.

Finally, with *Myself and Strangers,* I was taken over by delightful Ann Close, who has been so in tune with my voice that any awkwardness or errors remaining in the book derive entirely from my own ineptitude.

Almost the only publishers I have dealt with have been Knopf and a handful of regional presses in the Southwest, so I can't speak with authority about the current state of publishing. As an outside observer, I think the worst thing that has happened has been the depersonalization of ownership, which often means that a long-established house in New York may now belong to a potentate or consortium located somewhere in Europe, in accord with the corporate globalization we are currently told to admire. This has often led to a gap between writers and those who handle their books, in contrast to the times only a few decades ago when great editors were almost as well-known as great writers, and loyalties were personal and strong.

Knopf, of course, is now owned by Random House (which is owned by whom?) but is still one of the very few publishers that somehow, by hook or crook, have held on to many of the old practices and ways.

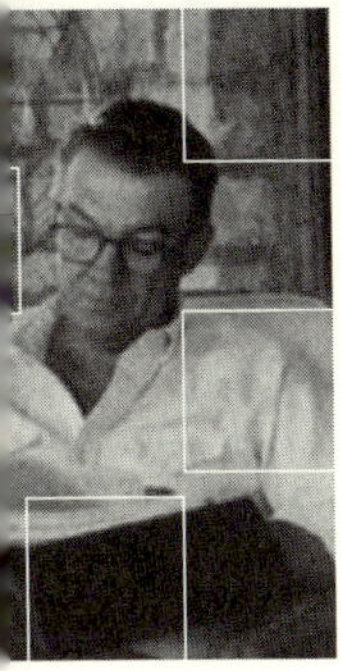

PART TWO

Friends

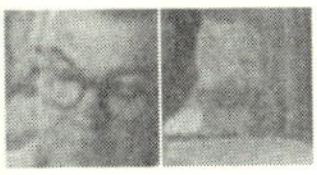

John

BILL WITTLIFF

THE FIRST TIME SALLY AND I and the kids went to Hard Scrabble I had to ask directions from a thorny old gentleman sitting out in front of his house on the side of the farm-to-market. "John Graves. Yeah, that's that fella writes those books." I said it was. "Hell," he said, "if I was to write a book, wouldn't be a marriage left in Somervell County."

A mile or so later we turned left on to a dirt road as directed, drove through a low-water creek, then past a neighbor's pig yard where grunting mud-caked hogs lounged in old pockmarked porcelain bathtubs and urinals half-buried in the dirt. We opened and closed a gate, then drove on down the road a little way to Hard Scrabble. There was a barn and a small rock house, both built by John. There was a canvas-covered canoe turned upside down on the rafters (not the canoe from the journey that became *Goodbye to a River;* that one had been given to a friend years before and wrecked in some mishap).

At the end of the barn there was a little room where John wrote on an old upright typewriter. There was a spittoon beside the desk with splatters on the floor all around where John had shot and missed. And of course there were books on the shelves and a long row of neatly labeled notebooks wherein John kept his farm records and notes on various—and mostly country—interests: cows and fences and honeybees and grapes and the like. Eventually these notes would be expanded into a number of articles written for *Texas Monthly* and later gathered and reworked for *From a Limestone Ledge.*

Outside, below the house, there was a garden and an apiary and a compost so ripe you could warm your hands by it. There was a woodpile out back, where one day I happened to find one of the two paddles John had used on his *Goodbye* trip. A cow had stepped on it, broken it in several places, and John had simply tossed it away, a tool no longer useful. (It's back in one piece now, and in the Graves archive at the Southwestern Writers Collection at Texas State University in San Marcos.)

And of course there were the animals: Blue the dog, Doorbell the Spanish nanny goat and her big brown randy billy goat son William, the ponies Lady Bird and Penny, chickens, other Spanish goats, and a small herd of cattle.

There was White Bluff Creek, where Graves girls, Helen and Sally, would take our son, Reid, and daughter, Allison, to skip rocks and wade—and where Helen and Sally now take their own children on visits from homes far away.

All in all Hard Scrabble was—and is—what local country folk might admiringly call "a good place."

In the evenings we'd have supper out on the screen porch, then talk for hours, long after Jane and Sally had sent the kids off to bed. (I teased John for oversleeping after one such evening. "Well, damn women, anyway," John said. "Keep you up all night talking, then don't get you up in the morning.") If it happened to be a Saturday night and the wind was blowing just right, we might hear ghostly whiffs of fiddle music coming from the little dance hall the Graveses' neighbor with the pig yard had built out in his pasture just for the pleasure of his extended family. And if we stayed up long enough—and we usually did—we'd sometimes hear the foxhunters running their hounds through the creek bottom and blowing on their cowhorn bugles just as their kin had done down through the generations before them.

The Graveses always had several projects going and usually within an hour or two of arrival we'd just naturally get folded into them. On one trip we kibitzed as Jane designed Christmas china for Neiman Marcus; another trip she was designing playing cards and candles. (Incidentally, it was Jane who invented the inflatable car buddy called the Silent Partner.) There was a weekend John and I repaired a water gap that had washed out during a flood. Another weekend we slaughtered a goat to make sausage, then made a mess of it with too much salt. This was somewhat corrected—but not entirely—by remixing it with several pounds of pork. On one trip John sent me up a tree to cut off a limb on which one of his hives had clustered after swarming. I did as instructed, and John, down below, caught the swarm in a cardboard box. Over the years there've been many trips, many projects; I can't go out there without thinking of what old Mister Charlie Goodnight said of the pull of his own varied pursuits: "I'll be damned if I could ever find time to lie in the shade."

Hard Scrabble and John. It's where for more than thirty years now I've gone for good conversation, for inspiration, for friendship—and in times of crisis for advice. It's where I go when I need to be reminded that life—and the principles by which one lives that life—matters and matters hugely. This is not something John preaches. John doesn't preach. You just sort of get it by osmosis.

I'm not alone in this. Several generations of writers—and readers—have been drawn to John and his books for the same nourishments.

It would be impossible, I think, to overestimate John's continuing influence on his fellow writers. He has been the master for a half a century now. His writing is the mark by which the rest of us scribblers measure our own.

Every culture, it seems to me, gets a handful of writers each generation or so who have the talent and ability to reach beneath the surface of things into those deeper currents that run through us all as fellow members of the human tribe. That is why great writing can be universal—why all great art in any field can be universal. It touches the commonality in all of us. It links us one to another. It links one generation to the next and to the next, and to the next. At its most universal it can link one man's experience of a river or a patch of land to all rivers and all patches of land in the world. That's what John did in *Goodbye to a River* and in *Hard Scrabble* and all of his work.

The ability to write with such reach is a rare gift, but having the gift doesn't mean the work comes without effort. The gift of great talent may get you in the boat and put you out on the water, but you've still got to row the sonofabitch yourself.

No one knows this better than John—and no writer I know works harder at building his own symphony of words and thoughts and feelings to express himself than does John.

And another thing. I've never known John to publish anything large or small that didn't come up to his own standards of quality writing and thought.

There's something else about John. I'm not sure what it is, but you just feel better after reading his books or being around him. You feel somehow enriched, enlarged, renewed . . .

You feel—and for me this is exactly the right word—you feel blessed.

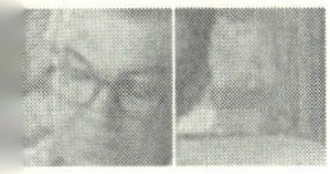

John Graves

A Tribute

RICK BASS

WHAT EXHILARATES ME about John Graves—the father of Texas writing—and what sometimes discourages me as well, is that there isn't anybody else even remotely like him. No one else writes like he does, nobody thinks like he does, nobody else moves through the world quite the way he does. As with few other writers I can think of, a knowledge of his books conveys among his shared readers a kind of wonderful visa—the commonality of having been witness to an invigorating and incomparable mix of elegance, grace, intelligence, and occasional cantankerous, good-humored, sideways grumbling.

Graves' 1960 classic, *Goodbye to a River,* showcases these qualities, along with a structure as free-flowing and enduring as its subject, the river itself, with a river's attendant range of metaphor, both simple and complex. That book stands squarely in the pantheon of works such as Aldo Leopold's *A Sand County Almanac,* and these two books should, in my opinion, be required reading for every policy maker and student of environmental matters. *Goodbye to a River* should also be required reading for all students of literature.

Comparisons to Emerson, Thoreau, and Leopold are easily made, in reading Graves' reflections upon and awareness of the natural world and humanity's place and context within that relationship; but the more I reread his work, the more I realize that which was never really beneath the surface to begin with, and which should have been obvious: that the values and themes of his work are those of the self; of generosity, moderation, and all the usual complex paradoxes of being human. Critic Tom Pilkington has praised the style of Graves' work as being not one of clamant declaration but rather one that insinuates itself gracefully into a reader's consciousness, in which reading the text has much the pleasant sensation of sitting next to a river, perhaps, watching and listening to it, absorbing it, or staring likewise at a campfire. Graves' work is as elegant in its philosophy as it is in rhythm and observation and language, and admirers respect it also for the manner in which he has looked at our past and celebrated the authentic and the specific while refusing to buy into—to hold accountable—the comfortable but rarely examined myths and injustices and dangerously brittle sentimentalities of the past. What I think I personally admire most about the work, in addition to the mastery of the sentences, is the liveliness and cleanliness of the spirit. In *A John Graves Reader,* Graves spoke of his English and birding instructor at Rice, George Williams, and of what he taught Graves with regard to a certain kind of purity in one's writing, "of awareness of excellence and strong feeling about it" and of "gladness and delight" (200).

This to me seems the secret braid of Graves' work—the "graceful insinuation" of which Pilkington speaks—in which the struggles and challenges and joys of the self, both isolated and yet connected also to community (the community of family, of Texas, and even of the United States), are dealt with, again and again. There will be no strident declaration, no foolishly static announcement of stasis, but instead, always a dynamic examination of the movement of history, place, and even our own—especially our own—individual moods, desires, fears, and loves.

In Graves' work, such examination is almost always riverine in approach. A typical run-of-the-mill John Graves masterpiece sentence, or masterpiece paragraph, will celebrate the authentic and time-tested durable, while at the same time refusing to buy into, or to hold accountable, the comfortable but seldom examined myths, as well as brittle and dangerous sentimentalities regarding the past.

We see this day-and-night wrestling in yet another classic passage from *Goodbye to a River:*

> One waxes pessimistic? Not so much . . . There is a pessimism about land which, after it has been with you a long time, becomes merely factual. Men increase; country suf-

> fers. Though I sign up with organizations that oppose the process, I sign without great hope. . . . Islands of wildlife and native flora may be saved, as they should be, but the big, sloppy, rich, teeming spraddle will go. It always has. (58; Graves' ellipses)

I don't mean to take away anything from his earlier masterpiece when I say that I find *Hard Scrabble,* published fourteen years later, an equally powerful book, and in some ways even superior to the first. The sentences in *Hard Scrabble* are a virtuoso display of Graves' style, manifesting an even greater depth and breadth of philosophical concentration that is surely attributable, in part, to the author's being somewhat older and, yes, somewhat wiser—but also, perhaps, to the difference in structure in the telling of the *Hard Scrabble* story, which is about making a rooted commitment to place, as opposed to the freedom involved in getting in a canoe and following the run of the Brazos River, with history always moving alongside, as was the structure of *Goodbye to a River.*

(Even in *Goodbye to a River,* a prescient reader might have been able to see the book that would come next, forming in Graves' mind like a crop in the soil or a tree in the forest—Graves' earlier goodbye not simply to a wild, undammed run of the Brazos but to other freedoms, and youth itself.)

The advance of middle age and deepening of experience, set in humble personal scale against the senescence of the frontier, is the buried structure of *Hard Scrabble,* as is the theme, initiated in *Goodbye* but developed further in *Hard Scrabble,* of identifying that which can be controlled, versus that which cannot. And of the importance of understanding the difference between the two, and the glory as well as the ultimate insignificance of that vast space between them. The struggle to exist in that space-between-the-two produces history, in the case of Texas, and art, in the case of John Graves.

Larry McMurtry has stated that John Graves has done the most to mediate between the past and present as they've meshed—or failed to mesh—with one another in the Southwest. In *Hard Scrabble,* Graves mentions his "sunny disposition" and writes, "Bells still toll for one and all—and, God knows, for the land" (264). And yet, at the end of *Hard Scrabble,* he writes that "while finding much that seemed sorrowful and wrong and reaching stout disaccord with some main forces of the age, I have been barred always from glumness by the rather ridiculous fact that I've liked so many people I've known and have always been so bloody glad to be alive" (263).

Knowing Texans' fierce and extraordinary pride in John Graves, I like to think that when we honor him, we are honoring also the landscape—our landscape—on which he has reflected, again and again, in his life and in his writing. What a wonderful conjunction of fit for this writer to allow himself to settle in at the farm he calls Hard Scrabble for the duration of his life and to give himself over to the personal exploration of, and carving and shaping by, time and landscape. Not control or mastery over a life or a landscape: but a dignity and craftsmanship exerted, at the very least, upon one sentence, and then another, and another. A gift to the community, in that regard, and a guideline for the self.

> Neither a land nor a people ever starts over clean. Country is compact of all its past disasters and strokes of luck—of flood and drouth, of the caprices of glaciers and sea winds, of misuse and disuse and greed and ignorance and wisdom—and though you may doze away the cedar and coax back bluestem and mesquite grass and side-oats grama, you're not going to manhandle it into anything entirely new. It's limited by what it has been, by what's happened to it. (237)

Sentences detailing this exploration, this intelligent and curious yielding, have emanated from him, over the years, with the music of White Bluff Creek itself, running over timeworn limestone, trickling in pools, eddying, redistributing ideas like sediment, carving out new banks, sometimes tearing out old water gaps, sometimes honoring old boundaries, other times proposing new ones.

In his books, a reader will find explorations on building a stone house, the energy and imagination of children, immigration practice and policy, goats and snakes, Comanches, beekeeping, the evils of feral hounds, the approaching physical diminishment attendant to middle age, and all the unavoidable mortality—stuff facing a man or woman who works with livestock, or a garden, or the land in any fashion, for that matter—or with literature.

(Something that never ceases to amaze me is the physical and artistic strength it must take to write the sentences Graves makes—the linguistic vigor! A writer of a more rushed nature, and possessing infinitely less talent, might write something like, "I am ambivalent about poisonous snakes." In *Hard Scrabble,* however, Graves writes, "Though I am of Eve's own distant get and lack special affection toward legless fanged reptiles and have a wary respect for their powers, I lack also the loathing some people feel for them" [111].)

Even far from home, when in Spain, Graves observed that

> land mattered, and even in peasant villages in foreign mountains I had cared to know that a man owned a patch of terrace with vines and olive trees, and what it produced for him, and how the grazing was for sheep and goats on the gnawed slopes thereabout. I had never managed to purge myself of the simple yeoman notion, contracted in childhood from kinsmen looking back to a rural past, that grass and crops and trees and livestock and wild things and water mattered somehow supremely, that you were not whole unless you had a stake in them, a daily knowledge of them. (42)

Land matters, in Graves' work and world—as it has always mattered to Texans—and excellence matters. Perhaps one of the things that causes Graves' readers to bond so fiercely with his work is that by excellence alone, his writing provides us a code of manners that possesses the reassurance of durability and integrity—artistic, environmental, historical, and personal.

In wonderful literary paradox, much of the strength of Graves' work comes, I think, from the fact that although his work is constructed upon real things—stones and stone-house building, screen porches and foxhunts and cedar-whacking, and the migrations of cranes and plover—the matrix and even the foundation of these essays are ghosts and spirit: not just of the Comanches and the Paleolithics before them, but of other people and places Graves has known and loved, the ghosts that helped steer and shape him toward Hard Scrabble. Again, to me, Graves' world of dirt, bone, blood, stone, fires, floods, ice, wind, stories, horses, deer, goats, and always, our tiny but vital living relevance amidst the motion and history of these other enduring nouns—accommodating ourselves within that ancient architecture, into the space we must call community, self, and history—these landscapes and inhabitants that he writes about, then, are comfortable and familiar to me: so much so that in the early years I would again overlook the obvious, that these are stories and sentences that provide a direct map from the heart into the world—any world—and provide us instruction on how to move with passion and yet as much intelligence as can be mustered, through the wonderfully beguiling and paradoxical terrain of our lives.

Aldo Leopold noted that to possess an ecological awareness is to understand that we live in "a world of wounds," which reminds me of Graves' comment, voiced even more poetically: "We will be nearly finished, I think, when we stop understanding the old pull toward green things and living things, toward dirt and rain and heat and what they spawn" (*Goodbye to a River,* 262).

When Graves writes in *Goodbye to a River* that "older, one knows himself an excrescence upon the landscape and no kinsman to any wild thing; one hears the bass drumbeat and the gabble of the rapids below and the roar of the rain and feels abrupt depression and wonders why he barged out alone" (37), I am tempted, like some line-editing literal-fundamentalist, to expostulate that such a passage is commentary on the loss of frontier and wilderness, and on the crazy-making collapse of a bridge between lonely-versus-alone—one of the grand estrangements of this and the previous century, from the land itself, as well as from one another . . .

But again, I have to remind myself that Graves is, above all things, a gentle man, a family man, living on a hardscrabble farm, sometimes just beyond the reach of an ungentle world, making some of the wisest and most beautiful sentences the state—indeed, this country—has ever known. Whatever else that gets thrown into the mix is our own interpretation, our own hungers. His truths, his sentences, are paradoxically of-the-moment, specific for the wedge of time in which they were written—and yet as enduring, too, as stone itself.

John Graves' work will, I suspect, become even more important as years pass: for what a powerful lesson it imparts, informing us of the quality and pace and patience and frustration inherent in a good and respectful relationship between one person, one family, and the land.

We love John Graves and his work because he is a great man and a great writer—and I can't help but think part of the zeal with which Texans, particularly, love him and his work is also an indirect or subconscious homage to our love of homeland, the genius loci he articulates so splendidly. In a culture not always renowned for a tradition of being able to articulate the more subtle, less warlike, even tender emotions, Graves' work is a conduit between us and our ancient attachment to the land and the older, more enduring world of stone and sky, antler and bone, feather and toil; and reading his works, we understand more deeply some of the strange and wonderful and complex relationships between our land and our history, as well as within and between ourselves.

I believe that Texas is in transition from a culture in which the land was viewed as the primary source of wealth to one in which knowledge is seen as the source of wealth or empowerment—knowledge that surely now must include an awareness of our natural history and sustainability. As an activist, I'm inspired by the reverence Graves brings to the land. As an artist, I'm inspired by the reverence he brings to the language of his engaged relationship—his partnership—with the land.

I worry often about the future of Texas' wildlands, and Texas' open spaces, though I like to think I know better than to try to brandish Graves' art as a manifesto to instruct other people how to think about land.

I suspect also that if I tried to engage John in any such discussion about the social and cultural benefits of using literature for a kind of activism, his good eye would get a little fidgety, even a little glazed, and he might glance over my shoulder toward the Booker pasture, where a goat might be bleating, or a beehive might be in urgent need of repair, with the day getting longer and warmer already. It's likely he would remind me that "all" he ever wants to do with his pen is to make beautiful sentences, and that he sure, by God, never intended for any of his books to be set upon by activists of any mien. He might excuse himself and climb up on his tractor or his four-wheeler, preparing to head out to one corner or another of the postage stamp of the hardscrabble ranch to which he has committed himself in the third-smallest county in Texas.

When I consider the future of the wild landscape that has so often been one of his mediums—the other half in the equation of the human heart—I try to keep in mind Graves' epigraph to *Hard Scrabble,* which comes from Thomas Traherne's *The Centuries,* I, 22:

> It is storied of that Prince, that having conceived a Purpose to invade Italy, he sent for Cineas, a Philosopher and the Kings friend: to whom he communicated his Designe, and desired his Counsel. Cineas asked him to what purpose

> he invaded Italie? He said, To Conquer it. And what will you do when you hav Conquerd it? Go into France said the King, and Conquer that. And what will you do when you have Conquerd France? Conquer Germany. And what then? said the Philosopher? Conquer Spain. I perceive said Cineas, you mean to conquer all the World. What will you do when you have conquerd all? Why then said the King we will return, and Enjoy our selvs at Quiet in our own Land. So you may now said the Philosopher without all this adoe.

No more ado. I am proud that John Graves is ours. We are all proud that John Graves belongs to Texas and are smart enough to recognize the good fortune of this rare gift he has provided to an entire culture—past, present, and future.

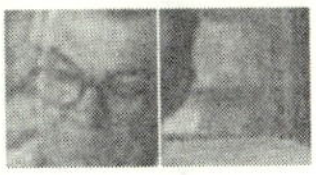

John Graves Tribute, November 11, 2000

WILLIAM BROYLES

THE MAN HAS BEEN TO WAR and been wounded in terrible combat. The wound has taken half his sight, and he sees less but also perhaps he sees more. Anyway he has already seen too many people die and before the book is finished will see his first daughter born. When his wounds heal and they give him a new eye, he wanders the world and lives in places with names that sound like music and whose history is written in every building, centuries of it. That man returns to a part of Texas where history has rested lightly and left not a trace.

He takes a canoe and points it into the current of a river that is about to be dammed and changed forever, the way the man and his world have been. Small wonder that after so much turmoil he is drawn to quiet, after so much history and so many crowds he yearns for solitude, for something that could be his and his alone. A piece of the natural world. A piece of Texas.

Ernest Hemingway never mentions World War I in his classic story "Big Two-Hearted River," but it is there, up in the thickets, beneath the surface, back in the deep water. John Graves doesn't dwell on his war either, may even claim that he'd laid those demons to rest in his wanderings through Mexico and Europe, but for anyone who has also seen combat it is there on every page. The brief fleetingness of life, the savoring of it, the love for what small fragile piece of it is yours, that gratitude just for life, for living: the combat veteran has all that buried in him like shrapnel working its way to the surface. That too is with John when he sets his canoe into the current of the Brazos and heads downstream.

And when he steps out, he goes home, and then, with the tools of his trade, words crafted together, one by one, he takes that stretch of land and the people—Indians, Anglos, Mexicans—who coursed over it and of course himself too, and sets them down on his pages. Part colloquial, part literary, like all his work, the book is robust and rural and deeply aesthetic, all at once. His tools bring a vanished past and a vanishing present to robust life.

The strong young man who paddled his canoe down the Brazos is over eighty now. A genuine old coot, still full of beans and listening for the sandhill cranes flying overhead, but feeling his age.

The river flows on, like time, sweeping all its sons away. But John's book is forever. It will be read as long as books are read. It is his gift to life. To all of us.

ONE OF THE DRAWBACKS of being a writer is the words you read the most are your own. For someone who loves to read great writing, this can be an all but intolerable burden. The best cure is to set yours aside and read a master.

Ask any writer why John Graves is so important, and the answer is, because he takes language, which we waste out in torrents, language that can be twisted and parsed and made to mean this or that. He takes it and distills it into honesty. To make the simple sound sublime, that is the trick. Few of us can do it, ever, and usually by happy accident. John can. It's a hard job, which may be why we don't have nearly enough of him. But what we have, we cherish.

John once told me that being in *Texas Monthly* made him feel like an armadillo that had wandered onto an interstate highway. His columns gave us a civilized, literary consideration of what is this oft-invoked and little understood quality called a sense of place.

John, we thank you. Mister John Graves.

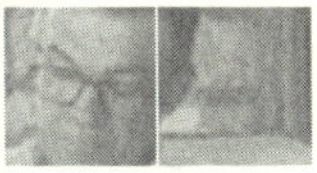

John Graves

From Prairie Gothic: The Story of a West Texas Family

JOHN R. ERICKSON

I REMEMBER SITTING on an airplane and watching the man across the aisle from me. He had oriental features and was reading a newspaper covered with Chinese characters that had no more meaning to me than chicken tracks. Yet those marks on the page caused him to smile and frown and held his attention during a flight that lasted two hours.

This left me thinking about the wonder of written language and the miracle that occurs when the human mind transforms those lines of type into mental pictures. Printed words can cause us to laugh, cry, think, remember, and shake with anger. They can alter our blood pressure, dilate the pupils of our eyes, raise the hair on the back of our necks, and cause our breath to quicken. Books have started wars, brought down tyrants, altered history, and caused people to fall in love.

Words have a power that is almost mystical, and our ability to transform scribbles on the page into feelings and actions is one of the spiritual qualities that sets us apart from our dogs and cats and defines us as humans. Sometimes the direction of a person's life can be changed by what he reads in a book.

I can point to several books that have had a profound effect on me. Stories from the Old Testament gave me the heroes of my boyhood. When Mrs. Smith, my fourth-grade teacher, read *Tom Sawyer* aloud to our class, it hit with the force of revelation that reading need not be a joyless experience, that a gifted writer can trap the sounds and nuances of the spoken word like butterflies and turn them loose to fly out of a page of printed type.

Mr. Haley's biography of Charles Goodnight opened a door on my Texas roots, and John Graves' *Goodbye to a River* gave me a template for combining the love of words with an affection for one's soil.

I don't know if my life would have turned out differently if I had never read *Goodbye to a River,* but it might have. I think my cousin Mike Harter was the first to call my attention to it, and my wife, Kris, gave me a copy of it for Christmas in 1969. It made a huge and lasting impression. Here was an author who wrote on subjects that were often shrugged off as "regional," yet he wrote about them with such precision and wisdom that his sentences resonated in my imagination. His slow, careful stalking of the truth might begin with observations about a horsefly or a Spanish goat, but somehow it turned one's thoughts toward the stars and beyond.

Texas novelist Marshall Terry has described Graves as "a stylistically elegant writer" and "a whole human being. . . . He is who he is but there is just a slight ironic edge to him that, mostly playfully, warns you against taking too seriously what an 'old crock' (his term) like himself might utter" ("The Republic of Texas Letters," 143).

I met John Graves just as I had met Mr. Haley, showing up unannounced and uninvited—a practice I have come to disavow, now that I am an aging man of Texas letters myself. But in those days, I was on a mission and had no shame.

It was in the fall of 1973, and I had driven down to Austin to meet with Bill Wittliff. Today, Wittliff is best known as the author of the screenplay for *Lonesome Dove,* but in 1973 he was building a reputation as a photographer and owner of a small publishing company called Encino Press. He had read my *Through Time and the Valley* in manuscript and wanted to publish it through Encino Press.

That didn't work out, and the book was published five years later by Shoal Creek Publishers, but at the time I was elated. I felt that, at last, I had become a real author.

The book described a fifteen-day horseback trip I made down the Canadian River valley in 1972, and I explained to Bill that I had gotten my idea for the book's structure after reading *Goodbye to a River.*

Bill didn't seem surprised. Books that imitated John Graves had almost become a separate category in Texas literature, as Graves was without question the writer most admired by other Texas writers. We all wanted to imitate his precise, methodical style of writing, and few ever succeeded.

Bill asked if I had met John Graves. No. Did I want to? Of course. "On your way back to the Panhandle, stop by Glen Rose and visit with him. Tell him I suggested it."

Around two on the afternoon of October 7, I drove into the little town of Glen Rose, south of Fort Worth, got Mr. Graves' phone number out of the directory, and called him from a pay phone. After several rings, he answered. As rapidly as possible, I explained that I had read and admired his work, that Bill Wittliff had suggested I drop by for a visit, and that I was the great-great-grandson of Martha Sherman, whose story he had recounted in *Goodbye to a River.*

I held my breath and waited through a moment of silence. "Well, come on out. I'm not doing anything special." He gave me directions to his place outside of town, which he called Hard Scrabble. I found my way with no trouble, but the rocky road to his house almost destroyed my little Ford Pinto.

When I pulled up to the house, a man wearing khaki pants, a faded blue denim work shirt and a railroader's cap came out of the barn and walked toward me. I was surprised that a man who looked so ordinary had written a book as fine as *Goodbye to a River.* He resembled the men you might see in a small town café at lunchtime—welders, farmers, mechanics, carpenters, bricklayers.

He wasn't what I had expected, this man who held degrees from Rice and Columbia. We shook hands and I followed him to the house. He fixed us glasses of iced tea and we sat on the screened porch, groping for conversation that would justify my invasion of his sanctuary. It came slowly at first. John Graves was no chatterbox, but Mrs. Sherman's story gave us some common ground and then we moved into subjects that seemed to interest him more: his bees, goats, and cattle and his various projects to restore native grasses on his four hundred acres of rock and cedar.

Then we moved down to his study, a small room in the northwest corner of the barn. There was a wooden desk against the north wall, holding an ancient manual typewriter and heaps of letters, bills, and scribbled notes. He apologized for the mess and said he was going to straighten things up one of these days. He sat in a chair at the desk and used a big brass spittoon on the floor beside him.

By this time, we had warmed to each other, and we talked through the entire afternoon, covering a wide range of subjects: books, authors, Texas history, coyotes, birds, carpentry, farm machinery, hay, poetry, dogs, family history, the seasons of the year, religion, guns, and writing. Without the slightest hint of pretension, he made references to Milton, Shakespeare, Joyce, Hemingway, Faulkner, Jung, Freud, Dobie, O. Henry, Dos Passos, Mailer, and Bellow. It appeared to me that he had not been much influenced by Texas literature: "I like most Texas writers, but if you want to know whom I admire, I would say only Katherine Anne Porter. She spent her life trying to prove she wasn't from Texas, but her early works were set in Texas and those were her best." He said his writing style had been most influenced by O. Henry—"although I hate to admit it"—and James Joyce.

He lamented that he was not a very disciplined writer and hadn't produced much. I pointed out that anyone who had written *Goodbye to a River* didn't need to write much else. He smiled and said that he did his writing in snatches. Sometimes he'd wake up in the night with a complete passage in mind, jot it down, and go back to it later. He preferred to do his writing in the morning and to do physical labor the rest of the day.

He showed me some black-and-white photographs that Bill Wittliff had taken of him. There were three of them and I noticed that each appeared to show a different man: a university professor, a Southern laborer, and a Texas rancher. And stranger still, the John Graves I was looking at in person didn't show much resemblance to any of them. How did he explain that?

"I've always been lucky that I don't have a face people remember," he said. "If I look like four different people, maybe I am."

Around dark, Jane Graves, John's wife, drove in from town with their two daughters, Sally and Helen. She was a kind lady and seemed glad to meet me. She told us to come up to the house for a drink and some supper, and we moved back to the house. After supper, we drifted back out to the screen porch and resumed our conversation deep into the night.

At one point Mr. Graves stopped talking and cocked his ear. "That's a screech owl . . . no, two of them. Before the night's over, they'll be up around the house." Later, he heard the baying of a hound in the distance. "That's Kenneth's dog. They're running foxes tonight."

Shameless to the end, I hung around until midnight, and by then it was too late to start driving back to the Panhandle. Mr. Graves was kind enough to invite me to stay the night (what else could he do?), and I made a bed on the couch. When I left the next morning, I got the feeling that he had enjoyed our visit but also that he would be relieved to get back to his bees and goats.

After that, we kept in touch through letters. I had gone to cowboying and was collecting rejection slips from New York publishers. I wrote him sprawling four-page letters filled with souped-up, overheated prose, letters I saved as carbon copies and now find embarrassing. He wrote back one- and two-page gems of precision-built sentences, hacked out on his manual typewriter in the barn:

> I am glad if our day together meant something to you; I found it pleasant also. I am, as you will have discerned, not a very august type and probably the best of what I am and whatever I know has gone and will go into my writing. But occasionally one hits upon a younger friend who is enough like himself—in background and in thrust and perception—that some communication is possible, some illusion of being able to pass along relevant observations. It is a good feeling. (March 30, 1974)

In my letters I expounded on theories of writing, whole mountains of them, and he wrote back his quiet, sensible advice:

> I still believe that the best writing pulls in one way or another toward spoken language and the old short hard powerful Anglo-Saxon vocabulary. But like most rules this one was made to be broken when you learn enough to be able to break it right, and it is always necessary to take into account people like, say, John Milton, to whom it would have been repugnant nonsense from the start.
>
> I know that for me at least to be able to maintain a sense of spoken language in writing is absolutely necessary, like Antaeus touching the earth, but I feel best about my

> writing when it is going sort of on tiptoes, touching earth but not rolling on it. (September 14, 1974)

And again in 1976:

> If I and my work have meant something to you, that is very pleasant and I appreciate your generosity in saying so. Influence from other writers works on us all, of course; it is part of the continuity of language and literature. (November 6, 1976)

Recently, browsing through my file of John Graves letters, I came across a short handwritten message he sent in 1979:

> The cowdog piece was really fine. Keep it up. Regards, hastily, John G. (August 7, 1979)

I don't know to what piece of writing he was referring, probably something I had published in *Livestock Weekly* or the *Cattleman.* It must have been one of my earliest efforts to write in the voice of Hank the Cowdog. The first book in that series didn't appear until four years later.

I can't excuse the impertinence I showed in meeting J. Evetts Haley and John Graves, but I have treasured the time I spent in their company. Both are writers I admire and both of them helped to steer me back to my Texas roots . . . back to the stories my mother told me about the Shermans.

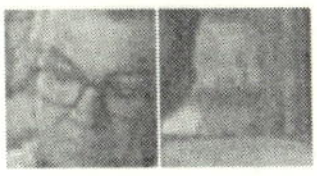

Texas Past, Texas Present

BILL HARVEY

Texas Past

No other place holds for me the magic of the Upper Brazos River. It was the favorite and frequent destination of my father and grandfather, both excellent outdoorsmen, who began taking me fishing in the early 1950s. We would rise early and point west from Fort Worth, first through Weatherford and then Mineral Wells to a crossroad's blinking light in the tiny town of Graford. My father drove with my grandfather on the front seat to his right, while I dozed on quilts covering the exposed rear seat springs of Dad's blue Ford sedan. There, in the near dark, I watched for falling stars through the car's rear window and listened to the tinny melodies of pre-FM western swing.

In early spring of the year, we minnow-fished for white bass in the Brazos below Possum Kingdom Dam, taking full advantage of that species' biological migration upstream to the impassable. But summer was my favorite because it meant catfish, caught on trotlines set after dark and checked every hour or so until sunrise. I especially liked camping there under the Comanche moon, because upon its rising over the river, its light chiseled the profile of an Indian in the limestone cliffs that rose above. He watched us in silence and vigilance as we fished in a river over which he and his people had once held complete dominion.

Older and alone, I canoed, fished, swam, and wandered that

stretch of river until my sixteenth summer and then did not see it again until returning from naval service in the spring of 1977. But I missed the Brazos terribly. It was a place and time like no other in my life, and upon returning there, even now, I still sense the faint smell of their pipe tobacco in the river's morning fog and hear their voices in the shallow riffles of the Brazos. How does such a place hold us so firmly in its grasp?

Thinking back to those days spent with the men of my family, it occurs to me that the places we hold most dear as adults are quite often the places where we were happiest in our youth. I mean, after all, there are friends who speak with fond remembrance of childhoods wrested from cornfields and two-room farmhouses in Nebraska. The Brazos River of the 1950s, as I knew it, was a place of endless wonder and adventure, a landscape that seemed to me just as wild as it was the day Anglo settlers came to Texas in the early nineteenth century. But that was the temporal romanticism of a boy born after the Brazos River Authority had, in the spirit of progress and rural electrification, already tamed its wildness. For me, the dam at Possum Kingdom was a wonder, humming with power and mystery. For others, it was a reminder of change rigidly fixed in time by a tall wedge of concrete and steel sunk between the rock walls of the river.

When John Graves returned to the Brazos River in late 1950s, it was no longer the river of his youth. He had known it long before any government of, by, and for the people flipped the switch on turbines tucked deep within Morris Shepard Dam and long before nearby highlines crackled with electricity destined for cities over the eastern horizon.

He realized that the "old" Texas was passing and that its future was blueprinted in part by plans to construct five dams on a relatively short piece of river: his river. So he set out to revisit a stretch of water that he, too, had known as a youth and that would surely be passing. From that trip, of course, came one of Texas' literary treasures.

It gradually came to me that aside from the wonder of the stories and philosophy found in his body of work, his writing represents both an important documentation of "Texas Past" and insight into what would become "Texas Present." It is clear that he was prescient in understanding that technology, engineering, and population growth would mean dramatic change for Texas. Although he could not know the magnitude of that change, his references to population expansion were prophetic as the state morphed from a rural to an urban population within a generation after World War II. Moreover, he clearly recognized that the growth of Texas' population would be dependent upon the availability of water and that additional water was dependent upon additional reservoir construction. In effect, water and population formed a positive feedback loop simply because population increase meant a need for more captured water. But water planners have never been satisfied with meeting current need and are always about planning for future growth, as we would expect, really. So more water was captured, which spurred more growth that in turn required more water. Still, Graves' inherent pragmatism reconciled his love of things wild with the stark fact that change, although perhaps painful to observe, is what it is—unrelenting, undeniable, and inevitable.

Part of the immense power, for me at least, of John Graves' writing in general and *Goodbye to a River* in particular is that its detail and description allow comparison of the ecological changes that have occurred over half a century in Texas. He is a link to the Texas that was and cannot be again. For example, the detail of his descriptions of flora and fauna lead me to believe that if John did not describe a plant or animal (for example) that occurs in the Brazos River today, then it was not there in 1959 or that he at least did not make that observation. Conversely, he references natural resources that are no longer to be found there. His writing, then, allows us to lift the lid off the box that holds our collective resource management and to tally our successes and failures. Without question, John is one of the finest writers to have come from Texas, but I would add, he is also one of the state's finest naturalists.

The sheer romance of *Goodbye to a River* beckoned me for twenty years, and so in the spring of 1997, I set out to retrace Graves' river course, to spend three weeks or so on the Brazos as he had done. I wanted to go for many reasons, to remember as well as forget, to experience the solitude and silence that were hard to find in twentieth-century Texas and are even harder now in the twenty-first. There were other questions: How had the river changed in almost half a century? Would any of it be recognizable from his writing? Had that Comanche, and my wild courage, evaporated with my youth? Was he still alive, and, if so, where might he be found?

I found Graves through an editor who had ushered his latest collection around the publication process, and he responded to a letter of self-invitation with grace. We spent most of a hot July afternoon going to the post office in Glen Rose and then retiring to his back porch to talk about Texas, the Marine Corps, and saltwater fishing. Eventually, conversation turned to his trip on the Brazos and the prospects for mine. He had taken the journey alone (save his pup), and I suggested to him that it might be a good idea to take a friend or two along for different parts of the three-week float. He answered immediately, "No, if I were you I would go alone. *It will sharpen the experience.*" He smiled broadly and added, "If you do that, you will find out how much you enjoy your own company, and you won't feel the need to keep anyone else occupied."

We parted in early afternoon with a handshake and a promise to see each other again in the fall or early in the next year. I asked if he might be interested in joining me, if for just a day, but he told me that his "knees just weren't up to it, but maybe we could make that run together another time." So, in the fall of that year my canoe slipped, as his had, into the water just downstream of the Possum Kingdom Dam, and I set out alone on a three-week search for Texas Past and Texas Present, at least a small part of it, the part that I wanted to remember. I traveled the river much as he had done, with the exception of the passage through what is now Lake Granbury, traversed in a kayak when the wind whistled sharply from the southeast. Possum Kingdom to Glen Rose, one hailstorm, two groups of canoe-challenged Methodists, and three weeks alone.

Texas Present

The river has changed in many ways, and in others it remains essentially the same. Its course is confined by the limestone country it traverses, exactly as it has been for millennia, so the Upper Brazos lacks the meandering, oxbow-tied character of the river as it crosses the flat coastal plain below. Stream flow is constant, if only a trickle, around thirty cubic feet per second most of the time. Still, the river does flow constantly, water reluctantly allocated by river authorities after long years of bio-battle established water as a necessity for all wildlife, all the time, in all the state. Not much water, maybe, but water *is* water, and sometimes just a trickle is enough for the fish and wildlife to prosper.

Still, the species and populations in the Brazos have changed remarkably from those described by John in the middle part of the last century. One in ownership of even the most untrained eye does not travel far before noticing that every cottonwood tree along its course appears to have been gashed near its base, the upper parts of the tree withered as the bark is stripped away and the underlying wood exposed. Some have been gnawed in half, while still others, attacked but too large to conquer, have been left in rodential frustration to survive, if survival is possible after such an attack.

The Brazos is replete with beaver, busy as reputed in their single-minded task of ridding soft-wooded trees from the entirety of the shoreline. On the second morning I was awakened by the gobble of turkeys and rose in the dark to photograph the sunrise on the cliffs across the river. In the early sunlight, a flight of perhaps twenty turkeys glided across upstream, looking from a distance like an archaic squadron of Lancaster bombers. Returning to my campsite, just over a low gravel hill, I spotted the only beaver I actually saw. My absence had lured him into the eddy of the river, where he circled my red canoe with interest and then disappeared with a slap. John did not mention the presence of beaver in his writing nor did he see any during his trip. They simply were not there.

In a state where beaver were rare, they now thrive, largely as a result of changes in water management and the slow stream release from innumerable floodwater-retarding structures built on private lands to ease erosion and provide water for livestock. They remain as industrious on private lands as they do in the public domain, burrowing underneath the banks of man-made ponds and dutifully hewing limbs to clog spillways and irritate their landlords. Who could have foreseen that the science of land terracing and hoarding rangeland precipitation would bring with it the large-scale return of a species symbolic of the American West?

Other species have returned as well. My binoculars found at least one osprey on the river each day, and on seventeen of twenty-one days, at least one golden eagle floated above the cedar trees. Five days brought sight of one or more American bald eagles, and on a single occasion a golden and a bald eagle floated above the river together, poorly camouflaged by the hundreds of buzzards that rode the updrafts of afternoon. Graves noted what he thought was the inevitable passing of eagles; they were birds that needed "big space, big time and big solitude" for their breeding. Insecticides played a part in it too, the reproduction of so many raptors affected by bioaccumulation of chlorinated hydrocarbons and the resultant eggshell thinning. But, somehow, society succeeded in halting the decline of its symbol, and breeding pairs now nest in Texas, triggering traffic jams when the birds choose to nest near state highways.

In some respects, we have been pretty successful in game management. There are more white-tailed deer, turkey, doves, and people in Texas today than at any time since the first land impresarios began herding immigrants up the Brazos River from the ports of the Texas coast. Those species that thrive in the presence of humans—white-winged doves, raccoons, and coyotes—appear to be quite satisfied with the current state of urban and suburban affairs. But those wild things that really do need big space—bison, antelope, bighorn sheep, bears, and wolves—have not fared nearly so well. The last of Charles Goodnight's herd of bison are tucked neatly behind the barbed-wire fences of a state park, and red wolves are gone from Texas. Still, restocking of antelope and sheep has been successful on the scale that humans can address, and black bear numbers are slowly increasing in the Trans-Pecos.

I suspect there are probably fewer ducks, though snow geese (another species for which Graves held a special romance and concern) are so plentiful now that their breeding grounds in the most northern reaches of the hemisphere are in danger of being denuded, and the daily bag limit for hunters in pursuit of snow geese is astronomical. Ducks, on the other hand, have suffered as the prairie potholes have dried up or have been converted to the very agricultural lands that feed geese in their southern migrations. Who could have predicted that the grain monoculture of the Midwest would result in so many changes in the birds of autumn on the Brazos?

Freshwater mussels, bivalves with colorful names like "pearly mussel" and "heel splitter" are virtually gone from the Brazos, disappeared from a stretch of river where they once were as numerous as the stars. Some say that these filter-feeding invertebrates were poisoned by agricultural runoff, others say the dams on the river changed the water chemistry faster than the mussels could adapt, and some scientists suggest that commercial "mussel hustlers" overharvested them for transport to the Far East and the cultured pearl industry. No one really knows why they disappeared, but they are gone. Once the delight of raccoons and curious boys, abandoned mussel shells now only rarely sparkle in the shoreline mud and then almost always in juxtaposition to the rather human handprint of raccoons.

The fish in the Brazos are much the same, with yet more species. Catfish, carp, sunfish, and freshwater drum will always inhabit these waters or at least as long as they remain habitable. Buffalo (the finned sort) still dart out from the gravel sandbars, leaving in their wake puffs of mud, and monstrous alligator gar still roll on the water's surface in the hottest days of summer. But the native largemouth and spotted bass of the 1950s—still slimmer and tougher than their reservoir counterparts—have been joined by a near relative, smallmouth bass, brought from places farther east and north to be stocked from hatcheries similar to that located below Possum Kingdom. Other nonnative fish have been purposely stocked in the Brazos, striped bass and rainbow trout, for example.

Game fish diversification came in an attempt to provide fishing opportunities in Texas, and for the most part these attempts have been successful or at least benign. But access to that man-made biodiversity is another matter altogether. Getting on the river now means staying on the river. The fragmentation of land in Texas has brought with it a new riverside landowner, one who is far less welcoming to strangers in canoes and to casual camping along the riverbank. Although Graves enjoyed and chronicled several forays out of the riverbed, he who today takes to the shore in search of legend or arrowheads runs the risk of a court appearance.

Despite the riverbed confinement, the very act of canoeing and camping along the Brazos is a far easier task, I think, than it was in the late 1950s. Maps and compasses are now the remnants of an archaic form of navigation, no longer necessary as constellations of satellites beam latitude and longitude to handheld GPS units. As long as the batteries hold out, one runs little risk of getting lost. Weather radios with severe-weather alerts remove the uncertainty of clouds on the horizon, and cellular phones mean instant communication. I often wondered what would have happened if John had been injured on his journey. Who would have known, and how would he have been found? But with GPS, a cell phone, and a credit card, one could have pizza delivered to Mount Everest if one so desired, and help can be summoned by the push of a button. Of course, one is not required to carry this technology along, but one finds it hard to argue with its utility.

Canoes are no longer canvas; rather they are now of more exotic materials, Kevlar and plastic, impervious to rocks and as stable as battleships. I did not build a fire in three weeks of travel, warmed instead by space-age fibers made from recycled plastic bottles and kept dry by materials that repel water and yet allow water vapor to escape from an overheated body. Food comes freeze-dried, and hunting for sustenance really no longer enters into the experience now unless one just wants to see how it feels. I did take along a shotgun, firing it once to take a mammoth squirrel that chattered at me from an overhanging branch. In homage to squirrels eaten in an earlier time by a different hunter, I cleaned, quartered, and fried it over a gas stove. It was *awful*—stringy, tough, and largely inedible. I don't recommend it.

Perhaps it is sufficient to know that we have won some battles and lost others, while some have come out about even. But in the long term, Graves' prophecy for Texas and its people will hold true, I am afraid. Those of us who live in Texas Present won't recognize Texas Future. Progress and growth, like motherhood and apple pie, are inherently good, and those wild things that disappear in their wake will not be missed by most, because most never had the chance to know them even in partial bloom.

Graves and I met again in March of 1998, just long enough to have him autograph the paddle I took on the trip and for me to give him the compass used over those three weeks. I thanked him profusely for his advice, that taking the trip alone had made all the difference in the experience. We walked back to my truck and talked for a moment before again shaking hands and wishing each other good luck. We would see each other again, we hoped.

As I started to leave and paused for a moment at the end of his drive, I watched him turn back toward his barn. He walked the slow, deliberate walk of a man his age, and as he passed through the doors and faded into the shadows, I wondered aloud if he could possibly have any notion as to the importance of his life and his life's work.

So it is and so it was on our river. Days owned by solitary young men, loners by nature, melancholy and introspective, each bound to a place that disappeared before his eyes and was the victim of his own hand. At the end of their last day on the Brazos, they will feel it, that sadness, and realize that the passing of those they loved and the certainty of their own mortality is part of it. Yet, they will take heart in the hope of return and the promise that both the water and the words will still be there, each holding the remembrance of what was—and a reverence for what is.

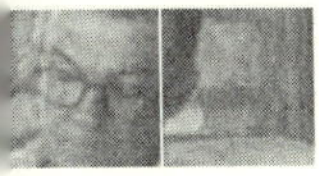

The Golden Age of John Graves

JAMES WARD LEE

ON A MORE OR LESS benighted panel discussion I conducted with A. C. Greene, Elmer Kelton, Benjamin Capps, and John Graves, I asked what they considered to be the Golden Age of Texas. I am not sure what answers I expected—probably something about the years of the Texas Cattle Kingdom between the end of the Civil War and the beginning of the twentieth century. Or maybe something about Spindletop or the days of the Republic. I think they all answered the odd and unhelpful question, but the only reply I remember is John Graves'. He said, "Fort Worth in the 1920s." For fifteen or so years I have wondered what he meant. Now I think I know. Some of his later writings may help to illuminate the answer. The first is his preface to Scott and Stewart Gentling's great portfolio of paintings of Texas birds. The second is in his recently published memoir, *Myself and Strangers: A Memoir of Apprenticeship*. The Gentling preface is reprinted in *A John Graves Reader* as "Self-Portrait, with Birds," in which Graves writes:

> In the simpler times I knew when growing up in Fort Worth, even we town youngsters had some almost unpeopled pieces of countryside, on the Trinity West Fork bottomlands and elsewhere, that were ours in exchange for a bit of legwork and a degree of sangfroid toward the question of trespass. Later on there were Depression country

> jobs in summer for a dollar or so a day and keep—wheat harvest, fence-building, and so on—and I can't remember a time when wild live things weren't a part of consciousness and when knowing something about them didn't matter. (3)

Graves was born in 1920 and spent what writers call "his formative years" in what was then west Fort Worth. Everyone talks of a person's "formative years," but nobody ever makes clear exactly when those years take place. Did Shakespeare spend his formative years in Stratford, or were they the early years after he went away to London about 1580 to work on the stage? I can't say about the great playwright, but I am pretty sure most people's formative years are those between birth and about fifteen or twenty. I have lived a long life, and yet, the things that happened to me in Leeds, Alabama, and in Birmingham between my birth year—1931—and the time I left Birmingham to go away to school—1945—are the years that haunt me and shape me and occupy much of my mind. Based on my experience and my ignorance, I submit that for Graves the Golden Years were the 1920s and a little beyond, maybe even up to the time he went away to Rice on the eve of World War II.

The things that impressed themselves on his consciousness during his early Fort Worth years lay fallow for a long time before he returned to his hometown and recaptured that past he so eloquently talks about in the essay on Texas birds. Reading the preface to the Gentling book and *Myself and Strangers* persuades me that the time Graves went away to Rice, was injured serving in the Marines, studied at Columbia, was married briefly, taught at the University of Texas for a short time, and set out for Europe to learn the writers' trade is what the Germans would call his Wanderjahre. It was a time of apprenticeship that Graves spent in a fog of selection and election before finding his true calling. He learned during those apprentice years that fiction was not his métier, and it was a hard lesson for him, one that may linger in some measure today if we can judge by his including a small amount of fiction in *A John Graves Reader.*

To some, an apprenticeship lasting well into a writer's thirties may seem excessive, but the war experience caused many returning combat veterans to take a longer time than most to readjust to a peacetime life. Therefore Graves' sojourn in Europe and his wanderings in Mexico are not all that different from what other veterans experienced following World War I and World War II. The experience of the American expatriates in Europe in the early 1920s reminds me a great deal of Graves' experiences in Mallorca and other places in the Old World. His long apprenticeship was not as fruitful as, say, Hemingway's, for Graves' stay in Europe did not result in great works. A fairly reliable source in Fort Worth who knew Graves' mother says that Mrs. Graves spent the fifties worrying that John would never "settle down and amount to anything." I think *Myself and Strangers* bears out the fears that Mrs. Graves had. The book details John Graves' years of drift and indecision. He is making his way with small writing successes and the disability pension he received for his injuries. He wanders from Mallorca to various parts of Europe, writing, agonizing over not writing, falling in and out of love, and spending time with the other expatriates who flocked to Europe after World War II, as well as with many Europeans of various countries. Throughout the book there is the constant sense of drift. There is the constant search for what he calls "the book." Once or twice, he breaks off his relationships with women because he cannot settle on one because he has not yet written "the book."

Graves' goal is to write fiction, though he does produce several travel essays for the money they bring. His failed novel, "A Speckled Horse," a part of which he reprints in *A John Graves Reader,* is, he hopes, "the book." He sends the completed manuscript to John Schaffner in New York and receives a "rather horrified letter listing in detail the reasons he disliked it." Graves calls the book "masculine, with hard edges" but says Schaffner's rejection "started me to thinking about it and reexamining it, and in the end I became dissatisfied with it myself and decided not to submit it anywhere, even though somebody would almost certainly have been willing to publish it. It was that good, containing long stretches of very strong writing. But it still wasn't as good as I had wanted it to be, and I had done all I could with it" (*Strangers,* 230).

Graves' reaction to the rejection is telling in many ways. It shows us the striving for perfection that marks his early career and is made manifest by his later successes with *Goodbye to a River, Hard Scrabble, From a Limestone Ledge,* and the many short pieces that have made him what someone once called "Texas' most beloved writer." Hardly anybody has ever quarreled with the perfection of *Goodbye to a River,* which became "the book" and which apparently has satisfied John Graves that he is indeed a writer of substance.

In *Myself and Strangers,* the three paragraphs following his comments on Schaffner's rejection, and his decision not to submit the novel elsewhere, answer many questions for me about Graves' Golden Years and bear quoting fully:

> So much for nearly two years of work that had been sporadic, yes, but full of belief in what I was doing. If you add in the months of thinking and note-making that led up to the writing, and the unproductive period of depression that ensued after I gave up the idea of publishing it, God knows how much time was involved. The whole matter threw me into a tailspin and I thought hard about abandoning my writing ambitions, because I viewed the long effort as a dead loss. I was getting along in years, but there was still time to go to medical school, or to study for the doctorate and turn myself into a genuine academic scholar.
>
> That mood did not last overlong, however. My "downs" have seldom seemed to do so, for there are always too many interesting things around to seize and hold my eyes and mind. . . .
>
> I had expected to move along elsewhere sooner or later, but my father came down with an esophageal cancer that required a horrendous operation, so I decided to stick around for however long a time I could be of help to him and my mother. And in the end this sticking around turned out to last forever. The years away from Texas, to my surprise, had accomplished something I had not anticipated or hoped for, allowing me to return to home grounds and family and social roots and to see them whole, and to live among them without either rebelliousness or chauvinistic pride. They were entirely mine, but were no longer a burden on my consciousness. (230–231; Graves' ellipsis)

I apologize for so much quotation, but in those paragraphs and in some that follow, I think we learn what Graves meant when he said his Golden Years were to be found in Fort Worth in the twenties. Back home after the years of wandering, the years that made Graves' mother—and probably Graves himself—despair of his ever settling down and "amounting to much," John Graves found the work that would occupy him, as he says, "forever."

Graves tells how, back in Fort Worth, he returned to many of the pursuits of his boyhood. He hunted and fished, he took nature walks with the local birding groups, and what may be most important for the writing of *Goodbye to a River,* he spent many hours of research in the city's Carnegie Library, reading up on the early days on the Texas frontier, on the struggles between the Indians and the whites, and on the general history of the region that is the subject of his book about a canoe trip down the Brazos. As Graves writes in *Myself and Strangers,* "I was no longer a speckled horse wandering to and fro among the bottomland myrtle trees. I was where I belonged" (231).

Well, almost. Actually it took Graves most of a decade to get back where he belonged, back to the Walden he created for himself on the four hundred acres near Glen Rose in Somervell County. But he was back in the Fort Worth of his Golden Years by the mid-1950s, teaching at Texas Christian University though he had no real ambitions as an academic. He bought the old wooden canoe that has since become famous, worked on it with paint and fiberglass, and took a trip down the Brazos River. His first trip in the early fifties was a prelude to the legendary one he took when the great Texas drouth of the fifties broke in 1957. And from that major trip came what Graves had so long sought in his Wanderjahre: "the book."

Goodbye to a River made Graves instantly famous, and its fame has spread from the date of its publication in 1960 until today. There is no need for me to tell a story that has been often told of how Graves became our Thoreau, how he has won every honor awarded in the state of Texas. There is almost never a statewide meeting or a gathering of scholars that does not want John Graves to appear. The Texas Book Festival, founded by First Lady Laura Bush, has given Graves its highest awards, the Texas Institute of Letters honored him with the Lon Tinkle Award for Lifetime Achievement, the Fort Worth Public Library made him a charter member of the Texas Literary Hall of Fame, and his photograph—sitting in front of a typewriter on his place at Glen Rose—graces the 1995 poster for Texas Writers Month.

Not too long after *Goodbye to a River* appeared, Graves gave up teaching and moved to the acres he bought in what was, and remains, a remote rural area fifty or sixty miles from Fort Worth. Better highways are allowing suburban creep to come close to Graves'

Hard Scrabble, the name he gave his property, but so far, he can lead the kind of life he chose for himself. He built the house and barns and sheds and fences himself. He has done what Thoreau planned at Walden Pond. Though I don't know that Graves has ever said so, I suspect that he, like Thoreau, decided to back life into a corner and strip away all that was not life and then decide whether it was good. He has not turned himself into a full-blown recluse and is still active at selected gatherings. But for the most part, he lives—perhaps I should say LIVES—on the Limestone Ledge he has written about so often.

John Graves is our Thoreau, our Aldo Leopold, our John Muir. Unlike many who have made a name as an ecologist, Graves has never taken a fanatical position against hunting and fishing, two pursuits he enjoyed in youth and well into middle age. He has done less of it in the years since removing himself to Hard Scrabble, but some of his writings mention his forays into nature with gun or angle. And unlike many ecologists, he never leads protests or preaches violently against the world that encroaches on nature. I know of no attack of Graves' that parallels Edward Abbey's assaults on "auto-tourism" in *Desert Solitaire.* John Graves lives the life that is an example to the serious environmentalist. He tends the land, nurtures it, uses it for his solace and reflection.

That patch of ground that is too small to be a ranch and too rocky to be a farm has become a place for pilgrimages. Glen Rose, once famous only for its dinosaur tracks along the Paluxy River bed, is now equally well known as the home of John Graves. I don't think Graves encourages acolytes, but he has been gracious to students of his work on occasion, and he spent a day with the *Fort Worth Star-Telegram* writer Jeff Guinn early in 2004 for a long feature in the newspaper. On my last visit to Glen Rose (not to visit Graves; I have never imposed myself on his solitude), I noted that there is no sign on the water tower announcing the town as the home of John Graves. Oxford, Mississippi, once considered painting on its water tower that the city was the home of William Faulkner. This was immediately after Faulkner won the Nobel Prize. The idea was quashed in favor of having a fish fry in the great writer's honor. I doubt that Glen Rose has ever even offered a fish fry in honor of its most distinguished resident.

PART THREE

Works

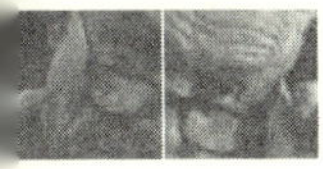

Haunted Landscapes

The Ecology of Story in John Graves' Texas

ALEX HUNT

IN TEXAS, environmentalism is a love for the land that cannot speak its name. While Texans are proud of their diverse landscapes of scenic beauty, land is foremost a commodity. This is true almost everywhere, of course, but in Texas, for reasons of cultural heritage and historical happenstance, the attitude seems remarkably entrenched. While the "Don't Mess with Texas" anti-litter slogan attempts to tap into Texas pride on behalf of the landscape, Texas has long encouraged entrepreneurs and corporate interests to mess with Texas with little environmental concern, even up to former governor George W. Bush's programs to encourage corporate voluntary controls on polluting emissions. As Pete Gunter and Max Oelschlaeger argue in *Texas Land Ethics* (1997), "When it comes to the land, Texas is a state of neglect," due in large part to a legacy of frontier exploitation. In my own Texas landscape of the Panhandle, feedlots, corporate hog farms, and Pantex rule the roost, and the Ogallala Aquifer, tapped by numerous wells for irrigation, industry, and residential use, edges toward depletion. While I may attempt to retreat from these concerns as I hike blissfully in Palo Duro Canyon State Park, these hikes typically tend to take me the other direction, further into the snarl of environmental issues. As I learn more about this landscape, and I understand what I'm seeing, the view becomes less scenic, characterized instead by neglect and absence.

In my learning about Texas landscapes, I owe much to my sense of

Texas history and natural history to John Graves, whose best-known work is the Brazos trilogy of *Goodbye to a River* (1960), *Hard Scrabble* (1974), and *From a Limestone Ledge* (1980). John Graves has for some time been lauded as a writer of Texas, the land, rural lifeways, and natural history but neither a nature writer nor an environmental writer in any political sense. More recent critical commentary on his work reveals some difference in opinion as to whether Graves might also be called a nature writer or even an environmentalist. This difference of opinion, however, is less over Graves than over what can be said to constitute nature writing and environmentalism. Larry McMurtry and many others have maintained that Graves is just too thoughtful to have something like an environmentalist politics. "He is popularly thought to be a kind of country explainer," McMurtry wrote in 1981, "when in fact he seems more interested in increasing our store of mysteries than our store of knowledge" (29–30). On the other hand, in her 1989 essay, Dorys Crow Grover explained, "In an ecological sense, and as a landsman working his home-owned ground, he belongs with the front-rank nature writers in his ruminations and observations about life in the edgelands or rural country rather than in a frontier wilderness" (5); this despite the sense that Graves, as she puts it, "seems to have little hope for better management of the natural resources" (6). In a 1997 essay, Craig Clifford noted:

> Graves is not the nature writer he's often considered to be, but someone who reflects on the entanglements of things human and things natural. He's no Roy Bedichek, no Annie Dillard, no Aldo Leopold. In a sense, he's less of a naturalist than Thoreau, although he's often dubbed the Texas Thoreau. Neither is John Graves an environmental activist. . . . By and large Graves has clung stubbornly, and wisely from an artistic standpoint, to ruminative, inconclusive considerations of human relations with nature. (576)

These assumptions—that to be "inconclusive" precludes being a nature writer or that to be an artist precludes being an activist—seem unfortunate and narrow, as does the sense that nature writing provides answers rather than mere entangled questions. Taking a more extreme position, one that seems overstated, Gunter and Oelschlaeger in their 1997 *Texas Land Ethics* characterize *Goodbye to a River* as a much-needed kind of book, the kind that presents "stories about real Texans in real places who articulate Texas environmental problems" (34). They describe the book as "an intensely personal and detailed account of the cultural and ecological changes wrought by the damming of the Brazos River" that helps urban Texans "grasp the ecological implications of the water flowing from their taps" (34). In his 1998 book, *State of Mind: Texas Literature and Culture,* Tom Pilkington remarks, somewhat more conclusively and correctly, to my thinking, that Graves' work has a thesis, which Graves states "over and over, in many different ways," which is that "nature does matter" and that "the character of a country is the destiny of its people" (48). Again, critics seem to differ on the question of whether Graves is a nature writer, depending on their sense of what a nature writer is and particularly the assumption that to be an environmentalist is to be polemical and to hold nature separate from and above culture. This is an assumption that needs questioning.

In recent academic discussions of environmentalist discourse, scholars have made the argument that in the well-intentioned rush to advocate nature and wilderness we have gone too far in the correct direction, writing ourselves as humans out of any acceptable or positive place within the natural world. William Cronon, to cite the most well-known example, writes that rather than wilderness idealism, "we need an environmental ethic that will tell us as much about *using* nature as about *not* using it." Such an ethic is essential because our ingrained nature/culture or wilderness/civilization binary construction "denies us a middle ground in which responsible use and non-use might attain some kind of balanced, sustainable relationship" ("The Trouble with Wilderness," 85). Cronon's criticism is applicable to literary and activist discourses that rely too much upon an ahistorical construction of the natural—"nature" being, after all, a very human construction.

In this context, John Graves should reach—deserves to reach—a new audience. Graves' work is the epitome of what seems to me a kind of hybrid creature called Texas nature writing. Texans are too steeped in lore and too aware of the blood-soaked earth beneath their feet to pretend, even fleetingly, that they might inhabit some Edenic wilderness. A contributing factor, to cite Tom Pilkington, may be that Texas is not known for sublime landscapes:

> For Texas writers, Texas is home, in the sense that it is the place where most of them grew up and that willy-nilly

> shaped their perceptions of the world. It is not, for them, a place of supernal beauty, a place that sets their souls aquiver. (For that kind of emotion, they ordinarily head for New Mexico or Colorado.) I think that, at some level of consciousness, Texas writers' primary allegiance is not to the land as a source of religious feeling—however broadly and loosely that term is defined—but to a land-based mythology that is the foundation of the Texas experience. (*State of Mind,* 39)

This "foundation," as we all know, can lead to a prideful kind of Texas nationalism associated with Confederate nostalgia and "Don't Mess with Texas"–type slogans on T-shirts and bumper stickers. A more recent favorite concerning George W. Bush's small coalition of the willing in Iraq is "Texas—it's bigger than France." But Graves is no cultural nationalist; he is, rather, preeminently thoughtful on his subjects of place, history, and nature. When one is thoughtful about these subjects, one quickly realizes how inextricably connected they are. Graves warns, for instance, at the outset of *Hard Scrabble,* that though his is a "place book" rather than a "people book," nevertheless "people inevitably edge into it from time to time." After all, as he explains, this is Texas, where the land "is weighted with human remembrances and ways of being, afflicted by them, rich with them, inseparable from them" (6). Graves knows that not only is the ecology of this place involved in human history but that the stories of the place continue to weight and shape it. In that stories affect the way people understand themselves and the way they behave, including the way they behave with respect to the land, there is in a real and material sense an ecology of story. In Graves' work, that sense of the ecology of story takes the rhetorical form of ghosts and hauntings.

Graves' awareness of ecology of story is evident in his thoughtful scrutiny of rural culture and folklore and its relationship to place and land. The stories that inhabit the landscape are a kind of haunting, as Graves suggests in *Goodbye to a River.* In the Palo Pinto country, through which Graves floats on his Brazos canoe trip, he tells stories of conflict and killing between settlers and Comanches: "Sometimes you take country for itself, for what shows merely, and sometimes it forces its ghosts too upon you, the smell of people who have lived and died there." This country, with "Comanche blood on the ground," is one that must be understood deeply in terms of its stories (36).

John Graves' landscapes are distinctive as instants of space and time composed of what was and what will likely be. Graves' Texas is clearly haunted by the violent history of western expansion, but it is also haunted by the future, by a looming sense of ecological change for the worse. Graves tends to speak the language of loss rather than of ecological crisis—for he is circumspect, never alarmist or polemical.

In fact, Graves, like certain of his critics, seems to share the assumption that environmentalism tends to be polemical. He writes of his book in the introduction to *Hard Scrabble:* "For the most part, I hope, it is unpolemical and does not seek to grind large axes or to give large answers." This work is "not the account of a triumphant return to the land, a rustic success story, but mainly a rumination over what a certain restricted and unmagnificent patch of the earth's surface has meant to me, and occasionally over what it may mean in wider terms" (5). Much the same could be said of *Goodbye to a River,* though its scope is slightly broader than the patch of land he names Hard Scrabble. Graves is clear that he wants not to be shrill but to ruminate. Of the impending loss of his beloved stretch of the Brazos to five more dams, he remarks: "When someone official dreams up a dam, it generally goes in. Dams are ipso facto good all by themselves, like mothers and flags. Maybe you save a Dinosaur Monument from time to time, but in-between such salvations you lose ten Brazoses . . ." (9; Graves' ellipsis). Graves' statement begins with a note of fatalism, but the remark about mothers and flags gives the ironic lie to the suggestion that dams are indisputably good. His ellipses suggest that he is ruminating, and that we should too. The loss of Glen Canyon to Lake Powell in 1963, an indirect result of the Sierra Club's successful defense of Dinosaur's Echo Park from the federal government's Colorado River Storage Project in the mid-fifties, has become a cautionary tale in environmentalist discourse. But Graves quietly reminded us in 1960 that unremarkable, unpristine river bottom should not be dismissed as unimportant. He's subtle.

Still, there is argumentation at work, subtle rather than shrill, more implicit than explicit, in Graves' work. One cannot simply discount his conservationist statements and his skepticism toward the kind of "progress" that is remaking the landscape. As he puts his canoe into the Brazos below Possum Kingdom, the dam is part of a complex, "a grim humming network of wires above squat finned transformers classified deadly by red-painted signs" (12). But because he is so thoughtful, Graves tends to seem ambivalent about progress, regarding it as an inevitable force that, in time, will play itself out, will undo itself. In *Goodbye to a River* (published two years before Rachel Carson's 1962 *Silent Spring,* a book based largely on the disastrous effects of DDT on bird populations), Graves notes that eagles "practically do not exist any more in our part of the country" (28). Graves says that he is not one who can appreciate species that adapt easily to humanized landscapes, that he prefers the wild animals: "the absoluteness of the spacious, disappearing breeds—of geese riding the autumn's southward thrust, of eagles, of grizzlies, of bison I never saw except in compounds . . . Of wolves . . . Of wild horses." But his rhapsody ends in ecological fatalism: "We don't deserve eagles; they will go" (29; Graves' ellipses). In *Hard Scrabble,* Graves ponders the fossil footprints of dinosaurs to be seen on his land and notes the way in which his own method is ill-suited to an environmentalist rhetoric:

> Clearly enough, things have been going on around Hard Scrabble for a good long while. In that perspective, a man's interest in any particular people's effect there, and his study of any particular community of wildlife and vegetation, and his groping efforts to "restore" the land to any particular sort of human use, are bound to look a little bit petty. And yet a man tries, anyhow. . . . (14; Graves' ellipsis)

Graves' way of trying—his particular, peculiar way of writing place; his engagement with history and folklore as elements of an ecology of story; his insistence on the human place in the landscape—is worthy of our attention and understanding. Graves is important from the standpoint of environmental writing because he teaches us of our embeddedness—for better and worse—in place. Yet the same can be said of many others to whom Graves bears comparison, including Wendell Berry and Gary Snyder. I want to suggest that Graves is uniquely important for his understanding of the role of stories, as a sort of ecological haunting, in shaping our flexible relations to place.

To illustrate this, I would like to focus for a time on a story that Graves tells more than once. In *Goodbye to a River,* he returns frequently to stories about Charles Goodnight, the Indian fighter and ranching pioneer of Texas. For Graves, Goodnight exemplifies the "old ones"—the pioneer Texans—who were products of frontier violence and the struggles to tame the land. It seems as if Graves feels the need to rescue Goodnight and his ilk from myth or at least a certain kind of myth of violent heroism that continues as "a raucous lie flooding out from bluely glowing television screens" (37). Instead, Graves wants to humanize such figures, which remain as the ghosts of the storied landscape. In terms of ecological acuity, Goodnight represents a type who—to a degree approaching the Comanches' "organic kinship to nature"—understood the country deeply (158). At the same time, however, this class of men and their descendants "have burned out and chopped out and plowed out and grazed out and killed out a good part of that natural world they knew" (159). This kind of pioneering and expansionism led, for instance, to the general demise of the buffalo, which along with predators like the wolf and mountain lion also haunt the landscape. Stories emerge, as one told by "a friend of a friend" of Graves who stumbled upon "a full-grown buffalo" that "lumbered off into the brush" (55–56). Graves remarks that its presence was unaccountable "unless it had escaped from one of the big ranches a good bit farther west, where well-to-do descendants of the old ones have a few small keepsake herds under heavy wire" (56). This reference to ranchers' buffalo herds leads back to Goodnight.

Considering the particular story of Goodnight's buffalo and Graves' use of it will, I think, illustrate his style of environmental writing and his environmental philosophy with some depth and clarity. This story is of great significance for Texans, westerners more generally, and even for Americans who have learned a certain corpus of myths of American nationhood that cohere around the frontier. The story is of Charles Goodnight, the frontiersman, scout with the Texas Rangers, and pioneering rancher of the West Texas southern plains. While the setting of Goodnight's story is a little beyond Graves' usual hardscrabble place, the connection is that Goodnight's first ranching enterprises took place in the Big Keechi country, and he lived near Black Springs as a boy, places Graves passes early in his float of the Brazos. But the story of Goodnight and the buffalo takes place near Palo Duro Canyon, where Goodnight later ranched at the edge of the canyon caprock and the southern high plains. In part, then, I admit that I am interested in Graves' story because of my own growing love and familiarity with this semiarid region and its history. More significantly, this story is of great importance to issues of history, race, and nature in Texas and beyond. And it is noteworthy that Graves returns to Goodnight often in his most famous book. The story is so important because it has to do with the transformation of the region by those Graves refers to as "the old ones" or the

"Anglo-Ams" who "tamed" the region, and in particular to do with the removal of the Comanche and Kiowa peoples to Oklahoma and the hunting to virtual extinction of the buffalo.

In brief, the story is that in the days after the Comanches were established on their Oklahoma reservation, a party of Comanche men, including some elders, traveled by horseback to ask a gruff old West Texas rancher—an old friend and onetime adversary—for a buffalo bull from the herd that the rancher kept. Goodnight—or a rancher of the same ilk and generation—resists at first but eventually gives in, presuming that they intend to bring the animal back with them to their reservation. Instead, they kill the buffalo with arrow and lance, in the way of a bygone era, before riding sadly away.

Graves first used this bit of folklore as the source for a short story. The story, called "The Last Running," was an important early success for Graves when it was published in the *Atlantic Monthly* in June 1959. It was subsequently included in *The Best American Short Stories 1960*, later published as a slim illustrated book in 1974 and 1990, and finally included in *A John Graves Reader* in 1996. In the meantime, Graves also included a brief version of the story, in a more anecdotal or folkloric voice, in *Goodbye to a River*. Graves comments on his use of the story in a couple of other places. He expressed some concern in a 1959 letter to his editor at Knopf—preserved in *John Graves and the Making of "Goodbye to a River": Selected Letters, 1957–1960*—while the book was in production. His concern over "the Charles Goodnight buffalo anecdote" is twofold. First, it is of uncertain origin: "I've heard that [story] about at least two people and am uncertain of its truth. It's been written down in another form in an obscure little book of memoirs somewhere, purporting there to be about Goodnight" (Hamrick, 26). But Graves is chiefly concerned that the *Atlantic Monthly* may object to his reuse of the story, though, as he notes in the book manuscript, "the form is different, condensed here and given as fact rather than fiction, though a little of the phraseology may be the same" (26). Much later, Graves discusses the story in a talk for the Texas Folklore Society that he gave in 1984. Here he uses it as an example of a writer's appropriation and "perversion" of folklore for his own purposes. The Goodnight buffalo anecdote, he remarks, "ties up a lot of historical meaning and feeling . . . and I have used it twice, once in a book in more or less factual, bare-bones form, and later in that short story where I could play with it and shape its meanings." Graves is emphatic that his use of the story had no obligation to historical or folkloric accuracy: "By the time I got through with it, I had made it so much my own that I didn't, and don't now, have the least idea of where I'd first run across it. By then it was purely mine. I had robbed somebody of it utterly" ("Folklore and Me," 6). But despite Graves' comments—in part a teasing of the friendly audience of Texas folklorists—he is well aware that a story cannot be "purely" one's own in this fashion; he has shaped it, but its significance, suggested by the cultural values evoked by the legend of Goodnight and the story of the buffalo, is a source of power that he taps into rather than something he owns.

Each version of the story is styled as appropriate to Graves' particular use in its context. The fictional story "The Last Running" is the more conventional or generic, a well-crafted short story. A first-person narrative, the story is a rather nostalgic one of cowboys and Indians who are, in turn, nostalgic about their respective frontier glory days. Both the rancher Tom Bird (who, in this version, replaces Goodnight, but who got his buffalo herd from Goodnight's and ranches somewhat south of Goodnight's former range) and his Comanche counterpart, Starlight, agree that they live in an inferior age. Though both old and ill, they know that in their youth they were actors on a legendary stage. In the immediate setting of the story, the two old men stand on a ranch located "in the canyon country where the Cap Rock falls away to rolling prairies, south of the Texas Panhandle" (*Reader*, 114). But Starlight and Tom Bird first met in skirmishes years before in "the Brazos country" and the "Keechi Valley near Palo Pinto" (117). In these places, in the 1860s and '70s, the men had been part of the bloody conflicts between Comanches and Texans. Bird is great-uncle to the story's narrator, who, Bird complains, is too young to have ever seen much "worth seeing" (114). The nephew regards his great-uncle, aged eighty-five in the year 1923, as "one of the real ones" (114). Tom Bird refuses Starlight's request for a buffalo. These animals, "the fourteen pampered bison," are penned in a "double-fenced pasture near the house," where Bird could "watch them from his chair in the evenings" (115). The narrator informs us that Bird "had bred them from seed stock given him in the nineties by Charles Goodnight, and the only time one of them had ever been killed and eaten was when the governor of the state and a historical society had driven out to give the old man some sort of citation" (115). The buffalo, we are made to understand, are not only valuable for Bird for nostalgic reasons but are important for historical and symbolic reasons to Texas. As Starlight wears down Bird's stubborn refusals, the Comanche elder appeals to times past. Americans of the present age, Starlight points out, talk of liberty, but "not one of you has ever seen liberty, or smelled it. Liberty was grass, and wind, and a horse, and meat to hunt, and no wire" (122). The hunt itself is by no means glorious, and the narrator reflects on the rather inept killing: "It was not fair. Fair did not seem to have much to do with what it was" (126). The killing is not ceremonial, either, but a chase that gives the Comanches a taste of the old ways, as Tom Bird explains: "Because old as they are, they ain't old enough to have hunted the animal that for two whole centuries was the main thing their people ate, and wore, and made tents and ropes and saddles and every other damn thing they had out of" (124).

After the killing of the buffalo—and Starlight settles for nothing less than the old bull named Shakespeare for their prey—Starlight gives to Tom Bird a lance with an iron point, the same point with which Starlight had menaced Bird in an earlier encounter in more dangerous times. The gift is evidence of Starlight's final comment, "We were there, Tom Tejano" (126). The old men's bond is based on this insistence of the reality of the past and their authentic participation in that history. The young narrator of the story notices that as the Comanche men ride off, Tom Bird is crying, and the story ends with the old rancher's salty curse: "'Damn you, boy,' he said. 'Damn you for not ever getting to know anything worth knowing. Damn me, too. We had a world, once'" (127). These final words reiterate the old man's feeling that his great-nephew, through no fault of his own, was a lesser individual for having been born too late. But the touch of self-blame at the end, and the rancher's sense that the world itself was once whole but is now fallen, is intriguing.

On a first reading of this story, without a sense of Graves' work as a whole, one could—and with reasonable justification—quickly write this story off as an example of what Renata Rosaldo has called imperialist nostalgia, in which an "attitude of reverence toward the natural developed at the same time that North Americans intensified the destruction of their human and natural environment" (*Culture of Truth,* 71). A prime example of imperialist nostalgia, after all, is Goodnight's preservation of a small buffalo herd at a time when the buffalo were being commercially hunted out of existence; in a remarkable silent film that Goodnight produced in 1916, entitled *Old Texas,* he uses the medium to valorize himself as the benevolent preserver of the "buffalo race." To romanticize Goodnight—as some historians and writers have done—as the protector of plains ecology is to perpetuate this imperialist nostalgia. For a Texas writer to represent an aging rancher and his aging Comanche nemesis as yearning for the good old days of free-range buffalo slaughter and interracial violence could certainly be called imperialist nostalgia, as well.

But the folkloric version of the story that Graves includes in *Goodbye to a River* offers a characteristically more ambivalent stance toward this tale of Texas history. "A tale exists," Graves begins, in passive construction, for as he explains, "I heard it once about Goodnight and once about another of the old ones who stayed alive long enough to get rich, and it may not be true of either of them. But it could be true—ought to be" (62). Graves begins *Goodbye to a River* with a prefatory note explaining that his book's "facts are factual" but that it also "has some fictionalizing in it." He thus effectively gives himself free reign to report, include, and improvise as suits him. His statement that the Goodnight story "could" but at any rate "ought to be" true, I think, not only indicates that Graves thinks it's a good story, but suggests—again—that the story is of great significance to the region and beyond. Graves continues the story, placing it on "the Quitaque ranch" when "Goodnight was old." Once, Graves writes, "a scraggly band of reservation Comanches, long since whipped and contained, rode gaunt ponies all the way out there from Oklahoma to see him" (62). Graves does not go into the backstory of the so-called Red River War that led U.S. troopers, under Colonel Ranald Mackenzie, to defeat the Comanches and Kiowas by burning their provisions and killing more than 1,400 horses. But Graves does summarize that history rather well and powerfully: "No buffalo had run the plains for decades; it was their disappearance, as much as smallpox and syphilis and Mackenzie's apocalyptic soldiers, that had finally chopped apart The People's way of life" (62–63). What Graves highlights here is the role of ecocide—the slaughter of the buffalo—within a larger genocidal process, as suggested by the "apocalyptic soldiers" who followed Mackenzie's orders in his scorched-earth campaign. While subtle, Graves' quiet words are deeply troubling in implication. They are crafted as incentive to read more of this history, to pursue these ghosts to other sources.

But in *Goodbye to a River* Graves romanticizes neither the Comanches nor ranchers like Goodnight. As to the disappearing buffalo, for instance, as we continue through the story, Graves says, "Jealously,

Mr. Charlie had built up and kept a little herd of them" (63). And in initially refusing the hunters' request, Goodnight first denies the Native peoples' moral claim to the land and its animals and then declares his own heroic mastery: "'They used to be anybody's that could kill one,' the old man said. 'These are mine. They wouldn't even be alive if it wasn't for me'" (63). In this version of the story, the rancher's ownership of the buffalo seems self-aggrandizing, and the decision to allow them a bull, which in the fictional version is the result of humorous exasperation and genuine friendship, here seems more the result of Goodnight's crisis of conscience. His decision gives the lie to his words. The ending of the story is largely the same in each version; in *Goodbye to a River,* Graves writes: "They ran it before them and killed it with arrows and lances in the old way, the way of the arrogant centuries. They sat on their horses and looked down at it for a while, sadly and in silence, and then left it there dead and rode away, and Old Man Goodnight watched them go, sadly too" (63). The "arrogant centuries" refers to Graves' treatment of Texan-Comanche conflict in a manner that lays a heavy share of the blame for that violence and removal on the Comanches' taste for war and unwillingness to compromise, a discussion in which Graves does romanticize them in unfortunately bloody terms.

It bears mention here, I think, that the Kiowa author N. Scott Momaday, in his autobiographical and ethnographic work of cultural memory called *The Way to Rainy Mountain* (1969), tells another version of the Goodnight buffalo story, as related to him by his grandmother, that reveals an alternative cultural perspective with key differences:

> The last Kiowa Sun Dance was held in 1887 on the Washita River above Rainy Mountain Creek. The buffalo were gone. In order to consummate the ancient sacrifice—to impale the head of a buffalo bull upon the medicine tree—a delegation of old men journeyed into Texas, there to beg and barter for an animal from the Goodnight herd. (10)

In this account, the killing of the buffalo takes on cultural meaning of which Graves seems unaware; for the Kiowa and Comanche peoples, as Momaday puts it, the end of the buffalo constituted nothing less than "deicide" (10).

I should say that I do not consider my knowledge of Goodnight and the buffalo by any means definitive, but rather I have an ongoing interest sparked in large part by Graves. In the various histories I have perused, I do not find the authoritative account of Goodnight and the buffalo. In this sort of case the truth is likely to be much like chasing ghosts: it is more a matter of gathering the stories than capturing the fact of it. And in any case it was not Graves' purpose to nail down the history so much as to make some use of it. Nor is it my purpose here to question Graves' construction of Comanche history, which is an account far more sympathetic and thoughtful than Texas writers have traditionally provided. But Graves was successful to the extent that he made me pursue a line of questioning, and that is what I am arguing is the essence of Graves' environmental rhetoric.

It seems to me, finally, that in his use of the Goodnight story Graves opens up a series of disturbing questions all interlocked with Texas history and the ecology of the land that he loves. The method, again, is to present place as haunted by the ghosts of history and lore. At another point in *Goodbye to a River,* Graves has a nightmare of murderous Comanches and Kiowas along the Brazos, which blends into thoughts of his service in the Pacific during World War II, where he had known fear. The killings along the Brazos "had been a long time ago, but the place was eerie in the fog." The barking of his companionable dog breaks the spell, "scattering ghosts with sharp sound" (40). Graves' invocation and disturbance of these ghosts in the landscape are his way of reminding his readership of what the earth has been and what has been made of it. The ghosts of Goodnight and the Comanches who may have come to him for a buffalo to kill, as well as the ghosts of the vanished buffalo herds of the Southern Plains, haunt this landscape, and Graves wants us to consider it. Such considerations do not lead to easy conclusions or polemical rhetoric on Graves' part, nor does he wish to provide easy answers for his readers. Rather than going on the kind of environmentalist tirade that Edward Abbey, in "The Damnation of a Canyon" and other writings, often did, Graves seems to think that understanding of landscape requires some knowledge of human and environmental history, that knowledge of that history implicates our individual consciousness and conscience in regard to landscape. This is why Graves feels that he must keep the ghosts of the landscape alive, lest we forget our role, our responsibility, in the nature of place.

Writing place is no simple matter. In *The Environmental Imagination,* Lawrence Buell reminds us that "place is related to complacency psychologically as well as etymologically; we reassure ourselves by converting abstract space into familiar place and subsisting in the unconsciousness of its familiarity" (261). Graves' ghosts and the bloody havoc they wreaked on the banks of the Brazos do not allow us that comfort. I am reminded of Keith Basso's description of Western Apache belief that people can be stalked by stories and that stories reside in places. Stories are instructive, reminding people through example of what constitutes proper and improper behavior, and stories are typically related to particular features of the landscape. So, explains Nick Thompson, when someone has told you a story, implicitly reminding you how to behave,

> you won't forget that story. You're going to see the place where it happened, maybe every day if it's nearby and close to Cibecue. If you don't see it, you're going to hear its name and see it in your mind. It doesn't matter if you get old—that place will keep on stalking you like the one who shot you with the story. Maybe that person will die. Even so, that place will keep stalking you. It's like that person is still alive.
>
> Even if we go far away from here to some big city, places around here keep stalking us. If you live wrong, you will hear the names and see the places in your mind. They keep on stalking you, even if you go across oceans. The names of all these places are good. They make you remember how to live right, so you want to replace yourself again. (Quoted in Basso, 59)

Although Graves is not emulating indigenous ways, I find that his use of folklore functions in a manner similar to this Western Apache idea of stalking with story. The story of Goodnight and the buffalo and the Comanche riders should stalk our consciousness in a manner that does not allow us to take place for granted and that requires us to think both about what is present in the landscape and what is absent or what has been absented.

If "The Last Running" smacks of imperialist nostalgia, the *Goodbye to a River* version attempts to haunt the landscape with a troubled and troubling history that in a nutshell shows us Graves' method of environmental writing. Rather than some sort of wilderness idealism, Graves implicates the scenery in a violent history of dispossession, death, and exploitation. Graves shows the land as, to borrow from Aldo Leopold, a biotic community and humans as, for better and worse, members of that biotic community:

> Neither a land nor a people ever starts over clean. Country is compact of all its past disasters and strokes of luck—of flood and drouth, of the caprices of glaciers and sea winds, of misuse and disuse and greed and ignorance and wisdom—and though you may doze away the cedar and coax back bluestem and mesquite grass and side-oats grama, you're not going to manhandle it into anything entirely new. It's limited by what it has been, by what's happened to it. And a people, until that time when it's uprooted and scattered and so mixed with other peoples that it has in fact perished, is much the same in this as land. It inherits. (237)

This certainly sounds like the work of a writer with excellent understanding of ecology, the study of the interrelationships between living organisms and their environments. Is this not also—remember the quagmire of critical assessments in this vein—the work of an environmentalist or a nature writer?

Obviously, I think so. And I find that Graves' brand of environmentalism and environmental activism comes not despite but through the very circumspection that others feel disables any environmental critique. At a 1983 conference on Texas literature, Graves spoke of writers he considers his immediate predecessors, the Texas trinity of Webb, Bedichek, and Dobie. In concluding his talk, titled "The Old Guard," he argued for the relevance of these writers' work, which is "still furnishing resonance, echoes, layers of meaning in our southwestern surroundings" (24). These "Old Three," Graves said, "believed, with differing emphases, in the lastingness of human dependence on nature and on natural connections" (25). While Graves does not count himself among the "ecology freaks" who discovered Webb's wisdom twenty years after his warnings, he does include himself in another category:

> We nature-heads are and always have been a fairly numerous body, including as we do maybe half or more of the poets who have written in English through the centuries, speaking in one vein or another about the links between

> men and earth. If I wanted to get up on a soapbox, which I don't, I could extend a quivering oratorical finger at you and could maintain at length—tritely perhaps, boringly without a doubt, but validly nonetheless—that upon awareness of such links may hang our grubby and sometimes glorious human species's very survival on this planet. (25)

I think that it is Graves' persona as what he dubs the "Old Fart," rather than any deep philosophical or aesthetic reasons, that restrains him from joining up, at least in spirit, with the environmental movement in more explicit ways. He wonders in *From a Limestone Ledge* "whether there is really much difference between these rather modish activities mobilized beneath the banner of ecology, and a lot of ancient practices and attitudes that have limped along . . . under a crude tattered ensign labeled Need" (58). Conservation and Thoreauvian simplicity, in other words, have always been necessary in difficult times, as country people know, and are good practices in all times. What "Old Farts" and "nature-heads" have over "ecology freaks," evidently, is a story to tell rather than an activist's rhetoric. Despite Graves' evident distaste for that sort of oratory, he clearly regards his own writing as working toward the same ecological goals but with less alarmist talk, more advocacy of thoughtfulness.

Nevertheless, in some of Graves' lesser-known essays, as in the previous example, I find him explicitly environmentalist in his statements. I wonder why Graves did not see fit to include in his 1996 collection, *A John Graves Reader*, some excerpt of his lengthy 1971 essay on Texas water use, "Texas: 'You Ain't Seen Nothing Yet,'" or the fine essay published in *Atlantic Monthly* in 1975 entitled "The Hard-Used Land." The former essay on water in Texas, which surely was influenced by Graves' work on the Potomac River for Udall at the Department of the Interior from 1965–1968, is an ecological critique of mismanagement and pollution. If it is not exactly polemical, it is certainly clear. Graves speaks eloquently and forcefully on the subject of the effect of polluted rivers on marine life in Texas estuarial bays. These areas are "rich with life," but the estuaries "have been abominably mistreated," and "no one really knows yet how much damage has already been done, or how permanent it is, or how more damage might be averted" (33, 35). But Graves' most emphatically environmentalist statement of which I am aware comes in the article "The Hard-Used Land." His annotation of this article in a bibliography of his work briefly states, "Commissioned and all right as I recall, but now dated. The tribulations of the Texas landscape" (Hamrick, 92). His recall does not give it enough importance, because in this essay Graves links Texas frontier mentality directly to exploitive land use. He begins with a bioregional critique of human borderlines, concluding that from a bioregional perspective there is no essential "Texan-ness" to Texas. What matters about regional variance, however, is "natural vegetation and beasts and birds and the patterns of human land use, and the interplay among them" (91): an admirable statement of ecology. One fact that matters, Graves continues, is that many Texas regions are some sort of grassland, which spelled big trouble as American settlement ensued. The article is then divided into sections bearing the subtitles "Squandering the Topsoil," "Chemical Farming," "The Quest for Water," and "Where Is the Wilderness?"

As I suggested, the matter-of-fact way in which Graves links Texas frontier heritage to environmental despoliation in this essay is noteworthy: "Relatively brief history has stomped around in Texas with abrasive boots on" (92). People Graves terms "Anglo-Celtic southern yeomen" were "tough and alert" but also "unencumbered with ambivalent attitudes," and they "assaulted the land's fertility as their kind and kin had been doing on American frontiers for two centuries and more" (92). This sort of "leapfrogging to fresh land" after wearing out the last would be problematical enough were it not for the grasslands, which were delicate and increasingly arid as settlement moved west: "In vulnerable places irreplaceable topsoil gradually vanished—a sort of cumulative disaster, of which the most flamboyant symptom was the Dust Bowl of the 1930s" (93). Considering the loss of ecological integrity, habitat, and wildlife, Graves—approaching Texas heresy, I should think—blames frontier-legacy agricultural practice as that force which "subjugated Texas" (94). Though farming practices have improved, Graves thinks, the age of "chemical fertilizer" is not without its dangers, because "the effects of it radiate outward" (95). And though industrial irrigation seems a boon, the overdraft of reservoirs, especially on the delicate High Plains, is frighteningly unsustainable: "On the High Plains the disproportion [of use vs. recharge] is horrific, and the Ogallala [aquifer] has been sinking in recent decades like straw-sucked Coca-Cola in a glass" (95). High plains agricultural success is "essentially a form of frontier exploitation of a limited resource, like nineteenth-century lumbering and mining and move-along farming and ranching" (96)—more heresy. Finally, in "Where Is the Wilderness?" Graves blames Texas land policy for privatizing the territory to the extent that little "wilderness"—by which he means a reasonably sized section of land left in an undeveloped state that could serve for wildlife habitat—remains. That wilderness that does exist is thanks to the feds, in the form of national parks and wildlife refuges. And finally, Graves concludes with a hallmark of environmental writing, the dire warning and injunction to get smart, qualified as befits Graves' signature circumspection:

> Reality lurks somewhere ahead, ready to confront us again, and despite astronautics and all that, reality is still primarily the earth that shaped us and feeds us and sustains us and will accept our bodies when we die. That the Texas land and the American land should have been sorely abused by history was inevitable: men always abused new land when they could manage to do so, and have had a hell of a good time at it; and we on this continent had better tools for the job than most other civilizations have had. That we will continue to abuse it in the future may be somewhat less inevitable. One hopes so, for the destination of such a course seems all too clear.
>
> The main hope, I suppose, is that we will at last grow up. (97)

These essays are important evidence that Graves has always had environmentalist inclinations, but they are less important than his Brazos and Hard Scrabble books. I am not coming full circle to agree with the critical assessment that important literature cannot be explicitly environmental in its politics. Rather, my view is that *Goodbye to a River* is Graves' most powerful environmentalist statement, though admittedly powerfully understated. Graves method of landscape circumspection, finally, speaks more powerfully of his environmental ethos than does his environmental oratory, in which he rarely indulges. Graves' method implicitly asserts that we have to understand the Brazos bottomland in terms of, for one example, Goodnight and his life and legend and in terms of how people have retold that legend and made sense of it. Just as we must understand the land in order to understand what is becoming of the people, we have to understand the people in order to understand the land. We must understand fully the ecology of story in order to understand what happened to the land historically, culturally, and ecologically, and why it happened.

In the end, it seems to me that Graves' writing gets us somewhere in furthering our understanding of a central ambivalence in environmentalism and nature writing: where does the human intersect with the natural in a positive rather than a destructive way to show us that one can be simultaneously regionalist, humanist, and environmentalist? I think Graves offers us an admirable answer. If we cannot hold this writing as environmentalist in its significance, then we simply have been considering nature writing and environmentalism wrongly. If environmentalism is not compatible with profound thoughtfulness, then we risk a pedantic and thoughtless environmentalism.

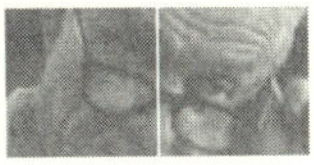

Goodbye to a River and American Environmental Literature

TERRELL DIXON

IN THE ALMOST FOUR and a half decades since its first publication in 1960, *Goodbye to a River* has become a classic of American environmental literature.[1] Even amidst the striking proliferation of books about nature and the environment during this period, John Graves' narrative of his trip down the Brazos River remains one of the most important books in the field.

This is due in part to its subject matter. From our perspective in the first part of the twenty-first century, this book's quiet protest against plans for new dams has an eerily prophetic quality. In a time when thoughtful citizens are becoming more and more aware of the value of water and have begun to rethink how we see rivers and dams, aquifers, water supply, water use, and water ownership, *Goodbye to a River* clearly speaks to our concerns. As it acknowledges these issues, it also reminds us of other values that come with free-flowing river waters, of their worth both as sites that can tell us much about our culture's history with the land and as wild places.

The book's importance, however, stems from more than its prescience about water issues. It is a decidedly local book, providing a much-needed focus on nature in a state that most often has promoted growth while ignoring its environmental consequences. *Goodbye to a River* does this in ways that bring some of the traditional values and concepts of environmental literature to bear on a specific Texas place and that incorporate these values into a vision of the natural world that is unique to John Graves. This application and extension of the perspectives of American ecological literature would not be nearly so effective, however, without what is perhaps the defining characteristic of *Goodbye to a River,* its style. This style—flexible, carefully nuanced, and superbly suited to the task of involving the reader in an appreciation of the Upper Brazos River country—is ultimately what makes this book succeed on such a high level and thus solidifies its place in American ecological literature.

John Graves clearly has his quarrels with Henry David Thoreau, but despite the gentle mockery of "Saint Henry" as a somewhat priggishly self-righteous, preachy voice, *Goodbye to a River* embodies some key features of what Thoreau espoused as our right relation to nature. Graves' Brazos, like Thoreau's *Walden,* offers the virtue of solitude. It is a place where "men and women are scarce," and his trip downriver is a welcome break from "the habit of people" (3, 34). The river trip with all the gear he carries is also a journey that leads Graves to remember the wisdom of Thoreau's exhortation to "Simplify, simplify!" (68).

How John Graves describes what he sees is also very much in the tradition of American nature literature from Thoreau to the best contemporary nature writing. The blend of evocative description with careful attention to the processes and cycles of the natural world that characterizes this narrative can be seen as he approaches Eagle Creek:

> That afternoon I got only to Eagle Creek, still probing uncourageously against weather's ire. Rounded gray-stone cliffs stand beside the creek mouth; in the river itself massive, split-away, rhombic blocks twist and slow the green current of a long pool. Big oaks gone red, and yellowed ashes rose precariously from slanted alluvial soil beneath the cliffs, piles of drift against their boles in prophecy of their own fate; it is on the outside tip of a bend, and in those places the river lays down rich sediment for maybe centuries and then in a fit of angry spate cuts under it and carries it away, trees and all. . . . A canyon wren was singing there; one always is. They love high rocks above water, and the wild falling song itself is like a cascade. (41; Graves' ellipsis)

Solitude and attentiveness to the natural world also offer the possibility of connection to a larger life force that drives the natural world that we see around us:

> But there have always been some of the others, the willful loners. And out alone for a time yourself, you have some illusion of knowing why they are as they are. You hear the big inhuman pulse they listen for, by themselves, and you know their shy nausea around men and the relief of escape. Or you think you do. (84)

While this "big inhuman pulse" is not exactly the Oversoul so important to the thinkers of nineteenth-century Concord, it is related to that earlier notion of a larger force informing and shaping the natural world, a force that we humans, if we choose to do so, can know. The narrative suggests that those who choose solitude amidst the natural world of twentieth-century Texas can connect with a larger life force that infuses the nature that they see and experience.

Goodbye to a River also shares with *Walden* the wish to redefine the meaning of land ownership. Graves' views continue Thoreau's argument, made as he contemplates the meaning of land ownership in the "Where I Lived, and What I Lived For" section of *Walden.* Ownership, true ownership, is more a matter of experience and observation than of money and legal title papers. Those attuned to the natural world possess the valuable part of the landscape:

> The Brazos belonged to me that afternoon, all of it. It really did. The autumn-blue sky (fair skies in Texas at other times of year tend to be white, bleached), the yellow-white air, the cedars and oaks green and gold and red, the rocks the size of buildings, the sun on my back, the steady, comfortable stroke of the paddling, mohair goats kowfl-ing at me from the shore when they caught my scent . . . Belonged to me and the whistling birds and the unseen animals. . . . People's sounds and a consciousness of them touched me from time to time . . . but it was fall, and they weren't on the river. It was mine. (Graves, *Goodbye,* 52; first ellipsis is Graves')

While quiet, complex, and persuasive reflection is certainly the dominant mode of *Goodbye to a River,* the book also includes some few outbursts of social criticism that do seem much like Thoreau. One example is this descriptive catalog:

> Under a cedar stood a table made from an old barbed-wire reel set on its side. Strewn thick about it were layers of that heterogeneous litter whose concoction is one of our glittering talents as a people: paper napkins and brown sacks rain-molded to grass and shrubbery; bullet-pierced beer cans brightly plated and painted against the rust that alone might have made them bearable; bottle caps and bottle shards; a yellowed latex memento of love's futility; tarnished twenty-two shell cases by the hundreds. (64)

Graves also observes that we are "a people whetted sharp to go places, to wear things out and move on, to take over and to use and to discard" (48). He argues that we have a pride in our destructive powers that prompts us to shoot the best that we have: "We don't deserve eagles; they will go" (29).

It is such ties to Thoreau and his tradition in American nature writing that led to comments like the one by Lewis Gannett, an early reader of the book, who said, "Call John Graves a 20th century Thoreau if you like" (quoted in Graham, *Giant Country,* 120).[2]

Such links, however, are only part of the picture; there are also important differences between these two nature writers. *Goodbye to a River* is obviously steeped in Thoreau's work and knowledgeable about his view of the world, but this same depth of knowledge also leads Mr. Graves to make quite clear the extent of his disagreements with him. He knows that people hunger for a "Texas Thoreau" (Bennett, "John Graves," 69), but that is not the writer he wants to be. As the narrative explores the differences between himself and his predecessor, *Goodbye to a River* carefully cautions the reader against such blanket comparisons as the one made by Mr. Gannett, and it develops Mr. Graves' own views on our right human relationship to the natural world.

"Saint Henry David Thoreau, incisive moral anthropomorphist that he was, implied that blood sports were for juveniles, not men, and was conceivably right" (*Goodbye,* 53–54). This, John Graves' opening statement on the question of hunting, is so finely balanced between its gentle mockery of Thoreau and its allowance for the possibility that he is right that it, by itself, might make it difficult to know where he stands. But a key to understanding how John Graves thinks is to notice how this narrative thread develops throughout the book, how the book then moves carefully away from this statement to disavow even the remote possibility contained in the phrase "conceivably right." Human nature and our relationship to the natural world, he argues, are, if only we let ourselves admit it, recognizably more complex.

What he sees as the "cramping contradictions" of human nature on this issue come through in his rich valedictory to a dove killed in a hunt. It opens with one of the more strikingly beautiful passages in the book:

> It [human nature with its contradictions] knifes through you, for instance, after waiting through a long golden evening for doves beside a stock tank in someone's pasture, watching your first bird coming in high and swift on the north wind, laying down knowing before you fire that you are on him, watching him contract raggedly and fall in a long parabola to baked hard earth and then going to pick him up—it knifes to feel suddenly in his warmth against your palm, in the silk touch of the feathers at his throat, all the pity of that perished gentle wildness. (54)

The other emotional dimension of hunting follows quickly. It is "a stone-hard exultation" that is "just as real" and "just as far down inside you." It prompts you to keep searching for "another bird, another shot" (54).

The chapter ends with his reminder that hunting connects us directly with what we eat. He tells us that "even Saint Henry had impulses to gobble woodchucks raw." Even when sports and ethics are ruled out, "eating does get into it" and "you still like meat in your belly" (54). His comments in turn take us backward for a moment to that night on the river when he shot, skinned, and ate a boar squirrel for dinner.

This disavowal of the one-sided, priggish preachiness that John Graves finds in Thoreau's views on hunting takes a further turn later in the book, with the shooting of a goose for food. The importance of these birds in his view of the world has been emphasized earlier when he says: "They sum up the autumn and sum up the spring and sum up all the wide surge of the natural world." He tells us, "I've always hoped geese would outlast me" (99). He chooses, however, to kill and eat this bird over a period of several days because "I believe the killing itself can be reverent" (167). He argues:

> To see and kill and pluck and gut and cook and eat a wild creature, all with some knowledge and the pleasure that knowledge gives, implies a closeness to the creature that is to me more honorable than the candle-lit consumption of rare prime steaks from a steer bludgeoned to death in a packing-house chute while tranquilizers course his veins. (167)

The sacramental sense of life and death made explicit here is enacted and refined all along the river trip as Graves talks to the proud owner of a powerful .207 rifle that he has gotten especially for deer hunting, as he sees squirrels, birds, and a deer and decides when to hunt and when to observe. Toward the end of the journey, his friend Hale berates him for killing only one goose when he could have filled the boat with them.

Fishing plays an equally important part in John Graves' journey down the river, and its role in his view of the natural world is developed with a similar care and richness. Perhaps the best way to approach this aspect of the book is to start with a photograph that caught my eye years ago. This brief sighting took place so far in the past that I am unsure whether it was an advertising brochure or a story in a fly-fishing magazine. I do know that it featured John Graves along with two other men (one a fishing guide) standing together, each man holding a fly rod. In the caption that identified the three fishermen by name and by profession; the line for John Graves read "Outdoor Writer." I laughed at what then appeared to be the misnomer of the caption because I *knew* what John Graves did: he was a nature writer, and in contemporary culture these are, of course, usually two very different things.

An outdoor writer will have a weekly column in the local newspaper telling readers about where to find fish and game, with some technical advice on what the hunter and fisherman should do once that bass or dove is located. We think of a nature writer, however, in very different terms. If the writing is done for a newspaper, the nature columnist writes about the natural world with an emphasis on nearby places where the reader can experience the natural world by walking, learning to identify trees and plants, and watching birds, butterflies, or other wildlife. If the nature writer writes books, we expect the emphasis in them to be on the celebration of wild places and the preservation of wildlife. An outdoor writer is part of the "hook and bullet" crowd; the nature writer is an environmentalist who watches and studies wildlife. Or so our usual assumptions go.

The narrator of *Goodbye to a River,* however, bridges this cultural divide by how he fishes as well as how he hunts. He meditates on the relative efficacies of the fly rod and the spin-casting rig and on fish native to the Brazos in comparison with the imported species that reside there. When he catches small bream with the fly rod, he—gracefully and without reference to the term—practices catch-and-release fishing by letting them go. He catches two nonnative white bass (with his spinning rig) and keeps them alive in the water as he moves downriver. When he catches a large black bass, those two fish are still healthy enough to be released. Since they do not taste as good as the native black bass, he turns them loose and cooks the black bass for supper.

It turns out, of course, that the caption writer was partially right, but the beauty of this book is that it goes beyond either category. The incorporation of the sportsman's role into the environmentalist writer's book is an easy, natural thing for John Graves, but it needs to be noted that it is a reasonably rare thing for contemporary ecological literature. The two other nature writers who come most readily to mind in this regard are Richard Nelson and Rick Bass, both of whom live in and write mostly about wilderness places, sites where it is easier to acknowledge the cultural relevance of hunting.[3] *Goodbye to a River* develops this more inclusive environmentalism in a constantly more highly populated Texas by sharing the narrator's reflections as he floats the nearby Brazos.

Today we live so far removed from any awareness of the origins of our food that Thoreau's rejection of hunting threatens to become not only a dominant theme in ecological literature but almost a commonplace in the larger environmental culture. We equate the hunt with destruction of wildlife rather than with knowledge of the natural world, protection of habitat, and reverence for the life of prey. There are reasons for this, of course: some hunting possesses none of those virtues and bases itself instead on the use of food as bait, then blasting away. In the language of *Goodbye to a River* the hunt then becomes reduced to a shallow act, "the climactic ejaculation of city tensions" (158). Much hunting, however, does incorporate a regard for the natural world, and ecological literature and the larger environmental movement are the poorer—in both numbers and breadth of vision—for their refusal to embody the kind of inclusiveness that emerges, always with quiet authority and complexly shaded points of view, in the pages of *Goodbye to a River.*

This highly effective but mostly low-key exploration of nature and environmental issues marks another key difference between the work of Graves and Thoreau. Thoreau's efforts in speaking "a word for Nature" (*Walking,* 1) feature an ongoing critique of the behavior and beliefs of the society around him. He often voices his beliefs in a language that is dramatic and by his own description "extravagant" (*Walden,* 303). John Graves deliberately chooses to build a quieter book for his reader, one that uses description, story, and historical anecdote to coax, rather than preach, the reader—toward acknowledging the value of the natural world. Social criticism, anger, and indignation do flare up in this narrative, but they appear only at intervals. In comparison, say, with Thoreau and with Edward Abbey, another twentieth-century river-minded environmental writer who is also often seen as part of the Thoreauvian tradition, the outbursts are rare. They serve as a frame for Graves' farewell trip down the river rather than as a constant refrain.

Goodbye to a River also exhibits the rarest virtue of environmental writing: humor. This emerges most often in how Graves characterizes himself, and it is both a way of engaging the reader and of emphasizing that this book does not want to be a heroic "Big History" or a "Bold Journey."

Some of the humor is tucked away in wryly self-deprecatory descriptions of himself: "When I was little, I used to think you could characterize families from the smells of their houses, but an early addiction to tobacco kept me from developing the theory" (70). However, most of the humor, like that in the nature writing of Robert Michael Pyle, comes from describing behavior on the trip that is resolutely unheroic.[4] Graves does not shy away from recounting the time that he drops a $200 borrowed camera into the Brazos or mentioning that he dropped a boot full of snowy wet sand into a pot of stewed fruit intended for breakfast.

The central and most distinctive stylistic trait of *Goodbye to a River* has also been a source of frustration for those who misunderstand it. In one of the most discussed essays on Texas literature, "Ever a

Bridegroom: Reflections on the Failure of Texas Literature," Larry McMurtry acknowledges that the book has a "lovely style" and that it is "a good deal more complicated than it is popularly thought to be," but then offers this description of the narrative:

> One of his most frequent rhetorical devices, used almost to the point of abuse, is to undercut himself: questioning a story he has just retold, doubting an observation he has just made, twisting out from under a position. Often he simply reverses his field and abandons whatever line of thought he has been pursuing. (29)

McMurtry's impatience with the narrative of *Goodbye to a River* can be partly attributed to context. It is part of an essay-manifesto written at a time when he was determined to separate himself from other Texas writers by stating, unequivocally, his views on what he saw as the failure of Texas letters. The quiet narrative of John Graves' river journey is at the other end of the rhetorical spectrum from the declarative, argumentative requirements of his own essay, and this context no doubt explains some of his impatience. Whatever the reasons, however, McMurtry's understanding of the narrative style of this book stops short and leads him to undervalue its stylistic accomplishments.

Graves has described himself as "a born English major" (Bennett, "John Graves," 65), and his river journey narrative possesses a kind of complexity most often associated with fiction, especially fiction in the tradition of *Tristram Shandy.* The quotation from that novel that opens *Goodbye to a River* announces more than this narrator's interest in the past and specifically those parts of our culture that are "hereditary." It also signals that the book will feature an associative and dialogical narrative structure that is somewhat like the novel.[5]

The narrative does, at times, appear to undercut itself; it definitely does return to previously told stories and themes, and it casts doubts on just-completed observations. However, a key to understanding the accomplishment of *Goodbye to a River* is to realize that it seldom abandons a theme. The important points resurface to become a thread woven throughout the narrative. The narrator's thoughts on such key matters as class and landscape, youth and age, gender and the river, the sovereign pulse of being, urban ownership of country land, asceticism, and so on never take their final shape in one single statement or declaration. They develop instead through a series of incidents and reflections along the river, a process in which various memories and thoughts associated with that theme are brought to bear on it.

This narrative proceeds, as it does in the development of the hunting theme, through a series of related reflections and incidents, each occurring at a different point on the river and each adding new information, or a different memory, or a new perspective on the continuing question, or a new shading of meaning to the previous considerations. For many readers this complex proliferation of perspectives is one of the major satisfactions in reading *Goodbye to a River.* It is also a major way in which John Graves develops the book's complex consideration of our human relationship to the rest of nature. Thus, when Graves finishes his reference to Thoreau's claim that hunting was "juvenile" with the phrase "and was conceivably right," that phrase first acts as a modest corrective. Its immediate function is to sand down the sharp, somewhat polemical edge in his own comments about Thoreau by softening the sarcasm of the phrases "Saint Henry David Thoreau" and "incisive moral anthropomorphist." This effectively distances his comments from any taint of the self-righteousness that he dislikes in other writers. However, the phrase, with its emphasis on the possibilities of the word "conceivably," also sets in motion the narrative's many varieties of dialogue—dialogue with himself, dialogue with the values of American culture, and dialogue with the beliefs of Saint Henry—about what hunting means.

Any apparent abandonment of the major themes of the book is thus only momentary. The narrative is at once recursive and forward-looking, so that an event or a thought that occurs to him on the river is often associated both with a previous event or theme and with those that will occur later in the book. Meaning emerges through an accumulation of nuanced bits and pieces that finally form a wonderfully complex whole. The prose, to borrow a phrase from the book, provides a narrative terrain that is something like John Graves' description of the river landscape itself, a "tessellated ecology" (37).

The interrelated bits and pieces of the narrative fit together to form a mosaic, an embodiment of meaning that is complex and inclusive rather than restricted and polemical. This way of shaping the meaning of his book forms the center of a style unique in American environmental literature, one well suited to involve others in caring about what John Graves has always known: the value of a river.

Notes

1. Those of us who think and write about John Graves tend to discuss his work in one of two ways. Most, like Don Graham in his essay on John Graves in *Giant Country,* locate him in the Texas writing tradition as the descendant of Dobie, Bedichek, and Webb (although scholars often see enough differences between his work and theirs that they feel the placement is a bit forced). Rick Bass, on the other hand, in this collection and in a review for the *Dallas Morning News* (April 8, 1990, J6) praises Graves as the "great father of contemporary Texas writing," suggesting that his work might tilt Texas writing in a more environmentally aware direction. I wonder, however, if our tendency to focus on John Graves almost exclusively in terms of the genealogy of Texas writing does justice to *Goodbye to a River.* It may tend to obscure somewhat the place of this book in the larger field of American nature writing.

2. This quotation also appears on the back book cover of *Goodbye to a River.*

3. See, for example, Richard Nelson's work of literary nonfiction, *The Island Within* (San Francisco: North Point Press, 1989) and Rick Bass' novel *Where the Sea Used to Be* (New York: Houghton Mifflin, 1998).

4. See, for example, Pyle's *Where Bigfoot Walks: Crossing the Dark Divide* (New York: Houghton Mifflin, 1995).

5. For a sense of how important the nuances of style in *Goodbye to a River* were to Graves, see *John Graves and the Making of "Goodbye to a River,"* ed. David S. Hamrick, 39–51.

Two Approaches to Ecology and Gender in *Goodbye to a River*

JAMES LANGSTON

WHEN CRITICS WRITE ABOUT John Graves' *Goodbye to a River,* they tend to examine how it represents place and whether or not it is some form of environmental manifesto. Craig Clifford, for example, worries that the book lacks an argument that readers may analyze. He points out, rightly, that Graves' work is more complicated than a "definitive statement about the Brazos River, about environmental protection, about being a Texan or being rooted anywhere" (576). For Clifford, Graves is not the nature writer some consider him to be and certainly not an environmental activist. He is, instead, someone who considers things, especially "the entanglements of things human and things natural" (576). Yet people do accuse Graves of being all the things Clifford says he isn't. For example, Pete Gunter and Max Oelschlaeger, in their *Texas Land Ethics,* use Graves to set the standard for ecological writing in the state:

> What we seem to need are stories about Texans in real places who articulate Texas environmental problems—real issues that unfold on the stage of history before our very eyes. One thinks in this regard of John Graves' book, *Goodbye to a River,* an intensely personal and detailed account of the cultural and ecological changes [which were soon to be] wrought by the damming of the Brazos River. Such a narrative helps urban dwellers in Austin and Dallas

> grasp the ecological implications of the water flowing from their taps. It comes from somewhere. And it has costs that go beyond the monthly water bill. (34)

The problem is that both views of Graves have validity: he merely considers, yet this consideration is somehow an impetus to social action despite Graves' apparent unwillingness to make an argument. Even his unwillingness is open to debate; Graves' sly, ironic tone leaves readers with a suspicion that he is winking at them when he claims that protecting the river is not his fight. People who have written about the work have focused upon these environmental questions.

When critics get together and talk about the book, though, the most intense part of the discussion usually arises from questions about gender. Why doesn't the sound of girls laughing belong on the river? Why doesn't he mention that his wife came along to take pictures as he sets off downstream? Why does he need to be the lone man in the wilderness? Good questions. In the discussions I've been part of recently, people tend to write off the machismo of the book, such as it is, to the era in which it was written and to apologize on Graves' behalf for this minor, forgivable, literary sin. This answer usually ends the discussion, but people haven't looked too convinced.

A better way to approach the question of gender is through an investigation of the other question, the one about ecology. With the rise of ecofeminism, critics have begun to look less at a narrator's attitudes about gender and to pay more attention to what the design of a literary work suggests about how collective groups of people should live in a landscape. The structure of the book, at first glance, is seemingly loose, shaped by the meandering path of the river itself and by the narrator's meandering line of thought. Close attention, however, reveals that Graves attempts to hold this openness together with at least two strategies, each having implications regarding gender.

Graves divides the book into two parts and emphasizes different narrative strategies in each, though both approaches are present and work together in both parts. In the first part, he makes an effort to present a variety of voices associated with the river. This strong dialogic quality privileges voices, including nonhuman ones, that Graves feels have not been heard by many and that will soon be irrevocably silenced. Ultimately, however, he finds this dialogic form insufficient by itself to sustain the themes he is trying to work out.

The second part is, primarily, an example of what Glen Love, in

"Revaluing Nature," calls "new pastoral." This form differs from "old" pastoral in that our aristocrat-disguised-as-shepherd is not going to an artificial green world with the sole purpose of recharging himself for a return to the city. In "Arden up the Brazos: John Graves and the Uses of Pastoral," M. E. Bradford argues that the book is a version of the old form, which he calls "hard pastoral," a form that pays tribute to a very real green world but accepts its mortality and the hero's inevitable departure from it. New pastoral, on the other hand, refuses to push Arcadia to the margins. It too attempts to examine various connections to a complex and real green world but does so in order to posit stable relationships with the modern natural world. *Goodbye to a River* meets this criterion.

Translating Juan Ramón Jiménez, Graves says, "Foot in one's accidental or elected homeland; heart, head in the world's air" (*Goodbye*, 254). Instead of offering himself as an example, he turns to some of the other human models along the river, past and present, and evaluates how well they live up to this ideal. Only when Graves weds the voices of the first form, dialogics, to the latter form, new pastoral, does he formulate an adequate defense of place and community. A closer look at each narrative strategy will illustrate their respective implications for ecology and gender.

Goodbye to a River, as the title tells us, is a work through which Graves speaks to a landscape. By speaking to it, he identifies it as a legitimate listener and locates it within a framework of discursive power relations. According to J. L. Austin, communication is not only a semiotic, linguistic, and symbolic medium but also a medium of power. An utterance not only may impart information but also may achieve (or fail to achieve) a desired effect (6–7, 99–109). By bidding farewell to the river, Graves intends to acknowledge ceremonially his relationship to what he calls "my piece of the river" and to bring that relationship to an adequate close. This acknowledgment, which is both speech act and journey, will allow him to reestablish himself and to come to terms with the river's impending doom. As listener, the river achieves an honored, if submissive, role in the speech act. What makes the book so compelling, however, is that Graves doesn't limit the conversation to his saying good-bye.

The Upper Middle Brazos speaks back to him through many voices, some natural and some human, both past and present. By empowering the landscape with voice, Graves attempts to insert it into discourse as more than just an inanimate sign or passive listener but also as a subject with the potential to defend itself by expressing its own value and right to exist. As Graves sets off on his journey, the rapids, birds, and days sing to him. The trees, soil, and stones speak of over a century of human impact on the local geography. They also speak of his own youth spent hunting and fishing on the river, of the tales he and his friends begged the "old ones" to tell them about local historical figures (7). Place-names, abandoned log cabins, and occasional arrowheads also speak of past human struggle. He tells us, "If the river has meaning for you, you can see [these stories] from the sandstone bluffs where the mountains drop away. You don't have to strain to impose the tales on the landscape; they're there" (140).

This tangle of voices, of course, manifests itself primarily as an internal dialogue. The reader can have access only to Graves' descriptions, interpretations, and responses. His persona acts as both medium and filter for the river's speech. But the river does have some control. Its linear geography, for example, shapes the flow of the narrative. Its history overpowers him: he continually apologizes to the reader for the river's surplus of violent Indian stories, claiming he can't help it if that's what the river has to say.

As a writer, he constantly confronts this tension between competing voices, a situation he views as conducive to good writing. In an essay on his literary predecessors, "The Old Guard: Dobie, Webb, and Bedichek," Graves reflects that this equivocal reaction is particularly characteristic of the writers he admires most. Looking at the work of Frank Dobie, he remarks that the writer's subject matter—the Texas rancher class, the brown workers they relied upon and exploited, and the land that these Latin cowboys animated with their oral tradition—had a tenacious hold on Dobie. According to Graves,

> that hold involved not only a fond knowledge for cowboy and ranching skills and a bone-deep affection for the brown people's lore, but also a need to reconcile his pride in the rancher class and his love for them with a personal effort to break free from their major limitations and faults. ("Old Guard," 21)

These limitations include "bossy piousness, censorship, racial prejudice, [and] rote genteel thinking," all of which are "inimical to human liberty and growth" (22). While Dobie never mastered this internal struggle, his effort to come to terms with his ambivalent feelings infused his writing with an energy Graves finds compelling.

For Graves, one generation further removed from his cultural roots, the conflict is less pressing but similar all the same. Graves comes from the Brazos River people, a puritanical, industrious folk with lingering traces of Confederateness. Some were heroic, some were louts, but almost all of them hated being told what to do, considered themselves true to their own values, and had the ability to endure tremendous hardships. As Graves floats downstream, their voices speak to him from the places where they lived and died. His response, like Dobie's, is mixed. He admires their grit and tenacity but dislikes their violence and judgmental self-righteousness. Ironically, what he admires most in them, their hardheaded drive to scratch out an independent life, leads to what he considers their biggest failing, their savaging of the land and its native people (fierce or friendly). Unlike Dobie, however, Graves does not feel the need to "break free," to be the "willing warrior" ("Old Guard," 22). Perhaps this distance arises from his inability to separate what he finds admirable from what he finds not so admirable. To condemn their faults would be to undermine their route to freedom and growth. Further, it would implicate Graves in one of their central limitations, bossy piousness.

This ambiguous connection to his people leads to an equally ambiguous relationship with the land. In order to cope with the tension that arises between his deep respect for the earlier generation of Brazos River folk (the people from whom he comes) and his own implicit role in their exploitation and wasteful management of the land (the place from which they come), he refrains from making polemical statements against them and focuses instead on negotiating an independent relationship with the river. This personal enterprise is troubled, however, by his knowledge that the river will soon be gone and his refusal to take an independent stand on the matter:

> It was not my fight. That was *not even my part of the country any more*; I had been living out of the state for years. I knew, though, that it might be years again before I got back with time enough on my hands to make the trip, and what I wanted to do was wrap it up, the river, before what I and Hale and Satanta the White Bear and Mr. Charlie

> Goodnight had known ended up down yonder under all the Criss-Crafts and the tinkle of portable radios.
>
> Or was that, maybe, an excuse for a childishness? What I wanted was to float *my piece of the river* again. All of it. (*Goodbye to a River*, 9; emphasis added)

When speaking of the river's destruction, he denies his cultural relationship with it. He may do so with a little irony, but there is a little truth as well. As he speaks of wrapping up what he had known, however, he confesses that it is his, that he is part of it. In order to bypass an uncomfortable stance condemning the dams and seeking to prevent their construction, he must temporarily deny his connection to the culture of this place.

When Graves disassociates himself from culture, the voice of the nonhuman landscape begins to dominate. As he meditates upon the effect the river is having on his body and mind, how it is "shuck[ing] off the gross delights" of the city from his senses, he realizes that those that are left are "few, sharp, and strong" (154). Graves, at these times, sees the river as a more independent entity, speaking to him, or to anyone who cares to listen, through its own unfettered voices: a bird singing, an animal track left in the wet sand, a breeze announcing a coming rain.

If he fails to understand the bird's song, it is because of his own ignorance (156), a lack in his identity. Culture cannot help him develop this "organic kinship" (158): "Your standard country lore about animals—about the nasal love life of a possum, or the fabled hoop snake—is picturesque rather than accurate, anthropocentric rather than understanding" (159). If he wants to fine-tune his ear, his only options, as inadequate as they may be, are "to try to tie it all together for himself by reading and adult poking," which, of course, is "never worth a quarter as much as kid poking" (160). We must also remember that these moments—when Graves sees the potential for connecting with the natural world, for understanding its voices—are moments that are overshadowed not only by his ironic dependence upon cultural discourse but also by the subsequent cultural connection to the river's destruction, a connection that he struggles to repress. The voices, for Graves, simultaneously depend upon each other and negate each other.

Nowhere is this paradoxical relationship more apparent than near the book's conclusion, where Graves attempts to achieve narrative closure. The final day of his journey sings to him, in the wrong tune, of unfortunate and defiant endings:

> I hate the Constitution and the uniform of blue;
> I hate the Declaration of Independence, too,
> And I don't want no pardon for what I was or am,
> And I won't be reconstructed and I do not give a damn.
>
> I'm glad we fought agin her and I only wisht we'd won
> And I ain't ast no pardon for anything I've done. . . . (295, 297; Graves' ellipsis)

As would seem fitting, this tune speaks not only for the ghosts of Confederate soldiers but also for the river, for the river folk, and for Graves himself. What we, as readers, are left with is the question of whether or not the voice rings true for all of the singers. Has the authoritative voice of the river given up fighting for its right to exist? On which side of the fight do the river folk stand? Has Graves, who claims it's not his fight, "fought agin her"?

The song, an elegy in which a group formally laments its own defeat, does not have the requisite authority to qualify as a successful speech act. Bradford argues that the "elegiac action" of the work, while limited, is itself a form of fighting: "An affirmative reminiscence—indeed any reminiscence not pointedly negative—*is* an injunction to reconstitute, an appeal to the spirit of Reaction" (952). While this reading may support the intent of Graves' voice, the effect is still troubled by the contradictory rhetorical positions of the other speakers. This confused act of communication is partially responsible for the contradictory responses to the book. Compounding the problem is that this speech act is in conflict with another one, Graves' "goodbye," which silences the river as listener as it vanishes from the speaker's presence.

In terms of gender, this silencing of the listener is duplicated on the last page of the book. "Somebody's wife" asks Graves, now at a party in town, "All by yourself?" In this place, the complexity of what he truly thinks seems inexplicable, and he responds, "Not exactly. . . . I had a dog" (*Goodbye*, 301). He excludes the woman from his primarily masculine experience with a voice that thinly hides a now silent and deteriorating internal dialogue. In effect, instead of recognizing the limitations imposed by the contradictions of his particular knot, as he would have Dobie do, he struggles compellingly, if unsuccessfully, to tie it all together and seems to settle in the end for cutting some threads and hoping the knot will hold. This scene is only a halfhearted attempt at closure, however, and one that is concerned with the dialogic content of the book, which is prone to evade narrative control. The scene is also more connected to the old pastoral than it is to the new. He has left the green world, temporarily, but he will return to it, permanently, in *Hard Scrabble.*

THE VOICES HE FINDS that speak to his own ends with the best effect are those of the new pastoral section. The primary metaphor that frames this section is the wind, which represents the world's air blowing across his homeland. The first voices are those of laughing girls and one of their parents, a man by the name of Potts. These are city people that romanticize life spent in the country. Graves moves quickly to more likely models for living on the river. Jacob De Cordova, a Sephardic Jamaican businessman, amassed a million acres of river land but lost it all when he tried to build textile mills on the river. John B. Christensen built a utopia called Kristenstad that boasted a "those-who-work-eat semi-socialism" (*Goodbye*, 260). It was destroyed by the Depression. Ultimately, he comes to modern-day absentee landowners, living in Dallas, who are "the cedar people's successor[s]" (279). He suggests that their so-called ownership is mostly good for the land. These moneymakers, like his friend Bill, are not likely to abuse their investments. What is most significant here, and probably most persuasive, is that these absentee landowners hire local people to work the land.

This brings us to Davis Birdsong, whose name recalls the voice of the river as manifested in an unknown bird's song, which Graves wants so much to understand. Birdsong likes the bulldozer, a "crushing agent of change" (269). After the cedar and juniper are cleared, the grasses have a chance to take hold and reestablish the soil. Birdsong likes change and improvement, but he also, like Graves, appreciates the history of the river. It speaks to him. He is an ascetic, willing to work in any conditions and eat whatever is put before him. He "quietly knows himself to be as good as any man" (275). In short, he has his feet in his homeland and his head in the world. It is Birdsong, not Graves, who becomes a figure of hope within the book for how things ought to be, both culturally and ecologically. With him,

Graves brings his various literary methods together and provides his reader with a positive model for living on the river.

Therefore, Birdsong provides us with another opportunity to consider gender. Obviously, he is rugged and manly, but he is not a lone man in the wilderness. When he comes across the ruins of his old home place in a dry creek bed, he recalls:

> We didn't *live* bad. . . . They was a garden patch under that artesian well and it'd grow might near anythang. I mean. And we kept a cow most of the time, and hogs. Good house. Plenty of wood to burn in winter. And old Maw she kept thangs right. (270)

Maw is Birdsong's grandmother, and it is she "who, alone against the lassitude of soil exhaustion and demoralization," held the family together (270). As Graves praises her, he states that although her husband had chosen the wrong place for them to live and although the "exhausted place had eaten at the fiber of her sons and daughters and grandchildren, those things weren't her fault, and she'd kept the erosion from going as far as it had with other families" (271). Just as Birdsong fights the erosion of place, Maw battled the erosion of family and community. Graves asks his reader, "Are we then praising the Noble Pioneer Mother? No. Just praising Noble Anybody who could shore up a clan's pride against cedar and bitter indigence" (271). He doesn't want to make her into a stock female type but does want to reveal her as an actual person and to use her and her grandson as models for the defense of both a place and a way of life. Because this concern is the foundation of his book, it is no surprise that he and his own family follow the Birdsongs' example, which is the subject matter of Graves' sequel, *Hard Scrabble.*

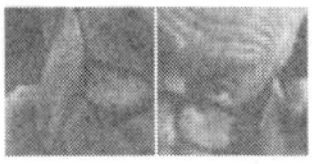

Boys' Stories

Beverly Lowry, John Graves, and the (Male) Texas Literary Tradition in The Perfect Sonya

BETSY BERRY

> What we have here is basically a picture of gradual but unmistakable decay, and the way things are going it won't take another ten or fifteen years to complete. You might say it's just civilization at work, the old naturally giving way to the new.
>
> ASTROV, IN ANTON CHEKHOV'S *Uncle Vanya*

IN BRITISH LITERATURE MANY novels seem to grow out of a literary relationship with a prior novel. Thus, in *Sons and Lovers* D. H. Lawrence appears to be rewriting Charles Dickens in several chapters; Graham Greene seems to be restaging Joseph Conrad; and so on. In Texas writing, however, such specific evocations of a prior work are rare. This is one of several reasons that Beverly Lowry's engagement with a specific Texas literary tradition is so welcome. This intertextuality can be seen in a number of her works, but most significantly in her novel *The Perfect Sonya,* published originally in 1987 and reprinted by Texas Christian University Press in 2004. How she came to Texas and how she came to write the novel is a story worth examining. Born in Memphis, Tennessee, in 1938, Lowry moved with her stockbroker husband, Glenn Lowry, to Houston in 1965, but it was not until several years later that she decided to become a writer.

She was not at first aware of a tradition in Texas writing, which, paradoxically, might seem a significant advantage for a woman launching a literary career. There was no anxiety of influence because there was no influence. In Houston at that time, she says, the only other writer she knew was Max Apple. She published her first novel, *Come Back, Lolly Ray,* in 1977, and in that same year she became a member of the Texas Institute of Letters, during friend Shelby Hearon's tenure as president, and suddenly she was thrust into an organization whose central purpose was to champion a Texas literary tradition. But it wasn't until her third book, *Daddy's Girl* (1981), that she took Texas as a setting for her story.

In an e-mail message to me, Lowry spoke of her take on "Texas authors":

> I didn't go back and catch up on the revered dead ones—Dobie, etc.—but began reading the living writers and found many of them quite exceptional. The tradition itself didn't mean a lot to me and when I hear conversations (less often these days) of the days when Willie [Morris] was in Austin and Billy Lee [Brammer] was the literary king . . . etc. I have to say they don't resonate with me. Besides, these are all BOYS' stories. (November 16, 2004)

One book, however, did resonate. That was John Graves' *Goodbye to a River* (1960). In *The Perfect Sonya,* her fourth novel and the second to deal with Texas as setting and theme, Lowry confronted what one might call the Gravesian tradition in Texas letters. A novel often tells a different story from an author's real-life feelings about her subject, and such certainly seems to be the case when one looks closely at how the figure of Graves is rendered in Lowry's novel. It is clear that Lowry offers a feminist critique of the Graves male persona in the long trail of the Texas literary tradition. In a brief sketch of the career of Beverly Lowry, Patrick Bennett sums up a widely held impression of *The Perfect Sonya:* "Some Texans judged the book a *roman à clef,* perceiving that the writer-professor walked and talked like John Graves, author of the classic *Goodbye to a River*" ("Laura Furman, Beverly Lowry," 153–154). Probably nobody outside of Texas, though, recognized that Graves was the basis for the character of Will Hand. To a reviewer for *Publisher's Weekly* Will Hand was simply the ex-husband of Pauline's aunt, and in the *Library Journal* review he is described as "a grizzled ex-professor." An online description of the book at Amazon.com cites Hand as a "professor and nature writer." This lack of recognition outside of Texas might suggest an exclusively Texas reputation for Graves, by the way. But most Texas readers, I submit, would easily recognize a Gravesian presence in the portrait of Will Hand.

Lowry herself, in her e-mail to me, makes it abundantly clear that Graves is the central figure behind the conception of Will Hand:

> Like most writers in Texas, I have been and remain a huge fan of John Graves. Laura Furman and I used to visit him in Glen Rose and he took us on walks around his land. We helped him feed creatures and usually he fed us a fine lunch. There are many things in the novel that I would not have known without these adventures. And anybody who's ever been to Glen Rose or John and Jane's place would know that the terrain of *Sonya* is basically the same as their craggy, wild, wonderful home place and land. Several real life men of my acquaintance fed into the character of Will Hand, including John Graves. They are all older than me and all, by my reckoning, appealing, intelligent and physical, which is to say, very sexy, as is Will Hand, at least certainly and forever to me.

However dynamic Graves might be in person, the novel interrogates the fictional construct in ways that are worth tracing in detail, and *The Perfect Sonya* performs different work from merely providing a novelistic portrait of a famous Texas author. What it does is challenge the whole of a Gravesian view of nature—and especially of women—as reflected in the rhetoric and staging of masculine and feminine desire in *Goodbye to a River*. Graves' view of external nature privileges masculine desire, and Lowry seeks to investigate that claim throughout *The Perfect Sonya.*

The novel's central action turns upon two visits to Texas by Lowry's protagonist, a New York stage actress named Pauline Terry. She returns the first time when her father, who was sexually abusive to her, suffers a heart attack. Her mother is an alcoholic, so Pauline carries plenty of psychological baggage in her adult life. During a visit to San Marcos, she comes into contact with Will Hand, an uncle by marriage and a former professor of hers "at the college in San Marcos." More importantly, Will Hand is famous for having written a book called *The Legend of Snake Creek,* which is the novel's equivalent of *Goodbye to a River.* He has also authored a second volume, called *Straddling the Fault Line.* Both of these books are among the prized possessions of Pauline's husband and acting teacher, Michael, and when he learns that his wife has to go to Texas to see her father, Michael is awestruck at the possibility that on her trip back to Texas she might actually reconnect with the great writer. Michael handles the Snake Creek book with fetishistic care, and he reads aloud to her: "I had not lived long on the creek when signs of ghosts appeared" (53–54). Michael declares it a "fabulous opening sentence" and asks Pauline, "Was there ever a better opening sentence than that?" (54). "Call me Ishmael" is one of a number that come to mind, but here Pauline agrees with her husband, pronouncing it indeed "fabulous" (54). Hand's opening sentence, by the way, seems to echo this one from *Goodbye to a River:* "Sometimes you take country for itself, for what shows merely, and sometimes it forces its ghost too upon you, the smell of people who have lived and died there" (36).

Once in San Marcos, Pauline meets up with Will. She remembers having been a student of his when Hand was teaching a course called "Rivers" in the science department. But she doubts that he will remember her. She sees him driving through town in his old pickup with a dog named Lotto.[1] Pauline trails after him, unseen, on a class trip to Wonder Cave, where he explains the mysteries of caves and geological eons. Will is very wise and, in his role as teacher, performs as "an actor plain and simple" who "had the knack—to spin and weave" (*Sonya,* 80). Afterwards, Pauline introduces herself to him as his niece and feels "like a child" (82). This is an important revelation because of Pauline's molestation by her father. Ironically, Pauline seems unable to keep herself from being attracted to older men—especially in the case of Will Hand, who is wise, measured, and an artist in the bargain.

Another direct Gravesian parallel would seem to reside in the physical description of Will Hand. Will has a bad eye, caused by a childhood accident with a BB gun. (Graves himself suffered an injury to one of his eyes during a combat episode on Saipan in World War II.) In the novel Will "walked in a kind of list, left shoulder leading" (82), which some might consider a fair description of Graves' carriage. Will lives on Snake Creek between the Blanco and San Marcos Rivers, east of San Marcos. (Graves, of course, lives on a farm near Glen Rose, a town southwest of Fort Worth.)

Upon visiting with Will at Snake Creek, Pauline falls under the spell of the lushness of the setting: "It was perfect. Uncivilized and perfect" (95). She also falls completely under the spell of Will Hand, who speaks with "that eloquent and self-conscious floweriness only men of Will's generation could get away with" (93). This floweriness really comes across more as portentousness, however, as is clear when she makes the mistake of asking Will why the creek is named Snake Creek. First Will rebukes her with a look: "He turned his good eye on her and silently scolded her like a child" (95). She is thirty-three, but Will seems hell-bent on casting their roles as man-teacher and woman-child.

"You didn't read my book," he admonishes her next (95). A clearer-thinking Sonya should have gotten in her car and driven off straightaway, but sufficiently chastened by the great Will Hand, she stammers and says that at least she had bought it (her husband, we recall, is the one who bought it). Then she plays to Will's vanity and asks him to summarize the book, which he is only too pleased to do. It's about a creek, some unspecified ghosts, some old Indian tales, and some other stories and legends that sound like the evocation of the past in *Goodbye to a River*. Pauline identifies two conflicting rhetorical modes in her long conversation with Will: he is a flirtatious tease or he is omnipotent, a disembodied echo over the great state of Texas, "like God." She thinks further that "he sounded like Charlton Heston as Moses. Which he knew" (99). Pauline should know better, but given her penchant for father/avuncular figures, she's truly a goner by now.

Then she serves up a question that he can hit over the fence. She asks him how his book did. She already knows but wants to flatter him by asking, and by golly he is ready to hold forth. He replies, "It did better than I had expected. It somehow struck people's fancy, especially young people. The times helped. All those environmentalists, romantics" (99). This could also be a pretty accurate account of the critical success enjoyed by *Goodbye to a River*.

Then Will speaks of *Straddling the Fault Line*, which was "not so successful commercially, although what reviews it got were positive" (99). In the Gravesian oeuvre, this book he describes could be *Hard Scrabble* or *From a Limestone Ledge*. At the moment, his career seems to be stalled, and Will tells Pauline he is *"pausing,"* which speaks not to the anxiety of influence but to the anxiety of success. It's a familiar problem for a writer, of getting the *next* book written (99), but as becomes clear in the novel, there is not likely to be a next book from Will's hand.

But Pauline has her own artistic calling, and it is time for those skills to be displayed. Her greatest role onstage has been that of Sonya, the dutiful, patient daughter in Chekhov's *Uncle Vanya.* Will, as it turns out, adores Chekhov. And that is the word he uses—"adore"—however odd a choice it seems for a man grounded so solidly in the Texas earth (105). Will entreats her to recite Sonya's famous last speech, and she is only too glad to oblige. Pleased by her recital, Will lapses into more autobiographical reminiscence, telling of his farming past, chopping cotton in West Texas, and in the omniscient narrative voice muses upon how men operate:

> Once again, he had deflected the intimacy they'd taken so long to establish and nudged the conversation back into the seductive and over familiar Texas rhythm of men making boasts to women, women listening, men tossing out kernels of wisdom and experience such as 'I can hoe as fast as I can walk,' to which the listener could provide no intelligent response. (109)

Once again she responds with childlike awe; "schoolgirlish" is how Lowry presents it (109). The tendency of the stereotypical Texas male and Texas male artist to reduce women to girls and to render them complicit in the process cannot be overlooked. Lowry's deconstruction of this familiar pattern is one of the real strengths of the novel.

Stimulated by Pauline's lovely stage presence and Will's Texas literary tradition, the couple make love in Will's modest homemade dwelling. The prologue to desire begins when Pauline demonstrates her skinny-dipping skills in Snake Creek, while Will, a living legend, stands watching from above. Whether he notices that "her nipples hardened," we are not told, but harden they do, as the third-person omniscient narration makes clear (115). After this, sex seems the sole resolution and will give them both something to fret about for some time to come. Will Hand likes his life pure and simple in a manly sense, a pickup truck, a dog, and a creek—and no domestic entanglements.[2]

Afterwards, he asks her to do more "scenes" for him (117). She complies with a smorgasbord of well-known theatrical turns: Juno, Maggie *(Cat on a Hot Tin Roof),* Lady Macbeth, Charlotte Corday,

Ophelia, Miranda, and Blanche DuBois. In any event Pauline and Will continue to spend time together on bucolic Snake Creek. Then a tremendous rain sets in. (Of this place and event, Lowry says in her e-mail: "Snake Creek and the flood are real, and really happened, but in Caldwell County where I then lived, not Glen Rose.") Will Hand, of course, sees all the signs of the upcoming storm and must "teach" Pauline about the complex vagaries of Texas weather patterns. It is also here that Will Hand shows again his commitment to dogs over cats. When Pauline hears his cat, Eggs (a connection with the female, perhaps?), crying to be let in, Will says dismissively, with that typical arrogance of the dog person, "She'll be all right. She's an outdoor cat" (129). Perhaps there is an echo here, too, of Hemingway's "Cat in the Rain," a story in which another domineering male figure has no interest in a cat being caught outdoors in the rain.

Now the two are stuck together, even though it is obvious Will would like nothing better than to put her in a taxi. Instead, Pauline and Will drive into town to get some food to ride out the rainstorm, and Pauline has another moment of vexation at men in general. She overhears a group of men talking on a porch about previous floods. Although Will does not speak to them, Pauline senses some kind of tortured, indefinable Texas maleness in them all:

> There was something between Will and the other men, some old argument that had gone beyond the need for speaking. Possibly the men didn't know what it was themselves. Whether they knew or not, it wasn't going to stop: the judgments, the competition, the need each felt to declare the unqualified rightness of his own life, each the center of his own closed world. (139)

Now that Pauline is squarely in Will Hand's world—that of nature—she proves herself unworthy of that high calling. She ignores Will's warning about steering clear of poison ivy! So now Will, at home in all of nature's incarnations, must show his homeopathic wisdom by prescribing aloe vera juice for Pauline's itch. Pauline professes never to have heard of its medicinal properties nor of the aloe vera plant itself, which seems odd to this reader, who has seen many an aloe vera as far afield as New York City restaurants. Aloe vera gel products used for sunburn and skin irritations are available at almost any pharmacy or supermarket. Still, it lifts Will's profile to be able to continue with the instruction.

The rain becomes a deluge, and Pauline remains in Will's small domicile, where she begins to chafe at some of his mannerisms and habits that had first attracted her. He sucks his teeth, and, worse for Will, he is "overprotective and possessive, like a nested mother hen" (145). Here is Pauline's assessment of him now: "His professional distance was beginning to get on her nerves, as was all the talk about nature and symbolism: lessons to be learned from the example of the universe. Wasn't that old news, really? Pauline nodded, but did not listen. He was beginning to sound like Serebryakov" (145). The reference is to the old professor in *Uncle Vanya*—a vain, pedantic, and boring character—a rather devastating judgment of Will, now Pauline's new lover.

But the rain stops, the creek's floodwaters subside, and Pauline too retreats, to her husband in New York, whereupon, in the fullness of time, she discovers she is pregnant. To Michael's inevitable question, she replies, "Don't ask whose, but I know. I'm not guessing" (161). There will not, however, be issue from Will and Pauline, as she has an abortion.

And her marriage to Michael ends as well. Her father, long in "vegetable state," finally dies, and Pauline is back once again in Texas, in Houston, to visit family and where she learns, with a shock, of several changes in Will Hand's life (163). At this point, a number of close connections with John Graves show themselves. Will Hand has moved from the San Marcos area to a place "up past Waco," where he lives outside of Eulogy (a fictional town) on "four hundred acres . . . nothing but limestone, rattlesnakes and rocks" (169). In other words, he lives on a farm exactly like the one John Graves has lived on and written about going on nearly half a century.

Another big surprise to Pauline is that Will has married a rich Mexican woman who owns a number of import-export stores in Houston, Santa Fe, and Scottsdale, Arizona. She spends a good deal of time on buying trips. (Graves' second wife, Jane, by the way, is retired from a career as a buyer for Neiman Marcus.) Pauline's source for all this new juicy information comes from her aunt Wanda, a sassy Houstonian in the real estate business—a woman who was once married to Will. Wanda takes a swipe at the expatriate years, when Will/Graves was in Europe and was drawn to the exoticism of Spanish women. Interestingly, there is a moment in *Goodbye to a*

River when Graves speaks exactly to this point: "Yes, ma'am, I too have heard the mermaids calling across the blue foreign waters, and once or twice at least I thought I knew what they were saying. On the river alone, though, mermaid thoughts seem not to stick to you deeply" (248).

Wanda also sums up her life with Will in a way consistent with Pauline's experiences. Wanda recalls that in her relationship with Will she was like an adjunct professor: "Well, that was what I was to Will Hand, adjunct. I could take a lot of other things but not that. Especially since what I was adjunct to was the entire, everloving natural world, rain, shine, birds and dooky, disasters and caves and you name it" (200). There are moments in *Goodbye to a River* when the preference of nature over women is made emphatic. Once, Graves recalls an earlier time on the river when he and his friend Hale were approached by two older "girls" who were drinking beer and flirting pretty heavily with the two boys. Graves muses: "What had bothered me then, besides the hot pubescent confusion, was a feeling that the women and the beer hadn't gone with the river, with the way I felt about the river and being there. Years and beers and women later, they still didn't" (109).

Here and now, in the presentness of floating down the river, Graves reveals how women have compromised his old-time closeness to his friend Hale. "Hale had been going partway down the river with me," Graves writes, "till business and his wife's opinion got in the way" (14). Another time in the book, Graves generalizes about the kinds of control women exert upon men. During a brief juncture on land, away from the river, he hears some men talking and describes it as "the talk of women-tended men magnifying the maleness of a three or four-day expedition away from their women" (81). Everywhere in the book the rhetoric of ownership and possession applies to relations between the sexes. Through the use of possessive pronouns ("their"), men own wives, and wives own men (although this latter formulation is put forth as a negative condition).

Will Hand's animus against women is a direct parallel to Graves'. Here is Will on the persistent conflict of women versus men: "Most women like people. And comfort" (110). Men, though, to Will, proudly, are loners, preferring nature over nurture. This preference, this theory that men have some privileged relation with nature, is an unexamined precept apparent throughout *Goodbye to a River*. The sole time that Graves permits a woman to be a lover of nature in his text is in a negative light. In a passage about the ecstasy of hunting, of killing, in this instance a dove, Graves writes, "all the pity of that perished gentle wildness. . . . No fiercely nature-loving female could ever have felt it stronger than I have, at times, and those people I care about hunting with feel it too" (54; Graves' ellipsis). Those people are men.

It is passing strange—but firmly within the mainstream of American literature—that Graves' masculinist ethic presumes a closer relationship between man and nature than the one between women and nature. How can hunting/killing connect men closer to nature than childbirth connects women? This is the question that D. H. Lawrence asks brilliantly in *Studies in Classic American Literature.*

So upon Pauline's second return to Texas, she goes to visit Will at his new home. He talks a lot about writing. He mentions that he writes little because there is so much work to be done on the land. He talks about the manuscripts sent him by aspiring poets. Seeing him in his second rural retreat, Pauline listens to him speak in a familiar rhythm: "His voice was warm, that special tone he saved for dogs and women" (196). Here the note of paternalistic chauvinism resounds once again. An obvious echo appears in *Goodbye to a River.* Upon meeting the wife and two daughters of a farmer named McKee, Graves writes, "I liked all three of them; tone filters through families from strong fathers as it does in business from bosses, and McKee's women were a corroboration of what I remembered of him. Even his dogs were" (102). The men-without-women theme runs throughout the river book of John Graves. He consistently sets up an unidentified imaginary female auditor against whom he is the truth-teller of male outdoor knowledge. "Yes, ma'am," he says repeatedly, no doubt borrowing the technique from Hemingway's genteel imaginary auditor in *Death in the Afternoon.* And the male self-approbation carries over to the final scene of *Goodbye to a River,* when, at a party after the trip is over, he explains to "somebody's wife" that he did have someone with him on the river—a dog (301). Note that this female character is not identified by name but as a "wife."

Pauline returns to Houston, then comes back to what Will calls his "rocky paradise" for a second visit (204). This time Hand talks about getting "so damned old" (204). He shows her with passion a greenhouse full of exotic plants, especially succulents, and she still can't recognize an aloe vera from an armadillo. But she has read his books, she tells him, and she even offers a distillation of their common themes: "Your books . . . , like your lectures, are to a great extent about the loss of water, the drying up of old sources" (208–209). She sees in Will's greenhouse the age-old Texas aim, to find new sources of water—in this case within Will's succulents—but it's no longer Will's old spirit. They're "just plants," he tells her (209). The implication of this exchange seems to me to be that if any theorizing's to be done, it's to be done by a man of the land. Not unexpectedly, Pauline feels like a "fool, trying to analyze his work" (209).

Later they take a walk around the perimeters of Will's farm, where Pauline sees for the first time his ingrained pessimism. In a wheat field on his property he finds a destructive pest, the greenbug, and points out to her that nothing can be done, the crop is ruined, that he will have to wait till next year for another crop. "Stunned by the force of his pessimism" (215), Pauline says they must do something to save the crop. But Will just laughs it off and says, "That's country life, Missy" (216). Later Will will say there's somebody in Stephenville who might know something about containing the greenbug, so here Pauline's energy perhaps has some positive effect on his dour realism.

When they go to feed the animals, Pauline is struck by the surge of life evident on the farm. The sight of a mare about to bear a colt prompts one of Pauline's sharpest insights: "On a farm, reproduction was everywhere. There was no way to avoid it. In the city, if you managed it right, you never even had to look inside a baby carriage" (223). A dust storm blows in, and at the onset of this atmospheric, the second storm they've experienced together, Pauline and Will have another of their edgy conversations. He reveals to her that he has had a heart bypass operation and is "not the man I was" (233). He doesn't write much, he says, he putters, and yet . . . the yet, she surmises, is that he feels the need to write a masterpiece. After this revelation he sulks. Will is still nothing if not a great sulker.

In the climactic scene of Pauline's psychological growth she agrees to spend the night at Will's house but will refuse his unspoken intimation to sleep together. Buoyed by a phone call offering a good role in a new play as well as the therapy she has been receiving from psychiatrist Russell Loving, Pauline is finally ready to discard the role of the dutiful daughter. For the final time, she sees Will in all of his limitations regarding nature and women:

> Will had what he needed, company for short visits only. More than likely Isabel [his wife] understood that this was

> as married as Will would ever be and that he couldn't bear to recognize the finished thing. He *had* to believe nothing was working out. Had to hold on to his eccentricities without defining or abandoning them. Had to deprive himself. Needed the antagonism. The goats, the greenbug, the loneliness. His side-kicks. (234)

Here all the limitations, for a woman anyway, of Will's commitment to masculine desire become absolutely clear. He is like some old-time cowboy, as the funny reference to sidekicks captures perfectly. Seeing Will objectively and without the constraints of sexual obligation is a good way for Pauline to assert her newly realized independence.

While she watches Will crawl under the house to fetch a bottle of homemade wine, she imaginatively visualizes his death from a heart attack at some unspecified time in the future: "The expression on Will's face is not one of unhappiness, exactly, only annoyance, as he thinks back over the projects he has not quite gotten around to, some half-finished, some not even begun. All the books he did not write" (240). Still, she comforts herself with the knowledge that he was "a man who knew exactly what he wanted" (241).

Pauline's ambivalence about Will here and elsewhere governs everything we know about him in the novel. But Will in the novel is not exactly the same as Graves in Lowry's life. Regarding Graves today, Lowry recalls seeing him recently in Austin, in 2004, commenting that "he commands the same attention and respect as ever, with his dynamite combo effect of great good self-deprecating humor, side by side with an innate seriousness he can only live out and through and keep notes on as he goes." There is Graves the man, and there is Graves in the novel. The novel, I submit, is at least as much an act of deconstruction as it is one of homage.

Texas letters, on the whole, could no doubt benefit from further novelistic explorations of the legends we live with. Lowry's interrogation of a classic Texas book reveals, challenges, and resonates.

Notes

1. Will sides with dogs over cats, as we shall later see. Texas letters (not litters) by and large split along that fault line of authors who prefer dogs versus

those who prefer cats, though so far as I know such a study has not yet been conducted. Graves' contribution to the literature of dogs is his collection published in 1981, *Blue and Some Other Dogs.*

2. The event is somewhat anticlimactic, however: "When he came, she hardly knew" (117). The second time they have sex, we are treated to a more detailed account:

> As a lover he was skilled. His erection was not as firm as a younger man's but that never mattered as much as men thought. He knew other things to do, lifted her buttocks just so, doing this and that with his hands and mouth. Unlike Michael, who collected her orgasms like trophies—even rating them, congratulating himself if she became particularly passionate—Will's attention seemed fixed on a more distant and somehow less exacting point. When he came, he ducked his head, moaned, as if in regret, and closed his eyes. (119)

This passage is stinging male-female repartee. Pauline lobs the first salvo, but Will makes a quick comeback by the mastery of his art (he's apparently not named Hand for nothing), but he's easily distracted from his task. By the end of the act, he is "in regret." This is the watchword of the whole passage. Regret in this context is trouble enough when it springs from a female source; expressed by a male, the term can assume cosmic proportions.

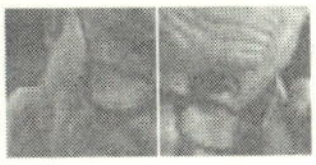

Of Dachshunds and Dashes

Subjects and Style in E. B. White and John Graves

DICKIE MAURICE HEABERLIN

I LOOKED FORWARD TO writing this essay once I decided on my subject because I have read with pleasure and taught with even more pleasure the works of E. B. White and John Graves. For over forty years, I have been teaching White's essay "Once More to the Lake." With freshman class after freshman class, I have been back, and back and back, to Belgrade Lake in Maine. Almost as often, I have taught Graves' *Goodbye to a River,* mostly to southwestern literature and nature writing classes. I even taught it at the University of Southern Maine when I did a faculty exchange. I have selected these and other works by these writers because I like what they write about and how they write about it.

Graves and White have many things in common. They each began their successful writing careers by publishing in the *New Yorker*—White with a regular column and Graves with a short story. They left the city to live in rural areas and write about their lives there. White moved from New York City to North Brooklin, Maine, in 1938 and wrote a regular column for *Harper's.* From it, he selected essays to produce his *One Man's Meat* and later the collection *Second Tree from the Corner.* Graves moved from Fort Worth to his land near Glen Rose, Texas. He wrote *Hard Scrabble* about his life there, and he wrote essays for *Texas Monthly,* selecting from these to fill his collection *From a Limestone Ledge.*

Their work might be compared to that of other writers from their own areas, writers who had returned from the city to write about rural subjects. In Maine, two that come immediately to mind are Louise Dickinson Rich, who wrote *We Took to the Woods,* and Bernd Heinrich, who wrote *A Year in the Maine Woods.* In Texas, the two that come immediately to mind are Stanley Walker, who wrote *Home to Texas* about his return to Lampasas, and George Sessions Perry, who wrote about his farm near Rockdale in *Tale of a Foolish Farmer.*

White lived on the extremely cold Maine coast, north of Bar Harbor, Graves in extremely hot Texas, yet they found common subjects to write about, particularly the animals they owned. Of the many animals they wrote about, the ones that most interested me, and most interest me, are the dachshunds, because I own and have owned dachshunds, right now two standard, wirehaired littermates, Barnaby and Clementine. The breed was developed in Germany and bred with short legs and powerful neck and shoulders to enable the dogs to go into holes and fight badgers. Because there are no humans down in the holes to help the dogs in this pursuit, the most successful dogs, and thus the breed, had to develop a great degree of independence and determination. Though not called on to hunt badgers here in the States, the breed has maintained those characteristics.

About my dachshunds, I can tell many stories—but won't. But I will quote my wife, Andrea, who says—sagely: "You don't see dachshunds in obedience competition." E. B. White said much the same thing when he wrote:

> Being the owner of dachshunds, to me a book on dog discipline becomes a volume of inspired humor. Every sentence is a riot. Someday, if I ever get a chance, I shall write a book, or warning, on the character and temperament of the Dachshund and why he can't be trained and shouldn't be. I would rather train a zebra to balance an Indian club than induce a dachshund to heed my slightest command. When I address Fred I never have to raise either my voice or my hopes. He even disobeys me when I instruct him in something he wants to do. (*One Man's Meat,* 160)

In another essay also in *One Man's Meat,* White tells us more about the behavior of Fred:

> Here he awaits the fall of an egg to the floor and the sensual delight of licking it up—which he does with lips drawn slightly back as though in distaste at the strange consistency of the white. His hopes run always to accidents and misfortunes: the broken egg, the spilt milk, the wounded goose, the fallen lamb, the fallen cake. His activities and his character constitute an almost uninterrupted annoyance to me, yet he is such an engaging old fool that I am quite attached to him, in a half-regretful way. Life without him would be heaven, but I'm afraid it is not what I want. (264)

John Graves, in talking about Blue and other dogs he had owned, mentions his concept of the "Nice Dog." Then he says that his dog Watty, a dachshund, was "emphatically not one" (*John Graves Reader,* 225). He goes on to tell about his Watty, also known as Passenger, Cacahuate, and Peanut:

> He started out all right, intelligent and affectionate and as willing to learn as dachshunds ever are, and with the nose he had he made a fair retriever, albeit hardmouthed with shot birds and inclined to mangle them a bit before reluctantly giving them up. He was fine company too, afield or in a canoe or a car, and we had some good times together. But his temper started souring when I married and grew vile when children came, and the job was finished by a paralyzing back injury with a long painful recovery, never complete, and by much sympathetic spoiling along the way. As an old lame creature, a stage that lasted at least five years, he snarled, bit, disobeyed, stank more or less constantly and from time to time broke wind to compound it, yowled and barked for his supper in the kitchen for two hours before feeding time, subverted the good sheep dogs' training, and was in general the horrid though small-scale antithesis of a Nice Dog. And yet in replication of my childhood self I loved him, and buried him wrapped in a feed sack beneath a flat piece of limestone with his name scratched deep upon it. (225)

Much of what Scott Elledge, White's biographer, said about White's attachment to his dachshund might also apply to that of Graves:

> During the many years that Fred had been his close companion, White had attributed to him a rich and real personality. Fred was "vile," gluttonous, and lascivious, possessing a "heavy charge of original sin." He was incapable of human love or loyalty, and he tended to deflate rather than build up his master's ego. But White admired him because he was "intensely loyal to himself, as every strong individualist must be," and because he loved life and was driven by curiosity. In Fred's individualism, in his loyalty to himself, and in his love of life and curiosity about it, White saw much of White. . . . (277)

White was an independent person—like Graves, an "O. F." (Old Fart), even as a young man, one wanting to live and write for himself, to choose his own path, unfettered by rules. About criticism of his manuscript of *Stuart Little* by Anne Carroll Moore, children's librarian emerita of the New York Public Library, White wrote:

> Her letter was long, friendly, urgent, and thoroughly surprising. She said she had read proofs of my forthcoming book called *Stuart Little* and advised me to withdraw it. She said, as I recall the letter, that the book was non-affirmative, inconclusive, unfit for children, and would harm its author if published. These were strong words and I was grateful to Miss Moore for having taken the trouble to write them. I thought the matter over, however, and decided that as long as the book satisfied me, I wasn't going to let an expert talk me out of it. It is unnerving to be told you're bad for children, but I detected in Miss Moore's letter an assumption that there are rules governing the writing of juvenile literature—rules as inflexible as the rules for lawn tennis. And this I was not sure of. I had followed my instincts in writing about Stuart, and following one's instincts seemed to be the way a writer should operate. (Quoted in Elledge, 263)

Given his fondness for independence, I find it surprising that White would have found the "rules" for writing in William Strunk's 1918 little book something to admire, but he did. When he revised *Elements of Style,* he made many changes. Strunk's precepts were not his. Elledge quotes White as saying that he could not "don the robes of solemnity at this late date" (330) and as saying that he did his own writing "by ear and seldom with any idea of what was taking place under the hood" (326). In his revision of *Elements of Style,* White wrote:

> The beginner should approach style warily, realizing that it is himself he is approaching, no other; and he should begin by turning resolutely away from all devices that are popularly believed to indicate style—all mannerisms, tricks, adornments. The approach to style is by way of plainness, simplicity, orderliness, sincerity. (Strunk, 69)

These are all elements exemplified by Rich, Heinrich, Walker, Perry, White, and Graves. But it is in the richness of the parenthetical structures that White and Graves are most different from the other excellent stylists (Elledge, 329).

William Strunk's third "elementary rule of usage" was "Enclose parenthetic expressions between commas." And that is the generic way of doing it. But among the other possible ways are, of course, enclosing them between parentheses, when they are quite off the subject, or between colons and periods. But the way preferred by writers who most frequently use parenthetical structures is to use paired dashes or a dash with a closing mark of punctuation. The dash allows the writer to announce boldly that he is going away from the main subject, that he is chasing rabbits. Dachshunds would love dashes. Using dashes is a declaration of independence, a way for the writer to put into his composition all of the nitty-gritty little things that make life interesting, whether near Glen Rose or Blue Hill.

A dachshund, in a hole alone, must decide for itself how to fight a badger—be independent, resourceful. Just so, must a writer be. Graves and White, exceptionally able, experienced, and competent writers, did not listen to arbiters of correctness, such as Ann Carroll Moore or William Strunk, did not follow their rules. Instead, Graves, a Texan, and White, a Mainer, each thought for himself, each a Maverick, seeking to and succeeding in writing clear, highly textured prose. Ironically, given their independent ways, each found the dash an exceptional tool, allowing them to provide the many asides that enlivened their prose.

Appendix A

Examples Showing Use of the Dash by John Graves in Goodbye to a River

Apposition

His Hernán Cortez was a man named Peter Garland—Captain Garland, they called him. (48)

Like someone in Tolstoy—Levin's brother, was it?—I'm fond of angling . . . . (208)

Feelings without knowledge—love, and hatred, too—seem to flow easily in any time . . . . (4)

But the squabbling had begun between their proponents and those otherwise-minded types—bottomland farmers and ranchers whose holdings would be inundated, competitive utility companies shrilling "Socialism!" and big irrigationists downstream—who would make a noise before they lost, but who would lose. (9)

He piled papers and maps on me, and instructions to see things he knew of and to look for things whose existence he suspected—Indian sites, beavers, and eaten-away silt cliff where longhorns' skulls and the remains of bison still came occasionally to view. (11)

I . . . finally carried up the other things from the boat—the map case and the shotgun and the rods and the food box, heavily full, and the cook box and the rucksack, all of them battered familiarly from other trips long before. (15)

There was very little Hollywood about them, and not much Fenimore Cooper. Rough, certainly . . . Mainly Southern, but not altogether, and even the Southerners heterogeneous in origin and type—rednecks and slaveholding younger sons from the cotton states, Texas-Revolutionary veterans from the older cattle counties far down the Brazos and the Colorado, hillmen from Tennessee and Carolina. (25; Graves' ellipsis)

All the murdered, scalped, raped, tortured people, red and white, all the proud names that belonged with hills and valleys and bends and crossings or maybe just hovered over the whole—Bigfoot Wallace, Oliver Loving, Charles Goodnight, Cynthia Ann Parker and her Indian son Quanah, Peta Nocona, Satank, Satanta, Iron Shirt . . . (7; Graves' ellipsis)

Nominative Absolute (Before a Relative Clause)

It was of that ungothic shape—roof peaked high along a ridge pole in the middle over three rooms in a row, and flattening fore and aft over the gallery and a rank of lean-to room—which the double log cabin's form had suggested to a log-cabin people abruptly presented with lumber. (69)

Extended Series of Adverbial Preposition Phrases

They lack the absoluteness of the spacious, disappearing breeds—of geese riding the autumn's southward thrust, of eagles, of grizzlies, of bison I never saw except in compounds . . . Of wolves . . . Of wild horses that have been hunted down in twenty years or so and have been converted into little heaps of dog dung on the nation's mowed lawns. And antelope, and elk grazing among the high aspens, an old bull always on guard . . . (29; Graves' ellipses)

What other brand of godliness, though, would you have substituted for it—in that time, in that place, in that people? (191)

Qualifying/Contrasting

We river-minded ones can't say much against them—nor, probably, should we want to. Nor, mostly, do we. . . . (8; Graves' ellipsis)

In that case they'd be letting out more—probably too much, he said ironically. (13)

It was a kind of tangential retribution for Moctezuma and the burned libraries of the Mayas—not that the Comanches thought of working retribution for anyone's wrongs but their own. . . . (19)

I would have been a headless-burgoo man—in fact am. . . . (33)

But it could be true—ought to be. . . . (62; Graves' ellipsis)

"Please, Buenas Noches," maybe one of them said. Maybe not—The People seldom begged. (63)

Change. Autumn. Maybe—certainly—there was melancholy in it, but it was a good melancholy. (119)

Another time on the Guadalupe to the south—but this is supposed to be about the Brazos . . . . (161; Graves' ellipsis)

"Aw, naw," Bill Briggs would say mildly when we wanted to do something we had no business doing, like—tired of fishing—swimming in the river when it was running strong, or—tired of fish—swiping a pullet from a farmer's flock, or—tired of chopping hard resistant driftwood—trying out our ax on the big shade trees above the bank. (250–251)

Parenthetical

From there Hale and I—he was taking me out—drove across the stripped and eroded farming section. . . . (12)

They . . . left place names and casks and chests of gold at each night's stopping place—"Ef a man only had him a good witchin' stick"—but for the most part who they were and how many and when is unknowable. . . . (17)

Irked perhaps by my calm—people who fly around near the ground seem to require delight and awe from earthbound watchers—they banked into a tight circle and came back to buzz me. . . . (27–28)

There was a fine long piece of river below, deep but with a pull, and running somehow—a miracle—sidewise to the wind, so that the water next to one bank was sheltered and smooth. (31)

The big water scooted us on down—I know the "us" is an anthropomorphism, but in the absence of other company a dog makes a plural, and not a bad one either—and through a fine, pounding rapids. . . . (42)

Noun Modifying (Adjectival)

He was a six-month-old dachshund and weighed about twelve pounds, and even after he was grown he wouldn't be a very practical dog, but he was company, too—more concrete, perhaps, than memories and feelings. (16)

So that the pathos one is prone to see in their destruction—apart, different from the destructions of the other red peoples to the east—is not pathos at all . . . . (20)

But the river was pretty where I was—wide and clean and even-flowing, with curious, arching, limestone overhanging along the right shore—and after the rain had stopped I dawdled . . . . (43–44)

Interrupter between Preposition and Its Object (Single Dash)

If one had a modern-tragic view like—oh, Graham Greene's, one might make symbols out of those fingers. (121)

Repetition of Verbs

Then, within a century, they made themselves into one of history's great races of riders—and made riders too of the other plains tribes northward and westward to whom they traded ponies. (18)

Implied Causation

Skating about the canoe on clogged boot soles, I made the laborious rearrangements and tied things down again and tarped them again and then, unwilling to start out again in the day's unpromising monotony—it seemed somehow a waste of good river—walked followed by the pup into the valley above the crossing. (25)

And the claim did have a little poetic verity—the river winds hugely. (77)

Ewell knew, but one finds it hard to blame him—writing in Granbury, with that kind of people still around him—for not having set it down. (203)

People with children—it was Sunday—walked along a path by the river and looked at me. (291)

Setting Off Adverbial Clause

And I care about knowing what it is, and—if I can—why. (160)

Setting Off Direct Object

They tell too—the stories—of the subsequent squabbles among the louts themselves. (143)

Repetition of Subject and Verb

It knifes through you, for instance, after waiting through a long golden evening for doves beside a stock tank in someone's pasture, watching your first bird coming in high and swift on the north wind, laying down knowing before you fire that you are on him, watching him contract raggedly and fall in a long parabola to baked hard earth and then going to pick him up—it knifes to feel suddenly in his warmth against your palm, in the silk touch of the feathers at his throat, all the pity of that perished gentle wildness. . . . (54; Graves' ellipsis)

Appendix B

Examples Showing Use of the Dash by E. B. White in One Man's Meat

Relative Clause

These persons are feared by every tyrant—who shows his fear by burning the books and destroying the individuals. (139)

Relative Clause Complementing a Verb Phrase

I got out of bed at half-past six, thinking about dreams and about what a plowman had told me the other day—which was that he often gets the answer to his problems in dreams. He had a dream lately telling him what to do about my newly-laid-down field, where I didn't get a very good catch of grass. (192)

Relative Clause Complementing a Location

One morning a few months ago, during a particularly busy time, when I awoke I didn't dare get dressed: I knew that my only hope of getting an overdue piece written was to stay in bed—which is where I did stay. (141)

Apposition

From these animals and this land you will receive all the food you and your family need, plus forty dollars a month—$25 from eggs, $15 from cream. (142)

This protein is ordinarily provided (on profit-and-loss farms) by expensive concentrates bought at a grain store—laying mash, hog ration, etc. (143)

So down the back stairs noisily and out through the dewy field with Fred, my chore dog, to the chicken range, where I opened the doors of the shelters and watched my two hundred pullets, long pent up, come sailing through the openings like chaff on the wind—a black cloud of feathers and delight. (193)

You will be looking out of a window, say, at a tree; and then after a bit the tree won't be there any more, and the looking won't be there any more, only the window will be there, in memory—the thing through which the looking has been done. (193)

The fourth, fifth, and sixth graders were gathered in the schoolyard with their teacher, who had on trousers in honor of the event, and I wished that I could see again (and in trousers) some of the teachers I had had in grammar school—Miss Hackett and Miss Kirby and Miss Crosby and Miss Douglas and Miss Ihlefeldt and Mrs. Schuyler and Miss Abigail A. Bourne and Miss Sheridan. (194)

I being glad, as always, to be self-released from indoor work and glad to be visiting the old Herrick place, which is remote and quiet—an old tumbledown barn in a run-out field encircled by woods and overlooking a small secluded cove. (194)

As we lifted the tongue of the roll and stirred the thing, a mouse leaped up and ran the length of it, like a tiny dog performing a circus act. I thought how pleasant it would be to start life fresh on the old Herrick place, with a one-room shack and no appurtenances—no equipment, no stock, no pets, no family responsibilities, no program. (194)

But knowing myself as well as I do, I well knew that it wouldn't be twenty minutes before I would acquire or contrive something to establish the roots of complexity in firm soil—a cold chisel perhaps, or an inamorata, or a folding towel rack. (194)

Just hulks of men, these old fellows seemed to me—dry stalks, autumnal creatures, about to die. (195)

Qualifying/Contrasting

I have a wholly different picture of doomsday—or rather doomsmoment. (193)

Noun Modifying (Adjectival)

In no time at all I would destroy the old Herrick place by setting out a pansy plant or repairing a rotten sill. And then it would be just like any other spot—beloved but not removed. (194–195)

Nominative Absolute

It was, as I had suspected, made in one long cylinder—narrow ten-foot spruce planks bolted to a pair of old mowing-machine wheels, and the frame heavily constructed. (195)

Predicate Adjective Complement

This year we're going to try putting up rhubarb, which I am told is simple—just cold water, no processing. (196)

Series of Past Participles to Complement Main Verb

On my last trip, however, it seemed to me that people had remodeled their ideas too—taken in their convictions a little at the waist, shortened the sleeves of their resolve, and fitted themselves out in a new intellectual ensemble copied from a smart design out of the very latest page of history. (135)

Independent Clause of Summary

He added: "Our American youngsters spend all their time at the movies—they're a mess." (135)

Luckily I am not out to change the world—that's being done for me, and at a great clip. (139)

Prepositional Phrase of Time

A writer goes about his task today with the extra satisfaction that comes from knowing that he will be the first to have his head lopped off—even before the political dandies. (139)

Adverbial Clause of Contrast

Nobody knows this better than I do—although my neighbors know it well enough and on the whole have been tolerant and sympathetic. (143)

Noun Phrase

And remember also that the grain harvest comes at the same season as the canning—those 600 Mason jars that have to be filled. (144)

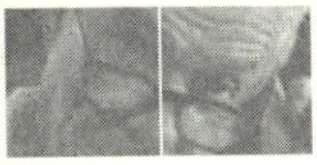

Brazos Bildungsroman

John Graves and Texas in Transition in Goodbye to a River

LISA SLAPPEY

Goodbye to a River is ostensibly the narrative of John Graves' 1957 canoe trip along a middle section of the Brazos River, from the base of the Possum Kingdom Dam in Palo Pinto County, Texas, to Somervell County, about 150 miles to the southeast. The three-week journey, though, becomes both a metaphor for the cultural changes evident in this stretch of North Central Texas and a fulcrum for the personal changes in Graves' life. Written initially as a magazine article for *Sports Illustrated,* then published in part in *Holiday,* the text itself grew into a three-hundred-page classic, not only of regional literature but also of the American frontier as Graves added a bricolage of local and natural history, anecdotes, canonical literary references, and moral ruminations to the bare bones of the canoe trip. More a mission than a leisurely float, the trip provides the structure for a personal and quite emotional memoir of what that piece of river has meant to the author. It is also, however, a scholarly exploration of the historical forces that have worked upon and against this riparian area of Texas. As Graves journeys down the river, he seeks to establish and determine meaning in his own life as well as in the life of his nation; both, it becomes apparent, are at critical junctures.

Although the stated urgency in this text derives from the "enraged awe" Graves feels regarding the proposal of a series of dams along the Brazos that would destroy the river, an examination of *Goodbye to a River* in the context of Graves' other writings suggests that the narrative contains elements of the Bildungsroman. The text diverges from the classic Bildungsroman in at least two important features—it is a quasi-autobiographical narrative rather than a novel, and the protagonist is not a youth but a grown man approaching forty—yet *Goodbye to a River* nonetheless demonstrates characteristics of the novel of formation. Specifically, the work functions as a version of the Künstlerroman, which chronicles the development of the protagonist as an artist. The manuscript of *Goodbye to a River* offers a diegesis of the moment of its author's birth as a fully formed writer.

True to the basic Bildungsroman plot, Graves is the wandering provincial who returns from his cosmopolitan experience with a newfound sense of belonging and purpose. His far-ranging education is to be distilled into local knowledge. To this end, the Brazos river trip serves as both a farewell and a homecoming. It marks the conclusion of Graves' personal picaresque and the beginning of his hardscrabble, settled, domestic life in rural Texas. After almost twenty years of travels, from college at Rice University in Houston to military service in World War II in the South Pacific and the struggling writer's life in Mexico, New York, and Europe, Graves returned to Texas for a visit and then remained when his father was diagnosed with terminal esophageal cancer.

The loss of the father, another element crucial to the Bildungsroman, runs as a thematic undercurrent through *Goodbye to a River.* In dealing with this loss, Graves must also determine his own inheritance as an artist, a man, and a Texan. The absence of the biological father in the narrative is made more striking by the presence of the author's literary forebears throughout the text and by the inclusion of the more generic Texas settlers whose violent relationships to people and place created the cultural milieu to which Graves finds himself heir. Graves claims intellectual and cultural descent from both the canonical giants (among them Sterne, Shakespeare, Joyce, Malory, Milton, Cervantes, and a healthy dose of Thoreau) whose references pepper his narrative and the Old Settlers and Cedar Folk who never read beyond the King James Bible. Writing from the intersection of south and west, Graves acknowledges that "there's nothing new in the idea that the frontier had continuing impact on our character" (144). Examining his portion of the frontier, subject to the violence of conquest like the rest of the continent, may shed light on who he is as a Texan as well as who we are as a nation of Americans.

At about the same time Graves returned to Texas, the Corps of

Engineers proposed a series of dams along the Brazos River between the already-completed dams at Possum Kingdom and Lake Whitney. For Graves, the act of damming the river constituted another instance of violence, this time against the country he loves. It was a continuation of human efforts to subjugate the land. While growing up in nearby Fort Worth, Graves took frequent canoe trips down the Brazos. This little stretch was *his* river, and the construction of dams would alter it beyond recognition. His father's illness and the river's plight combined to signify a son's loss of both his father and his childhood. In the face of such loss, however, the river became something tangible to hold on to, so that despite the changes, "it was still there, touchable in a way that other things of childhood were not" (7). The trip is itself a version of the picaresque, and the tale of the prodigal's return is couched in the largely epigraphic depiction of the questing knight as culture hero. The grail, for Graves, seems to be the discovery of the subject matter—the changing country and one's relationship to it—that would make his career as a writer.

In an appearance at the Brazos Bookstore in Houston in May 2004, John Graves replied to the question of whether he considered *Goodbye to a River* an elegy with, "I guess it is. I'm certainly not a celebrator of progress and change." Faced in 1957 with the prospect that the Brazos River would be changed forever, Graves took action by petitioning his editor to support an unusual writing project that would document what he anticipated would be the end of the Brazos as he knew it, before the Brazos River Authority turned it into a series of dams and lakes. Commissioned to write an article for *Sports Illustrated,* Graves set out in his canoe to revisit his childhood, to discover the region's past, and to say his good-byes. This resulting river journey was at once his homecoming and the beginning of his literary career.

In a letter to his agent, John Schaffner, Graves proposed the writing project and confessed, somewhat urgently, "I'd like to set my feelings about that river down now, before they drown it, and the framework for setting them down will be the trip" (quoted in Hamrick, 6). Graves' quest is a search for meaning, both historical and personal, along that part of the Brazos. Early in the narrative, he writes, "feelings without knowledge—love, and hatred, too—seem to flow easily in any time, but they never worked well for me . . ." (4; Graves' ellipsis). He has the feelings—he keeps telling us, "Either you care or you don't" (60)—and certainly a vast store of knowledge. The question becomes how to make the river and the author's journey meaningful to the reader. In the same letter to Schaffner, he admits, "I know that no one ever heard of those places, and there's not an oil well on the whole route, but it is as purely Texas country as you can find" (3). This place, then, unknown to the rest of the world, is home to Graves, and it is from here that he launches not only his canoe but his lifelong literary critique of how contemporary America came to be.

From the beginning of the narrative, Graves justifies to the reader his intention to canoe not the entirety of the eight-hundred-mile Brazos River but only "a piece of it that has had meaning for me during a good part of my life in the way that pieces of rivers can have meaning" (4). Cutting through Central Texas on its way to the Gulf of Mexico just south of Houston, the Brazos "slices across Texas history as it does across the map of the state" (4–5). Readers will have to know something of human and political history as well as natural history in order to know about the river.

Graves is willing to teach us on the journey, for in the writing process he has developed an academic expertise to complement his personal recollections and cultural associations relevant to the Brazos. His physical description of that piece of the river locates us in place and time. He is most concerned with "a hundred and fifty or 200 miles of the river toward its center on the fringe of West Texas, where it loops and coils snakishly from the Possum Kingdom Dam down between the rough low mountains of the Palo Pinto country, into sandy peanut and post-oak land, and through the cedar-dark limestone hills above a new lake called Whitney" (5). This early description posits the river as a living presence and permits us to recognize it as the main character in the text. It also introduces us to the notion that the river is subject to sweeping changes according to human caprice. Like the Concord and Merrimack Rivers, which Thoreau described more than a century before, the Brazos River and the country it drains bear the scars of human intervention. The grassy prairie is gone, with limestone hills from geologic time now covered in a recent growth of scrub cedar trees. Bounded by dams and man-made lakes, and threatened by the construction of more of the same, this piece of the Brazos already differs from the river of the author's youth and his memory. In some aspects, though, it appears deceptively unchanged, so that Graves is able to imagine that "when you paddle and pole along it, the things you see are much the same things the Comanches and the Kiowas used to see, riding lean ponies down it a hundred years ago to raid the new settlements in its valley" (5). At certain places, ignoring the presence of bridges, barbed wire, and submerged automobiles, this may even now prove true.

Unfortunately for the author, the Brazos, and certainly the Natives, "few people nowadays give much of a damn about what the Comanches and the Kiowas saw" (5). Graves concedes the rationality of this lack of interest, for "it is harsh country for the most part, and like most of West Texas accords ill with the Saxon nostalgia for cool, green, dew-wet landscapes" (5). However antithetical to Saxon desires, the Brazos country has its own beauty that invokes in Graves a different type of nostalgia for the lost physical and cultural landscapes of the Comanches and the Kiowas. Despite the river's unwelcoming aspects, Graves asserts that "it has meaning which makes it worth the trouble" (6), and it is the delineation of this meaning that will give birth to the autochthonous author.

This canoe trip will be a rite of passage for Graves as he contemplates, at age thirty-seven, the role of the river in his life, along with the direction his own life must take as his role changes with the impending death of his father and end of his extended bachelorhood. In his memoir, *Myself and Strangers,* an exploration of his personal and professional pursuits prior to his return to Texas, Graves makes explicit the split voices of Young John and Old John from the distance of half a century:

> In a few ways Young John the journal keeper is something of a stranger to Old John the gray-headed commentator and summarizer and square-bracketer. He was rather ill-read despite six years of college, naïve in several ways, sexually a bit randy, quite profane at times, and filled with inchoate, often frustrated ambition. And he was still carrying a pretty fair load of ingrained Texan-Southern provincialism. (xiii)

Already, though, in *Goodbye to a River* the author writes of himself as a maturing man in contrast to the boyhood versions of himself he recalls from previous experiences on the river. Distinguishing between Young and Older, he sees the former as one who "moves in upon the country and thinks himself a tile in its tessellated ecology," whereas the latter "knows himself to be an excrescence upon the landscape and no kinsman to any wild thing" (37). The mythic heroism attached to the narrative of western expansion fades with the maturing author's acknowledgment of his own participation in the destruction of the natural world.

The protagonist of *Goodbye* is perhaps a Middle John, able still to look back upon his own youth with some compassion yet cognizant of the changes that come with experience and with intellectual and emotional maturation. He is able to analyze and interpret his responses, particularly to situations involving violence or the threat thereof, with an almost clinical clarity. His attitude toward hunting, an activity he had enjoyed without reflection as a young man, is the most obvious indicator of Graves' maturation. Still feeling the itch to shoot, the author knows that in his youth he would have killed an eagle "for nothing, for pride of destruction that has marked us as a breed . . ." (29; Graves' ellipsis). This desire for destruction is as contemporary as it is deeply ingrained, and it is a sign that the nation, the breed itself, is far from mature. In one of the most violent scenes in the narrative, a mob goes to extraordinary lengths to slaughter an ancient, giant catfish in the Brazos. On this trip, Graves hunts and fishes only in order to eat and even then with some tinge of regret. Momentarily envious of the boys flying army helicopters, Graves refuses to shoot at the ducks they flush out and is ready to admit that "I'd had enough of the young, uniformed, harebrained business to last me three lifetimes" (61). Graves associates this change in attitude toward hunting with his military service, as if his own experience in World War II allowed him to reevaluate his relationship to other living creatures.

In contrast to his extensive discourse on the present and historical inhabitants of the Brazos country, Graves offers relatively little insight into his personal human relationships in *Goodbye to a River.* He even flirts, for instance, with the potential lure of the hermit's life. His childhood friend, Hale, an avid sportsman who does not share Graves' reverence for animal life, joins him for an overnight leg of the river trip, and even this seems like an intrusion on his privacy. Not until the publication of *Myself and Strangers* does Graves reveal some of the personal details missing from his Texas writings, including a failed first marriage to his college sweetheart, followed by a series of relationships of varying significance. Not long after returning to Texas, Graves met Jane Cole, the New Yorker who would become his wife during the writing of *Goodbye to a River* and whose photograph of the author, seated in his canoe, graces the inside cover of *John Graves and the Making of* Goodbye to a River. The marriage plot completes the Bildungsroman, and although Graves is a bachelor on this trip, he undoubtedly has more to consider during these three weeks than just the damming of the Brazos River. Facing these simultaneous endings and beginnings, Graves has arrived at a watershed moment in his life.

As he begins his journey down the Brazos, he harbors doubts about the timing, the weather, and his own preparation. Angered by his inability to identify the call of a bird in what he terms "that country where I belonged" (156), he realizes that his long sojourn away from Texas has left him disconnected. His body, softened by urban life in New York, complains in response to the cold, the rain, and the sheer exertion of paddling. He laments that in general, contemporary life has made it very difficult for humans to have an organic or even mystical relationship to the natural world, the type of relationship he imagines the Comanches and even the rancher Charlie Goodnight must have had, now that we live in a mechanized world, *on* rather than *in* country, in "the prickly machine-humming place that man has hung for himself above that natural world" (159). Graves seeks to reestablish for himself and for the reader a sense of connection to the natural world. He keeps pulling the reader into the text with the challenges such as "I can't give you three unanswerably good reasons why one should care a damn about what the land is" (32). In his moral universe, giving a damn is obviously the right response.

He makes us care by telling stories that show the river has a life of its own and that it has in turn shaped the lives of humans. Most of his stories are violent tales—of murder, rape, cross-cultural conflict of the frontier moment, and deadly disputes among poor whites who settled there. Knowing the river requires knowing the stories, and these stories are everywhere Graves looks: "If the river has meaning for you, you can see all of that from the sandstone bluffs where the mountains drop away. You don't have to strain to impose the tales on the landscape" (140). Instead of imposing tales, Graves seems to be allowing them expression.

Despite demonstrating little love for the "half-illiterate louts" who fought the Comanches and the land and each other, he concedes that they are part of his heritage (143). He must know where he came from before he can define himself. He writes, "Mankind is one thing; a man's self is another. What that self is tangles itself knottily with what his people were, and what they came out of. Mine came out of

Texas, as did I. If those were louts, they were my own louts" (144). In Bildungsroman fashion, his education and his travels have led him home to rediscover his own country and his place in it.

Throughout the trip, Graves relates stories associated with specific places along the route. As a boy he had relished the oral versions of these local stories, the "obscure and petty and always violent tales, hearsay usually and as often as not untrue" (7). Most have to do with local folks, others with those who found fame in West Texas, such as the rancher Charlie Goodnight or the captive Cynthia Ann Parker and her son, the Comanche leader Quanah Parker. These are most often frontier tales in which different cultures come into contact with one another. Such cultural exchanges are very often violent, even deadly as one way of life intrudes upon another, altering both forever. Again in his pitch to Schaffner, Graves concedes, "After you dig in the little county histories for a time, it begins to seem as though every curve of the river, every rapids and pool, must have some tale of murder, rape, mutilation, heroism, cowardice, attached to it from those thirty years or so of the last century when the fight was going on" (Hamrick, 4–5). With those glory days long past, the Brazos River remains for Graves a highly contested space as Americans struggle to exert control over the natural world and its inhabitants.

Graves' narrative foregrounds violence as the cultural imperative inherent in the conquest of the American West. Cultural changes in this part of Texas—including social, economic, and racial reconfigurations—have come not gently but brutally. At each site along the river, Graves tells of humans engaging in acts of violence against the land, animals, and each other. Beginning from the most recognizable type—human-on-human violence—the author works his way back to the impetus of his trip, the imposition of a series of dams upon the river. He dichotomizes the various acts of violence as antique and contemporary, near and far, colonizer and colonized, then shows that these supposed dualities function in fact as a continuum of violence throughout the history of the Texas frontier, a frontier that did not end with the last of the Indian Wars but that continues to reshape itself as both the land and the culture of its inhabitants are re-formed.

The story of the West, and indeed the story of America, involves an ethnocentric, aggressive colonial culture imposing itself upon and seeking to eradicate indigenous cultures. It also involves appropriating indigenous land in the name of nation building. Ethnocentrism—the Manifest Destiny notion that "we're better than you"—is the norm, whereas cultural relativism—the notion that each culture is a system with its own merits and flaws—remains largely the province of theorists. The foundational violence Graves depicts is echoed in Richard Slotkin's assertion that "the myth of regeneration through violence became the structuring metaphor of the American experience" (*Regeneration through Violence,* 5). Graves' violent stories impart much the same feeling that Patricia Nelson Limerick describes in *Something in the Soil,* so that "the person who contemplates these tales ends up feeling a kind of nondiscriminatory moral shock, unnerved by nearly everybody's behavior" (34). This behavior is more than simply a relic of the frontier.

By writing *Goodbye to a River* with "the Comanches and the stolen horses and the two little red-headed boys scalped and murdered always behind it all" (Hamrick, 5), Graves is able to explore radically opposed notions of belonging to a place. Although Graves certainly provides examples of Anglo depredations against Native peoples—the massacre of Choctaw Tom's peaceful group and the subsequent expulsion of Texas Indians across the Red River into Indian Territory are but two examples—this is not the only type of interaction between whites and Indians in the text.

The primary historical interhuman conflict in *Goodbye to a River* occurs between the Anglo settlers and the Comanches, whose territory, the Comanchería, they have violated. For the Comanches, the most significant cultural change came when they acquired the horse from the Spaniards, thus making possible the marauding Plains culture so familiar in the mythology of the West. Graves presents both Comanche and Anglo cultures as aggressively ethnocentric, then adopts the radical perspective of cultural relativism in pointing out the faults in Anglo culture as well as the merits in Comanche culture. He refers to the Comanches as they refer to themselves, as The People. He presents them almost longingly in all of their bloody and violent glory as engaging in "a kind of tangential retribution for Moctezuma and the burned libraries of the Mayas" (19). These Indians fight back as cultural conflict escalates into a war for supremacy along the Brazos, as "a new brand of un-Spanish whites had been moving in with the odd notion that *they* owned it, if they could grab it" (20). Graves describes the Comanche as "dominant in the world they had selected, rich in the goods they prized, dexterous, cruel, wild, joyful, unbearable, lousy, bowlegged, and magnificent"

(19–20). The People will not be silenced within the text. In one of his parenthetical asides, Graves challenges the reader: "*You* try to keep The People out of it, even now that we're through with them" (196). Their history sits along the river and upon the land, underwriting and informing all that comes after.

Although Graves forces the reader to see the extreme violence of the Comanches, including scenes of murder, rape, torture, and mutilation, he is also adamant in relating similarly egregious activities among non-Indians. He notes that the local religion is based on a vengeance not yet exhausted in the Brazos country: "Calvinistic fundamentalism and its joined opposite, violent wallowing sin, settled that part of the world and have flourished there since" (178). The North-South violence of the Civil War served both as an excuse for Texans to exterminate Indians while the rest of the country was distracted and as a breeding ground for the techniques and attitudes that would be useful in later acts of aggression. Violence between blacks and whites—including rape and murder—happens here along the Brazos, as well.

White-on-white violence, though, is the most common in this country and proves no less barbaric than any interracial outrage. The long-running feud between the Truitts and the Mitchells, for instance, like the battles between the Comanches and the Anglo invaders, is cause for a reevaluation of our notions of right and wrong, good and evil, when the conflicting stories make any form of truth so difficult to discern. Violence itself becomes the truth at the heart of the story.

These old violations, most of them from the 1800s, inform the contemporary narrative of the river journey. The stories are as immediate to the author, and therefore to the reader, as the water and the trees and the sandbars. They are connected to this place intimately. Graves, though, carries within him another version of violence, both contemporary and distant, in his remembrance of World War II. Most of his references to his war experiences are somewhat oblique, yet that sense of witnessed depravity is always present. Graves admits that the old-time violence in the Brazos country pales in comparison with "the violences two wars in two generations have wrought among our race. I once saw 4,000 Japanese stacked like cordwood, the harvest of two days' fighting" (143). His nightmare early in the journey melds the burbling sounds of the river into first drums and then Comanche, Kiowa, and finally Japanese voices pursuing him.

Graves' initiation into violence in a foreign war comes full circle when he connects his personal experience to the historical violence rooted in place.

Although he mentions nothing of the matter here, Graves writes sparingly in *Myself and Strangers* that as a young marine on Saipan he lost the vision in his left eye when a Japanese soldier exploded a grenade in front of him. In *Hard Scrabble,* a book primarily about the land on which he has lived and worked for almost forty years, Graves offers "An Irrelevance" for three tear-jerking pages, during which he holds the hand of a dying Alabama marine. The frontier violence has not burned itself out but has found new expression in new locales. The old stories, though, remain in place, and what they suggest to Graves is disturbing: "Meanings floated near the surface which have relevance to the murkier thing Americans have become" (*Goodbye,* 144). As he suggests to Schaffner, part of his fascination with the past involves "trying to relate it to this honkytonk present that has somehow grown out of it" (Hamrick, 5). By embarking on the solo river trip, the author has not dissociated himself from the contemporary world but has given himself the perspective from which to evaluate it.

Why does Graves place so much emphasis on violence in this narrative? Why not, he asks us, relate events to edify the reader? He confesses that certainly there were "sober, useful, decent" people and events along the Brazos River. The short answer may be that we need to know about the violence because it is always there. It is our inheritance as Texans and as Americans. The longer answer, as Slotkin later derives from Faulkner (the subject of Graves' master's thesis), may be that this is the legacy of our founding fathers,

> those who (to paraphrase Faulkner's *Absalom, Absalom!*) tore violently a nation from the implacable and opulent wilderness—the rogues, adventurers, and land-boomers; the Indian fighters, traders, missionaries, explorers, and hunters who killed and were killed until they had mastered the wilderness; the settlers who came after, suffering hardship and Indian warfare for the sake of a sacred mission or a simple desire for land; and the Indians themselves, both as they were and as they appeared to the settlers, for whom they were the special demonic personification of the American wilderness. (4)

Even if the "composite hero" has won and his pink Thunderbird has replaced the trusty steed and his brick patio home has replaced the well-built log cabin, it is all underwritten by the violence of the frontier, whether we want to see it or not (237). Graves interprets the relationship between violence against country and its inhabitants as a cumulative process in which those who come after bear the indelible marks of their predecessors:

> Neither a land nor a people ever starts over clean. Country is compact of all its past disasters and strokes of luck—of flood and drouth, of the caprices of glaciers and sea winds, of misuse and disuse and greed and ignorance and wisdom—and though you may doze away the cedar and coax back bluestem and mesquite grass and side-oats grama, you're not going to manhandle it into anything entirely new. It's limited by what it has been, by what's happened to it. And a people, until that time when it's uprooted and scattered and so mixed with other peoples that it has in fact perished, is much the same in this as land. It inherits. Its progenitors stand behind its elbow, and not only the sober gentle ones. Most of all, maybe, the old hairy direct primitives whose dialect lingers in its mouth, whose murderous legend tones its dreams, whose oversimple thinking infects its attitudes toward bombs and foreigners and rockets to the moon.
>
> I don't think this means only Texans. (237–238)

Our attitudes towards bombs and foreigners and rockets to the moon have a great deal to do with our attitudes towards land. Our proclivity for waste and destruction, often disguised as a desire for progress, is written upon the land. As the Old Settlers gave way more than a century ago, a new breed of whites moved into the Brazos country with no regard for humanity or for abstract justice. Graves describes them as "the cutting edge of a people whetted sharp to go places, to wear things out and move on, to take over and to use and to discard" (48). They used and abused the land, then abandoned the place when they saw better opportunities in automobile factories in Fort Worth, only to be replaced by absentee landowners. The result is a loss of connection with the land, and it is this connection Graves seeks to reestablish for himself and for the reader. Clearly, the place has meaning to him:

> If you are built like me, neither the certainty of change, nor the need for it, nor any wry philosophy will keep you from feeling a certain enraged awe when you hear that a river that you've always known, and that all men of that place have known always back into the red dawn of men, will shortly not exist. A piece of river, anyhow, my piece . . . (8–9; Graves' ellipsis).

This sense of outrage comes through most clearly when Graves addresses our collective violations against the land. He juxtaposes instances of violence among humans with those featuring injury to the land. He even associates the Possum Kingdom Dam, completed in 1941, with the outbreak of World War II (7).

According to Graves' version of what Americans have become and why, this foundational violence underlies our thoughts and behavior even if we can neither acknowledge nor understand it. By the end of the narrative, Graves has left the river and is at a cocktail party contemplating the events of the contemporary world. Sputnik has just been launched the month before, in October 1957. The civil rights movement is gaining momentum. The cold war is heating up. If we can see the roots of violence, then none of this is new, nor is it particular to Texas. Caught between lament for what is lost and dread of what may come, the maturing author witnesses his nation undergoing a painful and still-violent adolescence as America begins to deal with cultural changes, race relations, and a global power struggle.

Graves reminds us that the self is constituted through everything that has shaped it: stories, literature, myth, violence, decency, conflict always, and place. We have to locate ourselves within this complex nexus of culture, history, memory, time, and place. If a person "wants in some way to know himself, define himself, and tries to do it without taking into account the thing he came from, he is writing without any ink in his pen" (145). The Künstlerroman plot comes to fruition when the artist knows and embraces his origins. For Graves, the thing he came from is the Brazos country. Maybe this should give us reason enough to care: We are formed by and therefore never outside the very stories—and in fact the very violence—that Graves relates. This personal narrative must be personal to the reader as well.

Goodbye to a River ends with John Graves as an outsider in an absurd setting. The author is back in the city at a cocktail party trying to explain his solo river trip to a woman who has inquired whether he was lonesome on the journey. Off the river and sheltered from the elements, he is somewhat annoyed by the question:

> But it was a good place to be, and the thermostat on the wall was set at seventy-five degrees, and outside the windows the cold sleet mixed with rain was driving down at a hard slant, and far far up above all of it in the unalive silent cold of space some new chunk of metal with a name, man-shaped, was spinning in symbolism, they said, of ultimate change. In that place the stark pleasures of aloneness and unchangingness and what a river meant did not somehow seem to be very explicable. (301)

Graves has just spent three hundred pages making the river real and meaningful to the reader, and though he suggests it is inexplicable to "somebody's wife" at a holiday party, he makes clear to his audience—those who care—the river's relevance in the contemporary world.

From the almost forgotten landscapes of rural Texas, Graves finds his metaphors for "the murkier thing" (144) he has observed in Americans at home and abroad. He taps into the violence of western expansion to show how aggressive interactions among humans have extended to an utter disregard for the land and its inhabitants as Americans' demand for progress mandates a reconfiguration of the landscape that has morphed into an assault upon outer space. At the same time, he struggles to define his place within this landscape—as a son, husband, steward, and, most importantly, as a writer. As rivers and horses and land lose out to the cold war, Sputnik, patio homes, and pesticides, the writer John Graves comes of age at home in a real world worth saving.

Contested Landscapes

John Graves' Meditations on Hard Scrabble *Texas History and Ecosystems*

BARBARA J. COOK

> All things natural and rural being parts of a whole . . .
>
> JOHN GRAVES, *Hard Scrabble*

UNDER BLUE SKIES that seemed to reflect the hue of the spring bluebonnet fields, I drove north, with my husband, from Austin to the landscapes that are the subject of John Graves' written meditations. After reading *Goodbye to a River* in Mark Busby's Southwestern Studies class, I wanted to explore a region of Texas I had never paid much attention to. It was the stories that Graves tells rather than the landscape descriptions that drew me to take a closer look. We walked in the dinosaur footprints, drove past houses built of petrified wood, and explored the sleepy little town of Glen Rose. The Brazos was a little harder to access, but we managed to picnic beside a small creek that fed into the river. I write this essay eight years later and what stands out in my memory is the sense of a timeless landscape: A place exemplified by those footprints etched in Paluxy River limestone long ago and the way the locals incorporated the petrified wood found all over the area into building materials in a region that is scant on timber for house building. But as I have come to realize, a landscape is dynamic rather than timeless, and those dynamics reflect natural processes as well as human actions. By telling stories, Graves captures this reciprocal tension between human and nonhuman elements.

In *Goodbye to a River* Graves contemplates with quiet nostalgia the changing landscapes and contested histories along the Brazos from Possum Kingdom Dam to Lake Whitney. In his work there is a sense of the enduring qualities of the land, the river, and the peoples that have been a part of the history of this riverway. Born in Texas, he writes at a time of returning, and his meditations on history and the natural world are not so much a farewell as a search to define himself and the "thing he came from" (145). Graves writes in the belief that "the frontier had continuing impact on our character, [and] one slice of that frontier, examined, may to some degree explain the whole . . ." (144; Graves' ellipsis).

Graves' slice is the Upper Middle Brazos that meanders through the center of Texas. The Brazos is a river that "slices across Texas history as it does across the map of the state" (4–5). This was not an easy place to live—not in the 1800s and not even in the twentieth century. He often refers to the area as a hardscrabble landscape, and he later names the land, the place he calls his home years after his journey down the Brazos, Hard Scrabble. Graves writes that the name for the "something less than four hundred acres of rough limestone hill country . . . does reflect the way I feel about the work I have put into it and the existence it has imposed on other owners and occupants over the years" (*Hard Scrabble,* 3). A place is known through experience,[1] and Graves gives us experiential stories of the people who have attempted to come to terms with the "rough limestone hill country." At the same time, Graves constructs a sense of place for himself and offers readers the opportunity to experience vicariously a slice of rural Texas. Environmental historian Kent C. Ryden argues that although a place "necessarily has a physical geographical existence, our sense of place is primarily a narrative construction" (*Mapping the Invisible Landscape,* 77).[2] In a way the body of work Graves has given us is more than simple collections of stories; it is a narrative construction that organizes the reality of the human and environmental history of a small part of North Central Texas.[3] His essay of place speaks to the reader's own sense of place because it rings true. Thus, the understanding of the local geographical and cultural history is linked in the reader's mind to consequences of human and nonhuman interaction outside that particular region.

In *Goodbye to a River* Graves draws on folklore, historical events, and probably tall tales to construct a narrative of "his" part of Texas. Ryden's recent work on construction of invisible landscapes through study of material culture, folklore, and other local knowledge provides a lens through which to view Graves' narrative construction. In some ways Graves could be considered a traditional nature writer, but his texts provide more than a familiarity with the physical landscape. By bringing alive the stories of individuals who have inhabited the land over the last couple of centuries, Graves establishes "the meanings which people assign to that landscape through the process of living in it" (Ryden, *Mapping,* 38).

Natural landscapes have not always been considered in light of the historical. Currently, there is shifting theoretical ground in the fields of historical geography and environmental history. And nature writing has often been seen as a way to give voice to the nonhuman world. The nature writer seeks to speak for the natural world, evoking a pristine landscape devoid of human history, often bringing in humans only in an effort to conserve or preserve that pristine natural world. For instance, in *Arctic Dreams,* Barry Lopez contemplates the "heedless imposition on the land and on the people, a rude imposition" that human intervention has brought to the Arctic landscapes (xxvii). But even Lopez doesn't linger on those impositions; he goes on to question the way that "people imagine the landscapes they find themselves in . . . how . . . the land shape[s] the imaginations of the people that dwell in it" (xxvii). As Scott Slovic writes, nature writers explore "relationships between the human mind and the natural world" (17) and are primarily concerned with "interior landscapes, with the mind itself" (18). Early ecocriticism has a tendency to keep the human and nonhuman worlds separate—"contemplating something that is ineluctably separate from us, a world apart" (Ryden, *Landscape with Figures,* 45).[4]

Graves takes us in another direction—past imagination and landscape to the experience of a specific landscape. Ryden points out that human culture is often intimately intertwined with nature, both "shaped by it and shaping it in ways that, while they are interdependent and mutually informing, depend ultimately on the conditions that nature sets" (52). There is a symbiotic relationship between region and the people who occupy that region, and as Ryden shows us, many nature writers take on the role of both naturalists and folklorists. They listen

> carefully to people in order to understand their traditional uses and interpretations of the landscape, examining the landscape itself as providing clues to human culture. In so doing, they bridge the gap between the human and nonhuman that looms so large in American nature writing and ecocriticism; while fully aware of the deep and widespread harm that human beings have done to the natural world, they also examine individual landscapes on an intimate scale, showing how communities have constructed mutually sustaining partnerships with nature, suggesting through their literary examinations that humans can live wisely and well on the earth if only they will let nature take a guiding role in the development of culture. (66)

In order to understand the natural world of a region, it is necessary to understand the culture as it has evolved.

As Ryden argues, in some landscapes, "an understanding of the environment implies an understanding not only of natural processes but of the human lifeways, often subtle, often traditional, that those processes have informed and shaped over time" (48). His work draws on material folk culture in order to understand the praxis of landscape use. Graves does not necessarily look at material culture, although in *Hard Scrabble* (2002) there is much discussion of farm implements and adaptation of fence building to the local limestone underlying the thin layers of soil. Rather, Graves seeks to understand that praxis through historical accounts and folklore; thus, the narratives he constructs from the people's stories help us understand this particular slice of Texas. If we come to understand the tensions, conflicts, and struggles of the Comanches, Kiowas, and other Indians and the successive waves of white settlers, we are able to arrive at a fuller understanding of America's westward drive to achieve Manifest Destiny.

In the portrait that Graves constructs for us, there are few victims, merely proud individuals, formed by the past and struggling to survive in the local environment. Graves writes against the tale of frontier progress embraced by Frederick Jackson Turner. For Graves, the central saga of his narration is not transformation of "landscape from wilderness to trading post to farm to boomtown" (Cronon, "A Place for Stories," 1352). Rather, Graves peoples his stories with individuals, both Indian and white settlers and their descendants, and he contemplates their will to survive under shifting conditions and harsh environmental factors. He follows the changing farm and ranch economy in which the land is depleted and later slowly restored through human endeavors. His landscapes are contested in many ways—Indian and white, cedar and cedar choppers, grazing and grasslands, drought and crops, natural world and human world. "Hardscrabble" is a fitting term.

The stories in *Goodbye to a River* relate events that, according to Graves, may not have made "any notable dent in human history" (143). I doubt the Comanches would agree with this assessment. However, Graves does tell their story as one of

> a partly unnecessary, drawn-out squabble between savages and half-illiterate louts constituting the fringes of a culture which, two and a half centuries before, had spawned Shakespeare, and which even then was reading Dickens and Trollope and Thoreau and considering the thoughts of Charles Darwin. (143)

Although naming Native Americans as "savage" is not much used today, Graves softens that judgment by calling the Anglo-Americans semi-literate barbarians. The People,[5] or Comanches, are a topic Graves returns to again and again. The profile he constructs begins with their acquisition of the horse, which gave them a "barbaric wholeness" much like the "Tatars and the Cossacks and the Huns" (18).[6] According to Graves, Comanche life revolved around war, hunting, and "kindred proud patriarchal violences" (18).[7] Warfare was an integral part of their life, and a young man gained status and wealth by "displaying bravery in battle and by acquiring the spoils of war" (La Vere, 49). There were of course other tribal groups in this area of Texas—Kiowas, Caddos, Tonkawas—but this was the Comanchería—a vast area of the South Plains that included much of North, Central, and West Texas ("Comanche Indians," 1). The Comanches were probably drawn to Texas in the 1600s when they separated from their Shoshone ancestors. While proximity to the Spanish horses was one draw to the South Plains of Texas, they also found rich grasslands and abundant buffalo herds, both resources later depleted by the colonizing Anglo-Americans.

The Comanches were the dominant force for two "arrogant horseback centuries" until the influx of the white settlers (Graves, *Goodbye,* 19). Graves acknowledges the power and pride of The People, and he also recognizes "what his own people did to the Comanches" when they moved westward to Texas and sought to control land and region (19). The Comanches had come to terms with the Spanish, but after Texas won independence from Mexico, the influx of Texans made negotiation and accommodation more difficult. The two cultures clashed over land and differing worldviews. Those differences guaranteed violence. Many raids were conducted under the "Comanche moon" as a result of unfair trade practices and Anglo-American disregard of laws protecting Indian lands. Of course, these raids angered and terrified Texas settlers. Discounting any idea that the Indians may have had some justification for their attacks, Texans responded in kind, raiding Indian villages and often killing women and children (La Vere, 31). Sam Houston, first as president of Texas and later as governor, attempted to negotiate peace between the settlers and the Indians, but Texans "continually, often at their own risk, settled on lands claimed by the Indians" (32). La Vere writes that Houston at one time commented: "If I could build a wall from the Red River to the Rio Grande, so high that no Indian could scale it, the white people would go crazy trying to devise means to get beyond it" (32).

With every bend in the Brazos, Graves relates more of the area's violent, bloody history embedded in memory and local folktales but also "confirmed and partly straightened" by county histories and illiterate memoirs. The history is "part of the river. All the murdered, scalped, raped, tortured people, red and white, all the proud names that belonged with hills and valleys and bends and crossings or maybe just hovered over the whole" (Graves, *Goodbye,* 7).[8] The Texans desperately wanted the Indian land. Ironically, they would soon leave much of it behind.

Later stories tell of the continuing squabbles that occur among the "louts" themselves—lynchings, bootlegging, cattle stealing, Reconstruction, and family feuds. Sometimes the feuds ran so deep that courthouses were burned to protect the reputations of those who wound up in court (232). So many stories, but Graves "can't help it; the stories are there; [he's] not telling even a fourth of them" (131). "No end, no end to the stories . . ." (65; Graves' ellipsis). However, Graves doesn't write to perpetuate the myth of the West. He tells us that at times one could see individuals as "heroic in size and posture, and transmuted them into myth" (37). As a result many attempted to live the myth, and "it is this process that in this day has shaped the whole Western legend into a raucous lie flooding out from bluely glowing television screens" (37). Ironically, in the twenty-first century, although this myth is in question, we have a number of "new" western movies that attempt to present the mythical West to a new generation—*Open Range, The Missing,* and *The Alamo.* I guess they come from the "bag of fragmentary, jumbled, contradictory tales left over from the frontier," of which Graves gives us a bit (140).

We may ask (as Graves expects us to), was it all violence along the Brazos? As most depictions of the West prove, we need to know that the gentle hero wins in the end. We don't want to recognize the violence of our past history. It is true, as Graves notes, that the "gentler people did gain a kind of control" (237). But whether "the control they gained was deep and lasting, and wiped out the old evil roughness, and left space in every man for the Jean-Jacques Rousseau kind of good," Graves doubts (237). I do as well. "Neither a land nor a people ever starts over clean. . . . It inherits" (237). Continuing stories of heroic actions muddle our ideas and concepts of the world and lead to "oversimple thinking[, which] infects . . . attitudes toward bombs and foreigners and rockets to the moon" (238). (And, might I add, faith in military might and the necessity to impose American values on nations around the world.)

As Graves paddles around another bend in the Brazos, he encounters Rock Creek. Here he leaves The People behind for a little while and begins to ruminate on the worn-out land. He notes that after a rain, Rock Creek lets you know what "is happening to that country, and has been for a century" (131). Most of the tributary streams in this section of the Brazos drain sandstone country without much rich dirt, but Rock Creek (in 1958) "carries the runoff from the steeply up-and-down western part of Parker County which used to be an oak forest with grassed glades, and since the whites moved in with axes and moldboard plows and too many chattel ruminants, the western part of Parker County has been flowing down Rock Creek to the Brazos, and down the Brazos to the Gulf" (132). Graves notes that after the rain both the creek and that section of the river are as "thick as black-bean soup" (132). Around the feed store, old men brag about the land they've worn out. In the past the entire Brazos had run higher, steadier, and clearer because the "matted grasses of the plains to the northwest held their soil" (253).

Near the end of his farewell trip, Graves passes a new orchard project—four or five thousand acres of young pecan trees that have replaced the "tired homesteads that used to quilt the post-oak scrub" (223). The notion of wearing out and moving on does not apply to pecans, since they are a long-term investment. Money from the big city has moved in and scooped up the land, dispossessing the individual farmer: "The dispossession must bring much the same feeling the Indians used to have, a century ago . . ." (224; Graves' ellipsis). Philosophizing about the absentee possession of land, he wonders "if something in you believes that land is really owned more with head and heart, with eye and brain, than with pocketbook and title deed. . . . [But] there are people for whom ownership of land is only ownership, an investment" (262). One has to wonder which one leads to more stewardship of the land—wearing it out in order to subsist or protecting the land as an investment.

After early settlers wore out the land, they left it behind. It is a good thing, because after the 1880s, "the Brazos country needed rest" (265). The violence of the frontier had moved on. The money crop of cotton had exhausted the land; the cattle had eaten the grass from the slopes; the white limestone now shone through the sparse dirt layer, and the brush and cedar spread.

As Graves comes to terms with the end of his river trip, he laments what has happened to the region. The settlers sold out, moved to the big cities, or moved on to conquer the next frontier. The ones who stayed, the cedar people, clung to marginal freeholds and "slit-eyed exclusion of outlanders" (267). They are mostly "sort of more so. More Anglo-Am, more belligerent, more withdrawn, more hill Southern, more religious, or more hoggish in their sinning if they lack religion or backslide from it . . ." (267; Graves' ellipsis). They are all of these things because of the country they live in, and Graves tells us the stories that help us understand that becoming. Dorys Crow Grover calls *Goodbye to a River* "a synthesis of tale spinning, nature writing, and philosophical meditation" (19). It is also an understanding, an attempt at explanation. Grover argues that Graves has written a "Brazos trilogy founded on research into the natural history and myth of his region of north-central Texas" (5). She sees *Goodbye to a River* as a passage through a riverscape and *Hard Scrabble* as a passage into landscape (31).

In literary terms, I believe this trilogy constructs a continuing narrative. As William Cronon tells us, a good narrative must have a beginning, a middle, and an end. *Goodbye to a River* marks the beginning of the narrative, and along the river, Graves contemplates the violent frontier history. *Hard Scrabble* forms the middle, and *From a Limestone Ledge: Some Essays and Other Ruminations about Country Life in Texas* pulls the diverse threads together and completes the story. In this text, Graves reveals the bond between an individual mind and a particular piece of geography. In his introduction to the 2002 edition of *Hard Scrabble,* Rick Bass calls attention to the reverence Graves "brings to the language of his engaged relationship—his partnership—with the land" (xix). Bass thinks that "Texas is in transition from a culture in which the land was viewed as the primary source of wealth, to one in which knowledge is seen as the source of wealth or empowerment—knowledge which surely now must include an awareness of our natural history and sustainability" (xix).

Knowledge of the land's transitions is the theme of *Hard Scrabble,* and Graves tells us what that patch of land means to him and "what it may mean in wider terms" (5). Looking back on the rural past of his ancestors, he has the notion that "grass and crops and trees and livestock and wild things and water mattered somehow supremely, that you were not whole unless you had a stake in them, a daily knowledge of them" (42)—daily knowledge of the natural world and a stake in it. What are the broader implications? Although Graves seldom attempts to draw a direct connection from the local to the global, each reader is left to make that link.

The stories in *Hard Scrabble* tell of the effects on the land of human endeavors fueled by America's new land mentality. The Old World ideas of land nurtured through the generations gave way in the New World to a "guiding principle sanctified[:] use it up and move along. Wear out and get out . . ." (21; Graves' ellipsis). Good land to those moving West meant new land. The key to remember here is that cattle use up the grass, land changes, subsistence farming goes "down the drain" (21), the economy changes, streams grow more volatile, shifting from dry river bottoms to flash floods, and families move on. The frontier view of land was "deplete and leave" and thus included no attachment to the land. Cedar no longer controlled by the fire ecology of the grasslands became a lifeway for the cedar people, who "asked less of the land and of life than those who had come before; the land had much less to give" (31).

Graves points to the American farmer who exploits rather than values the land and argues that the legendary productivity of American farming is a fallacy. The production numbers are based on a "massively chemical, factory-farming technology that is itself an extension of frontier fecklessness, since it commonly exploits rather than nurtures the soil" (231). Not only are the numbers deceptive, but what type of produce do we find in such great numbers? Compare the tasteless supermarket tomato to the ones found at any local weekend farmers' market. The connection to the land and the fruits of that land are lost for us all. Through Graves' stories and meditations in this middle text of the Brazos trilogy, we again come to an understanding.

A rhetorical technique that Graves uses to invite us to join him in his meditations and philosophical moments appears near the end of a section or when he wants us to pause a moment. Graves ends a paragraph with a statement or a question that concludes with an ellipsis. This punctuation usually means something is left out; that something is space for the reader's thoughts or space to contemplate what else Graves might have said on the topic, such as this example: "And did not temperate unmarginal heartland Europe manage to get rid of a whole landscape of wild things a long long time ago? . . ." (230). Consider another: "Because westward ho, was the land not bright? . . ." (231). Finally: "He ponders such things, the muser, while his newer, useful self ponders other affairs . . ." (238).

One of the topics Graves muses about is bringing the land back to a healthy state. Restoration, or what Graves calls "backward progress toward what ought to be" (59), becomes his project for Hard Scrabble. He claims that the notion of making the place useful crept in on him "slowly with time, like arthritis" (164). Of course the land cannot be fully restored. The fertile grasslands evolved over thousands of years, but gradually Graves tries to do things right in his own way. Although not succeeding completely, it is "in the trying itself [that he becomes] a part of the land and the Way it works" (248). Reflecting on his relationship with this patch of land, Graves writes in an afterword added in the 2002 edition that his family who followed those early settlers found rocks and brush and a little soil along the creeks. But they loved it anyway and attempted to restore the landscape:

> The results of this one-family effort have not been spectacular, and after the family's younger members had departed to follow their own paths through life and their parents had begun to feel the bite of the years, the land started

> turning back into what the cedar-choppers and moonshiners had known, a diminished wilderness with a reasonably rich assortment of wild creatures and plants, but not much economic potential. (271)

To Graves, the effort still seems worthwhile.

In the third text of his trilogy, *From a Limestone Ledge,* Graves completes his narrative with meditations on the rural way of life he has found in the two decades of living on Hard Scrabble. Graves writes about cows and bees and making wine. He shares his compulsion to hoard junk, his tolerance for predatory varmints, his stubborn refusal to raise chickens the right way, his favorite dog, and his preference for visiting, and not living with, goats. He reminds once again that what he began with was a worn-out land in a region that even when virgin was never a land of surplus riches (181).

He writes of Texas as a transitional region between East and West, both culturally and climatically. Drought is a fact of life, along the ninety-eighth meridian, which runs through the center of Texas, marking less than thirty inches of annual rainfall and requiring that people adapt their lifestyles and crops to a land of lesser rain. Since nature doesn't recognize arbitrary lines on the map, drought and lush rainfall can and do occur on both sides of the ninety-eight. "Drouth has helped shape us Texans as a people" (168). Graves argues and goes on to talk of the twenty-two-year cycles that fluctuate between violent hailstorms and downpours and long dry spells. Texans expect the rain but know not to count on it; too many long droughts have occurred in the past. Ironically, the morning I read this section of the book, the *New York Times* headline lamented the lack of rain further west, the low water in Lake Powell, and the shortage of water in western states, created by booming development over the last two decades of unprecedented rainfall. The reporter didn't dare go far enough to call it a drought. Graves would have. Historical patterns of precipitation need to be considered, and I didn't need the ellipses to ponder the global implications of the stories of Texas droughts.

The surprising last chapter of *From a Limestone Ledge,* "A Loser," is about a farm auction in the upper West Cross Timbers bioregion. The newspaper ad that attracted Graves indicated there was to be a "disposal of everything on hand, including the farm itself—'125 a. sandy land, 45 in cultivation, rest improved grass and timber, 2 tanks, barn, new brick home 3 b.r. 2 baths, all furnishings'" (219). Although he knew such auctions to be "melancholy events . . . aromatic with defeat," Graves was lured by the possibility of acquiring an "Allis-Chalmers grain combine of the antiquated type that is pulled and powered by a tractor" (219–220). What he came away with instead was a sense of fragility of living and working on the land. He and the other bidders knew they could potentially be that man, that loser who

> sweated against the menaces of debt not to be covered by non-farm earnings or a job in town, of drouth, of a failing cattle or grain or peanut market, of having overextended [them]selves on treasured land or machinery or a house, of perhaps a wife's paralyzed disillusionment with the rigors of country life, and above all of the onslaught of sickness with its flat prohibition of the steady work and attention that a one-man operation has to have, or else go under. (228)

The Loser caused the men to view the fragility of man's struggle with nature and the land. Graves fled the sandy region and returned home to "black dirt and limestone country, where [he] could have a drink beside a fire of liveoak logs and consider the Loser's . . . troubles with equanimity from afar" (228). This is the way Graves chooses to end the trilogy, the way to ponder the global through the local.

I HAVE RECENTLY had two or three conversations about fragility— of culture, of languages, of ecosystems, of life itself. What Graves calls attention to is the centrality of nature's presence in landscape and in regional history. Currently, many societal decisions don't seem to consider the natural processes of ecological regions. There is a disregard for the fragility and limits of natural resources such as fertile soil, water, and oil. *Nature matters now!* History shows it always has. Ecologist Gordon G. Whitney observes: "The landscape is a historical document, a cumulative record of man's impact on the natural world" (quoted in Ryden, *Landscape,* 277).[9] But it is not a history parallel to human history. Rather there is one intertwined history. Cronon argues that the point of history is to come to terms with cultural values and that stories about the past are better if they increase attention to nature and the place of people in it (1375).

By ending the Brazos trilogy with "The Loser," John Graves demonstrates that human decisions and actions have irreversible consequences on the natural world and, as a result, on humans themselves. If the landscape tells stories of the past, humans can influence how the story ends and what values are revealed. Can we, as Graves suggests, attempt to restore the land, one place, one family at a time?

Notes

1. Experience of landscape is certainly not a new idea. For more background, see *Space and Place: The Perspective of Experience,* by Yi-Fu. He writes that "experience is a cover-all term for the various modes through which a person knows and constructs a reality" (8). Kent Ryden and William Cronon also discuss the connections between human experience, landscape, and stories.

2. Ryden is drawing on Barbara Johnstone here. See her *Stories, Community, and Place: Narratives from Middle America.*

3. Cronon argues that narrative connects but is not merely a sequence of events. Narrative has a beginning, a middle, and an end. Graves' first book, *Goodbye to a River,* is only the beginning; the story continues in *Hard Scrabble* and *From a Limestone Ledge.*

4. For background on nature writing and ecocriticism, see Slovic; Cheryl Glotfelty, introduction to *The Ecocriticism Reader,* ed. Glotfelty and Harold Fromm (Athens: University of Georgia Press, 1996); and Glen A. Love, "Revaluing Nature: Toward an Ecological Criticism." For later shifts in ecocritical theoretical thinking, see Patrick D. Murphy, *Farther Afield in the Study of Nature-Oriented Literature;* and Lawrence Buell, *Writing for an Endangered World: Literature, Culture, and Environment in the U.S. and Beyond.*

5. In "Comanche History," historian Lee Sultzman writes that "Comanches referred to themselves as the Nemenc, 'our people.'"

6. Evidently this image is not a romantic creation by Graves. In the WPA narratives, Allen Mihecaby recalls that his Comanche ancestors "were frequently termed the 'Cossacks of the Plains'" (36:259–261; quoted in La Vere, 78).

7. Sultzman confirms that the Comanches were a warrior society in which the men dominated. Women were not allowed to speak in council, and although the men were polygamous, the women were often not free to choose whom they would marry. Many accounts from the WPA narratives describe the men as fierce hunters who expected the women to perform the

rest of the work, including building the homes, carrying water, and gathering timber.

8. Some of the names Graves brings to life in this text are Bigfoot Wallace, Oliver Loving, Charles Goodnight, Cynthia Ann Parker and her Indian son Quanah, Peta Nocona, Satank, Satanta, and Iron Shirt, just to name a few.

9. Ryden is quoting from Whitney's *From Coastal Wilderness to Fruited Plain: A History of Environmental Change in Temperate North America from* 1500 *to the Present*, 2.

Kindred Spirits

John Graves and Texas Monthly

CORY LOCK

ONE WINTER DAY in 1975 William Broyles headed north out of Austin, on his way to the cedar country of North Central Texas. Broyles was the founding editor of *Texas Monthly,* Michael Levy's upstart magazine. Although the magazine's first issue had only been released in February of 1973, by 1974 *Texas Monthly* had earned a National Magazine Award, the Pulitzer Prize of the magazine world, for the "entire body of its work" ("*Texas Monthly:* Thirty Years").[1] Committed to bringing the state's best writers to *Texas Monthly,* Broyles had already published the work of Bill Brammer, Larry L. King, and Gary Cartwright (e-mail interview with Broyles, May 25, 2004).[2] Now he was on his way to Glen Rose to meet John Graves and, perhaps, add another distinguished writer to the ranks of *Texas Monthly* contributors.

Hard Scrabble, Graves' farm in Somervell County was the inspiration for Graves' second book, *Hard Scrabble: Observations on a Patch of Land.* Published in 1974, this award-winning collection of essays introduced Broyles and a host of other readers to the four hundred acres of farming-depleted land Graves had set about inhabiting and rehabilitating. Visitors to Hard Scrabble frequently remark how much they feel a part of the place, even after only a few hours. This visit was no exception. There Broyles found Graves in the process of building his home and gladly made his own small contribution by carrying several stones. As they toured the land, they spoke a little, but for the most part Graves was content "to let the land speak for itself" (interview). And that it did. By the visit's end, Broyles was more determined than ever to have Graves "write about what he had shown [him] on that first visit: about his life in the country, the simple themes and stories that would be made wonderful by his sensibility and his language" (interview).

This first visit set the tone for the decade-long relationship that followed between John Graves and *Texas Monthly.* Looking back on it, Broyles says of Graves: "He was everything I expected: laconic, focused, and careful with his words, but also the soul of hospitality" (interview). In Graves the professional and the personal merged. A retiring yet erudite and articulate personality transferred over to the carefully insightful essayist's persona. An initial connection between two men born of mutual affinity and kinship with the land influenced the subsequent attitudes all Graves' editors at *Texas Monthly* had with him and his work. Almost thirty years later, Broyles admits, "I can't think of anything I am more proud of than having him write for the magazine" (interview). It was this sort of respect, loyalty, and support for both Graves and the kind of rambling, rural-focused, poignant writing he produced that for years made Graves' column a mainstay of a magazine that was in most other aspects fast-paced and urban.

Texas Monthly and John Graves were on many levels strange bedfellows. The "New Journalism" that had originated during the turbulent 1960s and hit its peak during the 1970s had shaped the magazine. Such writers attempted to overthrow conventions of cold war journalism; they saw the "objective" reporters of the past as at best failing to challenge the status quo and at worst reinscribing social norms and hierarchies (Sherman, "'New' Journalism"). New Journalists, such as Tom Wolfe, Terry Southern, John McPhee, and Truman Capote, sought to break free from these constraints through innovative style and blatant personal investment in their stories. *New York, The Atlantic,* the *New Yorker, Harper's, Esquire,* and other such magazines became famous for their hard-hitting exposés that used creative language to bring personalities and conflicts to life (Arlen, "Notes on the New Journalism"). This work excited many *Texas Monthly* staff members, but they also saw the concentration of progressive, modern journalism on the East Coast, and to some extent the West Coast, as disappointing. *Texas Monthly* sought to bring such good, innovative writing to the Lone Star State (telephone interview with Suzanne Winckler, April 1, 2004).

Broyles initially suggested to Graves that he submit a single article, constructed much along the lines the magazine's other journalists were producing. In a December 23, 1975, letter he proposed a story on the arrival of the Comanche Peak nuclear power plant to Glen Rose. Broyles imagined the tentative project as "a biography of fear" (John Graves Collection). Graves rejected the idea outright, instead suggesting "a monthly or occasional column from a relatively rustic point of view" (December 28, 1975, John Graves Collection). Thus the column that was to become Country Notes was born, created on Graves' own terms and with a goal of exploring "rustic" subject matter far different from that of the rest of the magazine.

Graves made it clear that the style, too, was to be his own. On November 7, 1976, almost a year after the column's initial conception, Graves submitted his first two articles, "Coping" and "Treasure," along with an explanation of his stylistic aim: "The form I'm aiming at is a sort of thematic essay, not heavy on polemics or data or revelation and free to ramble a bit if a ramble presents itself. I'd like each to stand fairly well on its own feet, but with a little dangling sense of being part of a whole" (John Graves Collection). Graves' goal, a rambling, rustic essay, "not heavy on polemics or data or revelation," was the direct opposite of that of the New Journalists and, specifically, of the "biography of fear," nuclear-plant-comes-to-small-town variety that Broyles had initially proposed. Graves' first article, "Coping," a discussion of why people abandon city life to "cope" in the country, appeared in the February 1977 issue of *Texas Monthly*. Its explanation of why the relative self-sufficiency of country life matters, even at the expense of modern convenience, set the tone for the dozens of Country Notes columns that followed.

An Armadillo on the Freeway

Working with *Texas Monthly*, Graves often admitted to feeling like "an armadillo strayed onto a freeway at rush hour" or "a queer sort of maverick in that corral" (January 25 and February 7, 1980, John Graves Collection). Fast-paced, progressive, urban *Texas Monthly* and reflective, traditional, and rural Graves did make an odd match, but there was a logic to their connection. Most immediately, Graves brought literary clout to the pages of the burgeoning publication. Nominated for a National Book Award and the recipient of two of the Texas Institute of Letters Carr P. Collins Awards, Graves was truly a catch for the magazine, "an icon of Texas letters, with a built-in audience" (e-mail interview with Anne Barnstone, April 1, 2004). Yet just as important, the two were also united by a common devotion to good writing and to capturing a sense of the peoples and places of Texas.

In the 1970s, most of *Texas Monthly*'s staff members were only in their twenties and thirties. According to Suzanne Winckler, Graves' primary editor from November 1978 until the end of Country Notes in 1982, Graves was not just a man with a reputation conducive to selling magazines, but as an accomplished writer in his fifties, he was also an "elder" of sorts ("Texas Monthly Days"). Anne Barnstone, Graves' primary editor in 1978, calls him "old school, a courtly gentleman" (interview). Further, Graves was a man of the country whose struggles at beekeeping and adventures in animal husbandry seemed a world away from their Austin offices. Yet rather than complicating Graves' working relationship with staff members, these experiential differences gave Graves special privileges as a *Texas Monthly* writer. Winckler, for example, saw him as a "special case"; his "clean and . . . well-wrought" text needed little revision, and "the intimidation factor of an older, well-respected writer and younger editor" meant she was cautious when she edited his work (interview). Senior editor Broyles shared the same mind-set: "I like to think we took great care with every writer. But John, we were all a bit in awe of him. I would kid around with everyone else, but John deserved respect" (interview). All in all, Graves brought prestige to the magazine and, on a more personal level, "an older presence to a group of young, fairly cocky and self-assured people" (Winckler, "*Texas Monthly* Days").

Graves, who admits regular run-ins with editors of other publications, has repeatedly stressed his appreciation for what he called the "gentle editing" at *Texas Monthly*. Punctuation is a particularly sticky point with him; clearly he gives considerable thought to how he assembles language and objects to most compositional changes. "I really care about putting words together, how they're put together, and not only what they mean, but what their rhythm is and their sound," Graves explains. "These are things that depend very subjectively upon the author. Most magazines, and indeed most publishers, go by books of style . . . which [say a] comma goes in such and such a place, . . . a semicolon [in another place], and so on and so forth and all that. This is death to graceful writing" ("*Texas Monthly* Days").

Regarding his comma conflicts with other editors, he says: "If I put one in, I put it there because I want it there, and if I left it out, I wanted things to move fast . . ." (quoted in Bennett, "John Graves," 76). Yet though he is often vocal in protesting editorial intrusions, Graves calls his days at *Texas Monthly* "extremely pleasant," made so by Winckler and Barnstone, as they edited lightly and "got along beautifully" with him ("*Texas Monthly* Days").

Perhaps the only regular, notable conflict between Graves and his editors—one they hardly even remember today—was over his articles' titles. In a May 25, 1979, letter to an editor, Graves remarks, "I've quit trying hard on titles since you all have your own title context and rarely use mine anyhow" (John Graves Collection). Graves put up with such changes as part of the magazine publication process, yet when his collected *Texas Monthly* stories were published in *From a Limestone Ledge* in 1980, he retitled almost all of the pieces, replacing the catchy two- or three-word titles with longer ones expressing his dry sense of humor. For example, Graves gave a playful sort of dignity to the animals he described, as he changed *Texas Monthly*'s "Poultry in Motion" to "Some Chickens I Have Known" and "Goats Need Love Too" to "A Few Words in Favor of Goats." He became more self-deprecating and ironic by changing "Coping" to "Notes of an Uncertain Bluecollar Man" and "Fencing Myself In" to "More Than Most People Probably Want to Know About Fences." And, anticipating an audience more familiar with Texas literature than the general *Texas Monthly* reader, he replaced the cliché "Good as Gold" with "Coronado's Stepchildren," a nod to J. Frank Dobie's famous book *Coronado's Children.* As a whole, the new titles published in *From a Limestone Ledge* better reflect the tone of the articles themselves, which always maintain a sense of humor, no matter how serious the topic.

Graves' artistry within the Country Notes series depends on this sense of humor. In the *Texas Monthly* essays Graves laughs at life itself. For example, in his February 1979 essay, "Through All Kinds of Weather," he pokes fun at recent transplants to the West:

> What is certain is that our cities have grown dependent on . . . ameliorations, and if the energy shortage ever gets bad enough that air conditioners die en masse, a jaundiced non-cave dweller expects that the cloud of dust raised by Wisconsinites and Upper New York Staters and other dis-

> placed persons stampeding out of the Sunbelt for home will likely rival the one caused by Krakatoa when it blew in 1883. (118)

Graves' extravagant metaphors here, the description of Sun Belt newcomers from the north as displaced persons,[3] of the dust their departure could create as a volcanic eruption, and of himself as a "jaundiced non-cave dweller," exemplify his creativity and rich prose.

Graves caricatures the denizens of the region he loves even more often than he chuckles at outsiders. Some of the most memorable of such descriptions can be found in the October 1978 essay, "The Snuff of Dreams," one of Graves' famous treatises on tobacco:

> Some dippers who work outdoors alone or in masculine company, where niceties are not crucial, can pack in heroic amounts at a time and are often what is known as "front-lippers"—lowbred fellows who do not bother to tongue their load around to the side but leave it where it went in. Their frequent aspect—distended and blackened lower lip, jaw-wagging speech and a difficulty in shaping certain vowels, perhaps a trail of dried juice running down into stubble from one corner of the mouth—has been known upon sudden confrontation to set strong women screaming. (199–200)

Graves' descriptions are unforgettable because he combines accurate details, the bulge of a dipper's lip, or the tobacco juice trail dribbling from the mouth's corner, with fanciful exaggeration, "heroic amounts" of tobacco use and women screaming at the sudden sight of a "front-lipper." It is through singular phrases like these that Graves brings to life the people of his region: insiders and outsiders alike.

Alongside Graves' wit, and likewise present in virtually every one of his *Texas Monthly* essays, are also striking descriptions that address the more serious aspects of life. Graves is most poetic when depicting the miracles of the natural world, as in a passage recounting springtime bee swarms in his August 1977 essay, "Of Bees and Men": "A roar starts in the bee yard and a swirling tower of frantic, happy, golden bugs rises, to settle finally with their queen in a fat cluster dangling from some nearby limb, from which way station they will send out scouts to find a new abode" (124). Elsewhere, in the August 1978 essay, "The Loser," Graves gives a poignant description of a bankrupt farmer whose farm is sold at auction:

> He was in his forties, pale and slight and balding and with the pinched waxy look of sickness on him, maybe even of cancer, and as I watched his dark worrier's eyes swivel anxiously from bidder to bidder and saw the down-tug of his lips when something sold far too low, I knew very well who he was. He was the erstwhile lord of this expanse of wet sand and red mud, the buyer and mender and operator of a good bit too much machinery for 45 arable acres, the painstaking nurturer and coddler of those fat penned cows, the player perhaps of a tuba, the builder of a hip-roofed brick-veneer castle, 3 b.r. 2 baths, from which to defend his woman and his young against the spears of impending chaos. Except that chaos, as is its evil custom, had somehow stolen in on him unawares and confounded all his plans. He was, in short, the Loser. (114–115)

Just as in his humor, it is the details that Graves provides that elevate his prose. At times they make the subjects he describes seem otherworldly, as in the swirling tower of golden bees. At other moments, such as the description of the pale, slight, and balding farmer, owner of a three-bedroom, brick-veneer house and player of the tuba, who must face his life's work being sold at auction, they accentuate the pathos of everyday life.

Graves' editors at *Texas Monthly* clearly had a sense of this. As lovers of good writing, they cherished Graves' prose and felt honored to have anything to do with it. Today, Graves' abilities as a writer have not dimmed at all from Broyles' perspective. He claims, "I would have gladly crawled through a mile of barbed wire to get him into the magazine" (interview). And when one hears him describe Graves' prose, one believes it. Broyles explains that Graves

> takes language, which we waste in torrents, language which can be twisted and parsed and made to mean this or that. He takes it and distills it into honesty. To make the simple sound sublime, that is the trick. Few of us can do it, ever, and usually by happy accident. John can. It's a hard job,

> which may be why we don't have nearly enough of him. But what we have, we cherish. . . . His columns gave us a civilized, literary consideration of what is this oft-invoked and little understood quality called a sense of place. ("John Graves Tribute")

Here Broyles reminds us that it is not simply beautiful prose that wins the hearts of Graves' readers. It is Graves' ability to invoke the particulars of place, of what it is to be alive in one small corner of the world.

A Sense of Place, A Sense of Pace

Though the artistic goal of *Texas Monthly* was to publish great writing, it was, of course, equally necessary to market such material to an audience. Broyles admits that as a new publication, struggling to establish a core base of readers, *Texas Monthly* targeted "whoever we could get to buy the magazine!" (interview). Yet in this search for readership, *Texas Monthly* did have specific goals. Broyles explains: "We were trying to tap into a sense of place deeper than whatever town or neighborhood you lived in; something that was Texas and common to us all. And to that extent John's columns reached into some deeper place, the hardscrabble we had in our DNA" (interview).

In order to understand the readership of Country Notes, and of *Texas Monthly* as a whole during its first decade of publication, it is important to consider Texas' changing demography during this period. In 1940, Texas was still primarily a rural state; it had 6,414,824 inhabitants, 45.4 percent of whom lived in cities, while 54.6 percent lived in rural areas. In 1970 its population of 11,198,655 was 1.7 times that of thirty years earlier; 79.7 of these people now lived in the city, while only 20.3 remained in the country ("Urban and Rural Population"). Most Texans had either grown up in the country or had parents with a rural background, but they were now settled in the city. These were the people who made up the core of Graves' readership; as Broyles explains: "The more urban we were becoming, the more longing there was for our rural soul" (interview). Graves managed to convey the rural perspective to city dwellers by describing the practices and people of his own daily life. As such, Graves was part of a distinct Texas literary tradition of gentleman farmers, like J. Frank Dobie and Roy Bedichek, who not only investigated Texas' rural traditions but also embraced them as part of their present-day reality (Winckler interview). Graves himself was conscious of this tradition even when the column was only an idea. In a November 16, 1976, letter to Broyles, he stressed, "I have respect for old Dobie and Bedichek but I'm not trying to *be* them" (John Graves Collection, emphasis in original). Graves found his own voice but like Dobie and Bedichek sought to give "the urban reader a window onto that world and landscape" (Winckler interview).

One of the ways Graves gave his *Texas Monthly* readers a respite from their urban lives was through the pacing of his prose. According to Winckler, *Texas Monthly* had a general editorial policy that the author needed to suggest an article's topic within its first one or two paragraphs. Yet she cherished the fact that "John was able to write in a more organic manner," which "slowed the magazine down, at least on the pages where he was" ("*Texas Monthly* Days"). Barnstone stresses the same point regarding Graves' tempo: "John was definitely different. Not only in subject matter but in style—he trusted the reader to be able to hold onto longer thoughts" (interview).

Stephen Harrigan, a former staff writer and senior editor at *Texas Monthly* and author of the *New York Times* best seller *Gates of the Alamo,* saw Graves as a model for pace and tone. He explains, "John's pieces gave me permission to root around on my own and think about what I could write that was true to my own experience that would have the same sort of calm and same sort of depth of perception, ideally" ("*Texas Monthly* Days"). Like other *Texas Monthly* staff members, Harrigan recognized that the magazine was built on the principles of the New Journalism: "*Texas Monthly* made its reputation with big, giant, institutional, investigative stories about crime and politics and business." He recalls feeling "perplexed" because he could not produce these sorts of stories—nor did he want to. Reading Graves' work made him feel "as if I was no longer alone." For Harrigan, Graves' work was

> a validation of a certain kind of magazine article that wasn't necessarily built upon aggressive reporting and bringing down or building up some sort of massive Texas monument of some sort, but it was a way of, as one of his stories is called, "Noticing," . . . calm, clear awareness of the life

> going on around you and this wonderfully elegant prose—quiet prose, which was something that was, of course, very welcome in the magazine and valued, but was not at that time in American journalism. . . . There was this kind of model of *New York Magazine* and the New Journalism, and it was all about getting on the map, getting noticed, and the idea of not *getting* noticed, but noticing, was tremendously liberating for some of us, I think. It added to this necessary swagger that built this magazine . . . to the swagger it added *gravitas.* ("*Texas Monthly* Days")

Graves' expertise is noticing, pondering, considering. Broyles' successor as general editor, Greg Curtis, highlights this very quality in a 1994 *Texas Monthly* article, quoting Larry McMurtry's conclusions about Graves: "The persona he adopts most frequently is that of the man who considers. He may choose to consider a goat, a book, an anecdote, or some vagary of nature, but the process of considering is more important to the texture of his books than any conclusions that may get drawn" ("Uncertain Sage"). Graves shares with readers the digressions and speculations of a solitary man paddling along the Brazos River, or building a fence, or checking a cow's cut for screwworms. Temporarily relieved from the urban world's tempo, the reader can settle down to explore new ideas and chew on old ones.

The *Texas Monthly* pieces, most of which Graves published in only slightly revised form in *From a Limestone Ledge,* continue many of the themes of his earlier books, *Goodbye to a River* and *Hard Scrabble:* musings on the flora and fauna of the Texas landscape, discussions of the rhythms of rural life, and examinations of the intersections of the myths and realities of Texas history with present-day modernity. For readers struggling with the frustrations of modernity, his essays give hope of a Thoreau-like self-sufficiency. "Coping" is the subject of his first essay, and in a way it is what all of the Country Notes articles are about: "You go ahead and cope because you chose to be where you are and still like being there, and the coping is part of the bargain. And in it, too, you attain sometimes the pleasant illusion, rare these days, of dominating the world around you, technology and all" (101). Graves' topics in these essays oftentimes deliberately continue Roy Bedichek's reflections on fences, chickens, and cedar. Yet while Bedichek writes almost exclusively in the naturalist vein, detailing the habits of the mockingbird, eagle, and Inca dove, Graves focuses on the farm and all its habitants: cows, goats, bees, dogs, and man himself.

Of particular concern to him are the idiosyncrasies of the man of the country (and I do specifically mean men here; Graves tells us little of rural women)—his aspirations of self-reliance; his work constructing outbuildings, mending fences, managing livestock; and his habits—ranging from weather watching to treasure hunting to dipping. As early as September 13, 1977, Broyles was recognizing the import of such a focus:

> You're putting together a very important body of work on how man lives with the animals he has domesticated, a sort of high-toned Old McDonald Had a Farm. Just as in *Hard Scrabble,* where you showed what a man can make with land that other men have worked over and moved beyond, so in these stories you seem to be showing what a man can do with animals most of us have long since lost touch with. And it's not just a kind of atavistic oddity; it's very important. Anyway, I see something developing here that I like and am glad to be part of. One reason is that the stories may be "about" animals, but they are really about people. (John Graves Collection)

By writing about animals, Graves tells us about the rural farmer. By telling us about the rural farmer, Graves reveals aspects of human nature that are part of all of us. For example, in "Ol' Blue" in December of 1977, Graves mourns the loss of a favorite dog, even as he looks at Blue's successor:

> But he isn't Blue. In the domed shape of his head under my hand as I sit reading in the evenings I can still feel that broader, silkier head, and through his half-boisterous, half-bashful, glad morning hello I still glimpse Blue's clown grin and crazy leaps. I expect such intimate remembrance will last a good long while, for I waited the better part of a lifetime to own a decent dog, and finally had him, and now don't have him any more. And I resolve that when this new one is grown and more or less shaped in his ways, I

> am going to get another pup to raise beside him, and later maybe a third. Because I don't believe I want to face so big a dose of that sort of emptiness again. (203)

Broyles points to "Ol' Blue" as exemplifying what is best about Graves' essays:

> He was always using each one to explore another corner of experience. There were levels in each one; you might think you were reading about his dog and then discover you were in fact reading about a kind of love that we had all felt but never been able to express. (Interview)

"Ol' Blue" is a tribute to a lost dog, but it is also about the singularity of a loved one—animal or human—and the absence that surrounds such a loss.

Broyles saw Graves' Country Notes series as important work that directly served the needs of the growing magazine—both in appealing to and *educating* readers. On April 17, 1977, he explained to Barnstone: "Some teaching is needed in this column." Broyles underscored the need to address "reader ignorance" because "we don't, unfortunately, all have an easy acceptance with concepts like hybrid vigor, being further from the cattle industry than even John might want to believe" (John Graves Collection). Broyles recognized both the ignorance of most of the *Texas Monthly* audience regarding the specifics of country life, and more importantly, he saw such knowledge as significant to understanding both the history and the contemporary culture of Texas. The effect of this education is evident in letters to the editor that respond to Graves' *Texas Monthly* essays. In a letter of January 26, 1979, Gige Carlisle of Midland suggests this educational function is working: "After reading John Graves' article about our weather, *I* understand why my 89 year old grandmother, who spent her young woman years as the wife of a dry land cotton farmer in Central Texas, still 'watches the clouds' and follows intently the long-range weather forecasts" (John Graves Collection, original emphasis). Simply put, Graves' columns were helping readers understand the mind-sets and daily lives of country people, a population that was increasingly disappearing from mainstream discourse. This quiet interpretation, part didactic and part philosophical, is what Graves does best—teaching Texans (or at least reminding them) about their deepest selves, where they came from and, thus, who they are in the present moment.

This education was useful to native and nonnative Texans alike. Mark H. Slovek, of the University of Texas at Austin's Department of Astronomy, underscores the importance of Graves' rural perspective in a December 29, 1979, letter that responded to a reduction of Country Notes columns over that year. His articulate grievance is worth quoting at length:

> It is with some reluctance that I have decided not to renew my subscription to your magazine, which over the past two years I have frequently enjoyed. Not being a native Texan, I found the diversity of the topics covered in the magazine valuable to acquaint myself with the variegated facets of Texas culture, either extant or newly forming.
>
> My primary dissatisfaction arises at this point from the decreasing frequency of the "Country Notes" feature by John Graves. I eagerly scan each issue for an inclusion of his column, for it offers itself as a quiet counterpoint to the fast-paced writing describing some Texas city or political figure. I strongly feel that the latter style of writing has come to dominate your magazine, and detracts from the balanced nature it originally had. The Graves column describes a life style that truly has passed most of us by: perhaps in a sense it is appropriate that your magazine deal with less nostalgic days. However, the affairs of T. Cullen Davis and the battle between Houston and Dallas are matters of little import to me; I would rather know the way one man has achieved independence and happiness in a world which is increasingly offering less of both. (John Graves Collection)

Slovek suggests the educational value of Graves' column for *all* Texas as both a primer on state culture and a model for living in the modern world.

Slovek was not the only reader to find the style and subject matter of Graves' essays a sharp contrast—or even antithetical—to the rest of the magazine's material. When the *Texas Monthly* essays from 1977 through 1980 were collected and published as *From a Limestone Ledge,* this became particularly clear. For example, two Texas writers expanded on Slovek's suggestion that Graves' work elevated what they perceived to be *Texas Monthly*'s otherwise materialistic and insubstantial content. John R. Erickson, whose *Hank the Cowdog* series is today loved by children and adults alike, writes in January of 1980:

> You certainly did yourself, and the rest of us, a favor when you decided to write for *Texas Monthly*. . . . As I've mentioned before, it amuses me that you have managed to sneak these gems into a magazine whose slick, sneering hedonism is so repugnant to me that I can hardly stand to look through a copy. Strange bedfellows, you and *Texas Monthly*. But God bless them for giving you the time and space, whatever their reasons for doing it might be, to write about goats and chewing tobacco. (John Graves Collection)

Erickson goes even further to note he liked the pieces better in *From a Limestone Ledge*

> when I was not distracted by the visual noise of the magazine. One needs a lot of silence and a certain mood to enjoy John Graves. One doesn't want to guzzle or gobble, and much of *Texas Monthly*'s phenomenal success lies in the fact that they have discovered a regional market that guzzles and gobbles a lot of things. (John Graves Collection)

Marsh Terry, a novelist and professor of English at Southern Methodist University, likewise does not beat about the bush in reiterating Erickson's perspective in his December 8, 1980, letter:

> I have been reading slowly . . . your fine Literate Letters of Limestone Ledgerdemain. . . . This is a pleasure moreso because I did not read any of them in the *Texas Monthly* because it usually gripes me in the lower bowel right where my own private residues of Texas clichés [are] buried. . . . (John Graves Collection)

Terry, Erickson, and Slovek all associate *Texas Monthly* with what they believe to be the worst elements of modernity: consumerism, a frantic pace, hedonism, and a surface-level, clichéd approach to regional culture as a whole. Graves, for them, is the antithesis of this, a writer of substance whose thoughtful perspective on living seems an out-of-place, but welcome, addition to *Texas Monthly*'s "slick" pages.

The Exhausted Land

Yet, if Graves was so cherished by readers and editorial staff alike, why did the column wind down around 1982? Students of Texas literature have asked this question for years. It is easy to notice that while from 1977 to 1982 Graves published multiple essays every year, after 1982 he published infrequently. In fact, he contributed only five essays between 1983 and the present.[4] It is convenient to notice that in 1982 Greg Curtis took over Broyles' job as senior editor of the magazine and to infer some sort of causal relationship between the two circumstances. Did Curtis' rise as senior editor diminish Graves' presence within the pages of *Texas Monthly*, or was this merely a coincidence?

Evidence exists of a changing tone at *Texas Monthly* during this period. Winckler describes an ideological split amidst the staff at the magazine during the late 1970s and early 1980s. She believes some editors, such as Barnstone, Broyles, and herself, and some writers, such as Harrigan, Joe Nick Patoski, Jan Reid, and Chester Rosson, shared a specific concern with the natural world (interview and "*Texas Monthly* Days"). Curtis, she suggests, may have forwarded another perspective. Winckler explains: "Greg is a purely urban person. He never fully embraced what John Graves was trying to bring to the magazine. He had enormous respect for him, great friends. But purely urban, *Homo sapiens* focus [in contrast to] a staff that embraced the larger environment" (interview). Winckler describes this division as never hostile, but as a real thing that, in fact, contributed to her departure from the magazine.

As Winckler suggests, it is clear that Curtis respected Graves as a writer. Curtis says of Graves,

> We had a good relation, I always thought, and have been friends ever since then . . . Certainly, his was an important voice for us to have in the magazine. He wrote about important things in a way no one else did or could. And it was good for us at the magazine to have a relation with a man of his distinction. (E-mail interview, May 24, 2004)

Yet it also appears he did not approach Graves as a writer in the same manner as Broyles, Barnstone, and Winckler had. Graves' past editors loved and revered him as an icon of Texas letters. Curtis took a more objective but, perhaps, also more distant perspective on Graves and Texas literature as a whole. In "Uncertain Sage," a March 1994 Behind the Lines column in *Texas Monthly*, he remarks:

> For all the writing done in Texas in the hundred years since the closing of the frontier, there is finally no Texas tradition. We have not yet been blessed with a genius whose imagination is so great that it exerts a kind of gravitational pull on everything before it and after, as Faulkner's did in Mississippi or Yeats's did in Ireland. Without that we will remain a region of individual writers who happen to work in the same neighborhood but without much other connection.

The existence of a Texas literary school is open for interpretation—in fact, the issue has been repeatedly debated by critics for years. What *is* clear, though, is that editors like Broyles, Barnstone, and Winckler *do* see Graves as part of a distinct Texas literary tradition, while Curtis does not even recognize this tradition as existing.

Further, while Broyles, Barnstone, and Winckler find inspiration in Graves' rural focus, Curtis sees this concern for the rural as isolating Graves as a writer. For Curtis, it is a part of an old, dying perspective: "John's influence on younger writers is far less than one would suppose, given his skill, his accomplishment, and, at least in these parts, his long eminence" ("Uncertain Sage"). It is not that Curtis feels that Graves' style or subject matter is inferior or unimportant, quite the contrary. But Curtis sees Graves' focus on Somervell County as isolating him and perceives his agricultural concerns, as opposed to ranching, oil, or the urban, as unromantic and contrary to Texas mythology. Because of this, Curtis concludes: "It is probable, with small farms disappearing and our writers gravitating quite naturally toward cities, that no other writer will come along who knows enough about rural matters to continue the tradition or who cares enough to want to try" ("Uncertain Sage"). Broyles, Barnstone, and Winckler saw Texas' increasing urbanization as making writers like Graves all the more necessary—Curtis suggests that while, perhaps, such perspectives should be important to us, they simply aren't.

Curtis describes the same institutional split as Winckler, yet from a remarkably different perspective. In another *Texas Monthly* Behind the Lines column he explains:

> Of course, in time both Texas and the way we at the magazine think about Texas have changed. During the first ten years, which coincided exactly with the oil boom, we tended to reaffirm the Texas myth at the same time as we reinterpreted it for that era. . . . Covers of wide-open spaces were our most successful. . . . Texas has a history, a culture, and a special identity that we cannot escape and should not try to. But if the bust of the eighties taught us anything, it was that the same chimes cannot be rung forever. Oil will never propel the state again the way it once did, and "rancher" today is likely to mean someone from Houston or Dallas who likes to run a few head of cattle on the country land he bought for a weekend getaway. . . . Boots and hats will stay the same forever, but what is between them has not and will not. ("Great Days")

For Curtis, the rural focus—be it agriculture, ranching, or oil—is a thing of the past. Today *Texas Monthly* targets an increasingly urban, transitory state population that no longer has need of the "education" Graves once gave, because rural life has little relationship to their own present *or* past.

In 2000 Evan Smith replaced Curtis as editor in chief, and it is significant that he virtually echoes Curtis' perspective on *Texas Monthly*'s changing audience and attitude over the last thirty years. In "Great Expectations," the August 2000 Behind the Lines column published the month after Smith had assumed his position, he too describes the magazine's changing emphasis from a rural-focused myth to urban reality:

> The biggest change, of course, is in Texas itself. In the early days of *Texas Monthly*, the pitch to prospective readers went something like this: "We love Texas, and so do you. . . . Texas has a distinct identity that functions as a sort of connective tissue. Whether you're from Harlingen or Hillsboro, Lubbock or Lufkin, you care about the state as a whole—so you'll want to read our various takes on all things Texan." For such people, the "Texas myth" was a

> terrific draw, and it sold a lot of magazines (ads too). That was then. Today, many of our readers are Texas natives for whom the myth has meaning, but just as many are relatively recent arrivals lured here by jobs or that ephemeral concept known as quality of life. (9)

Texas—and *Texas Monthly*—changed significantly in the 1980s. It may have been that in 1982, as the oil bust began and the urban population of Texas surpassed 80 percent ("Urban and Rural Population"), Curtis as the new editor had enough perspective to recognize the winds of change and adjust the magazine's content accordingly—if not by direct veto of Graves' essays then by failing to seek out and encourage his contributions the way Broyles, Barnstone, and Winckler had.

Or maybe not. One of Graves' last essays for *Texas Monthly*, "The Exhausted Land" (January 1986), describes the depletion of Texas land through overuse. By this point, Graves too seems to have been finding Texas' land, as a source of inspiration for *Texas Monthly* material, exhausted. Around 1979 he began voicing a slight dissatisfaction with the column. In a May 21 letter to Winckler, he apologized for paucity of recent submissions. In doing so, though Graves mentions other factors, he goes on to say, "To a large extent also, though, it is the result of a feeling I've had about the recent pieces I've done for *Texas Monthly*. I think as the whole they've been pretty competent, but there is a certain echoing sameness in the slant and approach that has been bothering me, and I've been feeling around for a slightly different tone and realm of focus" (John Graves Collection). As he didn't find this new focus, it appears Graves began to reduce contributions on his own rather than producing more of this "echoing sameness." Curtis confirms this theory: "As to why the column wound down, I think every column has its natural life span. If memory serves, John wrote fewer of them as time went on and finally there weren't any. I don't remember any given final moment" (interview). And, in a 2002 panel discussion, Graves makes the same point: "When I ultimately tapered off from writing my country pieces for the magazine, it wasn't because of any disagreement between me and the editorial people. It was because I'd run out of material. . . . I found that I was getting ready to repeat myself, and I never have liked to do that" ("*Texas Monthly* Days"). Graves has consistently held that the termination of Country Notes was his own doing (telephone interview, June 28, 2004). If this is the case, why then does the question regarding editorial perspective even matter?

In our interview, Winckler emphasized how little students of contemporary literature consider the role of the editor in the making or breaking a particular writer—and that this omission affects literary analysis as a whole. "We think of writers as powerful people, but it's editors who are powerful," she explains. "It's editors who decide what gets published and what doesn't" (interview). Understanding the author-editor relationship yields considerable insight into any set of published works. Winckler feels it is to Broyles' credit that he recognized Graves as "another option to the urban life" ("*Texas Monthly* Days"). Barnstone concurs that Broyles' vision was a cornerstone to Country Notes: "Bill Broyles had the idea to stretch the magazine to include John's world, and it was a great stretch" (interview). Broyles sought out Graves, encouraged him to submit articles (to the extent of nagging him when submissions began to taper), at time suggested topics, and most importantly, found a place for such work within the pages of *Texas Monthly.*

Recent editors Curtis and Smith have made *Texas Monthly* a nationally recognized magazine, as evidenced by its National Magazine Awards for General Excellence in 1990, 1992, and 2003 ("About the Magazine"). In touch with who Texans are and where they live, Curtis and Smith have shaped the magazine accordingly. In 2000, 82.5 percent of Texans lived in a city, and *Texas Monthly* quite clearly caters to that urban population; its mission statement even says so directly. Further, during the past two decades, Curtis and Smith have brought in a number of important changes, such as new visual layouts and an increasing focus on Latinos.

Yet, when we compare the numbers of Texans living in the city today with those of a few decades ago, we find that the urban/rural ratio of Texans has not changed all that drastically; 79.9 percent of Texans lived in the city in 1970; 82.5 did so in 2000. Of course, the nature of these urban areas and the family history of their inhabitants have changed. Increasing numbers of us live in large cities and are more than one generation removed from country life. However, the fact still stands that Broyles' audience was not necessarily less urban than those of Curtis and Smith, just urban in a different way. Broyles' great achievement, in which he was aided by Barnstone and Winckler, was in making Graves fit into the magazine *despite* demographics. Today Winckler continues to assert that Graves—and a tradition of like-minded writers—is exactly what is needed to connect people to the land on which they live, the food they eat, and the drastic effects they have on the physical world (interview). And then there is Bill Broyles, who simply says of Graves, "He was and is and will always be one of my heroes" (interview).

Graves' relationship with *Texas Monthly* is educational to all of us. It underscores the influence of editors on the publication process as a whole. For those who mourn the diminishing influence of rural- or environment-focused perspectives in Texas today, the story is particularly important. It reminds us that it is only by making writers like Graves our heroes and, like Broyles, *finding* a way for their perspective to fit within modern life that we allow them and their subject matter—Texas' land and the way Texans inhabit it—to be more than an afterthought.

Notes

1. Adding to the prestige of the award, this was the first time a magazine with only one year of publication had won this award ("*Texas Monthly* Awards").

2. Such works include Bill Brammer's "Salvation Worries? Prostate Trouble" (March 1973) and "Sex and Politics" (May 1973), King's "Leavin' McMurtry" (March 1974), and Gary Cartwright's "The Lonely Blues of Duane Thomas" (February 1973), "Cops as Junkies" (November 1973), and "Rodeo Madness" (March 1974) ("Writer Archives").

3. This term references the tens of thousands of "displaced persons" of World War II. Primarily Jewish survivors of the Nazi holocaust, many displaced persons were housed in special camps before migrating to the United States and Palestine ("Vocabulary"). Graves made this reference even clearer when he revised the essay for publication as "Weather Between East and West" in *From a Limestone Ledge.* There he replaces the term "displaced persons" with the abbreviation "DP," which specifically originated during World War II.

4. These were in the years 1984, 1986, 1989, 1994, and 2003.

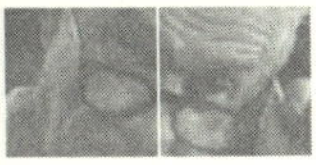

Auroras of Autumn

John Graves' Valedictions

DON GRAHAM

> Farewell to an idea . . . The cancellings,
> The negations are never final.
>
> WALLACE STEVENS, "The Auroras of Autumn"

A WEBSITE ON LEGENDARY Texans lists John Graves' birth date as September 18, 1888—the same year that J. Frank Dobie, Walter P. Webb, and T. S. Eliot were born. This would make him over 118 years old—a legendary Texan indeed. Fortunately for him and us, as of this writing, he's only 86 (born on August 6, 1920) and still at work, still crafting sentences that readers around the state admire. The regard with which Graves is held in Texas may say something about regionalism, pure regionalism as practiced in Texas: the rating and ranking of literature based on place and evocation of place. In this view Graves' reputation may ultimately be confined to Texas, as are, for example, the reputations of Dobie and Bedichek and Webb and George Sessions Perry and dozens of other writers cherished locally but not nationally. In Graves' case the reputation, the legend, the legacy, mainly derive from one book, *Goodbye to a River,* published in 1960 and continuously in print since. The work arrived at a propitious moment in Texas letters; the old guard of Dobie, Webb, and Bedichek were about to fade from the scene, and Graves' narrative about a canoe trip down a stretch of the Brazos River seemed to mark both the summation of and the end of something, of the land-centered ethic of Old Texas. In this one book Graves combined Webb's interest in history, Bedichek's in nature, and Dobie's in folklore into a seamless whole that was greater and more literary than any single work by any one of the celebrated Triumvirate.

Readers responded on several levels. They liked the elegiac tone that pervades *Goodbye to a River.* They liked the avuncular wisdom that Graves sought to impart. They liked the very muted ecological thrust of the book (called conservationism in those days), and Graves' ruminative manner managed to convey a sense of heartfelt worth to Texans with a strong and often sentimental attachment to the land. These include Old Farts (a favorite Graves term) who own a few acres and like to putter around on it, absentee owners who maybe run a law firm in the city and who romanticize how wonderful it was on a farm or ranch when they were growing up, and a wide assortment of Texans, mostly male, who like to hunt and fish. The book was also just literary enough, stuffed as it is with allusions to such authors as Milton, Chaucer, Laurence Sterne, Thoreau, Hemingway, and Shakespeare, to make readers feel they were getting a dose of culture with their wing shots and strings of crappie.

Graves was forty when *Goodbye to a River* came out, and before it, there was a long foreground of false starts inflected by trying to write from an expatriate perspective. Before he discovered his true subject, hardscrabble Texas, he spent a number of years abroad. In this he was like a number of other Texas writers. Katherine Anne Porter, Gertrude Beasley, William Humphrey, and William Goyen each lived in Europe for a time, and they all wrote their best work about a remembered Texas past, but none returned to Texas to live. Graves did return, of course, and he finally decided to color in his pre-*Goodbye* years by way of a backward glance, as Edith Wharton called her autobiography. Graves takes his title, he tells us, from a sentence in that longest of American novels, longest in that no one can finish it, Gertrude Stein's *The Making of Americans.*

The making of Graves' artistic development is the subject, mainly, of *Myself and Strangers: A Memoir of Apprenticeship* (2004). In it Graves surveys his beginnings: from his middle-class upbringing in Fort Worth (his father was a clothing merchant) through post–World War II years spent partly in Europe searching, he says, for himself and for his voice. He seems to have found himself abroad, but he did not find himself as a writer until he came home to Texas, where he embraced a deeply rooted provincialism, the stony ground and ethos of the small landholder that has formed the basis of his best work.

Before getting to the expatriate years, the book touches on Graves' education at Rice University, his service in the Marine Corps during World War II (he lost his sight in one eye on Saipan), a year or so spent in Mexico sharpening his Spanish, more education at Columbia University, a two-year marriage, and even a brief stint teaching freshman English at the University of Texas. His description of that experience helps explain the desire to go abroad: "A basically miserable, overworked, underpaid period, teaching indifferent freshmen and walking around full of guilt about the ungraded themes sticking out of my coat pockets. I was getting no writing done, nor was our marriage in the best of shape" (21).

The book moves through this material rapidly and then lingers on the years in Spain, Mallorca, and Tenerife with side trips to London and Paris; it concentrates on the "time between the autumns of 1951 and 1956" (xi), the key years of his expatriate experience. In the long run, his foreign adventures proved useful for life but not as much for the writing that he produced during that time.

Famous expatriate memoirs like Hemingway's *A Moveable Feast* are accessible to us because of the company the author kept. Hemingway met everybody, and nearly everybody he met was important: Stein, Picasso, Fitzgerald, Dos Passos, Joyce—virtually the entire roll call of Modernism. Almost every memoir of Paris in the twenties has the same cast of great characters, great because they were people who profoundly mattered: they were defining the twentieth century in painting, sculpture, literature.

But the people Graves met in the fifties were, by and large, nobodies. He says so himself, describing one group of "fellow countrymen" as "aimless, upper class, usually charming, heavy drinkers. They are really nobodies" (45). Not that there weren't major figures to be glimpsed, to be seen from a distance. The distance was self-imposed; Graves could have met them, but something in him kept him from doing so. In the case of Hemingway, his reticence is understandable. Once, in Pamplona in 1951, he observed Hemingway at a table surrounded by admirers. Papa was having a drink and demonstrating how to handle a bullfighting cape, but Graves felt that this giant of twentieth-century writing had probably become someone who would disappoint the acolyte. Graves was under the spell of Hemingway's early work—but then what American writer who went to Spain in those days was not? Later, Graves saw Hemingway in Harry's American Bar in Venice; this time Papa was surrounded by rich people, and he seemed very comfortable with them.

On Mallorca, that island of idlers where Graves lived fitfully for more than a year, there was a great writer who had dwelt there for many years and who bore the same patronymic. Robert Graves had himself authored one of the most important of World War I memoirs, *Goodbye to All That* (1929), and had subsequently established residence in Mallorca. But the book of Robert's that John admired was *The White Goddess,* a study of the essential role of the female consciousness as muse and inspiration. (Everybody admired it; Sylvia Plath and Ted Hughes virtually used it as a marriage manual.) Yet the American Graves never tried to make contact with the English Graves.

Eventually, Graves grew so tired of his fellow Americans on Mallorca that he wrote a highly critical sketch about them that was published in *Holiday* magazine. It was the only thing he ever wrote in anger, he says, and he felt bad about it. Some of those who recognized themselves in the article never forgave Graves (and he has not seen fit in the years since to reprint the piece). During all this time abroad, he was trying to write. He wrote two types of stories: "one for them and one for me"—"them" being the slick magazines that paid well, the "one for me" being the literary stuff that was slower to sell (and write) and earned little or no money (*Myself and Strangers,* 40). Graves would eventually concentrate all his efforts on the literary side. But even then he felt a lack. He needed a book; only that would provide the "status" or "touchstone" he required. This is one of the recurrent themes in the diary that Graves kept during his years abroad. "Time is moving along and I am farting around, writing halfassedly on insignificant stuff," he berates himself in December 1953, and then, the next month: "A book, a book, a book is what I need to write" (97, 111).

The book he pinned his hopes on back then never happened. In 1956 he completed a novel called "A Speckled Horse," but his agent didn't like it. Graves thinks the book was "quite masculine" for his agent's sensibility, which he describes as "gentle, civilized, and effete" (*Reader,* 291), but on the basis of the segment he chose to reprint in *A John Graves Reader* (1996), the agent seems to have been right.

Graves also seems to think that the novel was too much under the spell of Ford Madox Ford, a favorite of his at that time. Ford is one of my favorites too, but I confess to being unable to detect his presence in the portion of the novel that Graves publishes. To me it seems all Hemingway all the time. Here, for example, is a passage that sounds alarmingly like some of the worst moments from *For Whom the Bell Tolls:*

> Without his willing it, Hill's eyes flicked down the length of her body and back up again to her face momentarily, and something moved far down inside him. It had been a long time. He knew that she knew the thing had moved inside of him, and he knew that she liked that. (*Reader,* 311)

The memoir bogs down when Graves quotes verbatim from the diaries. One entry from August 5, 1953, is typical: "Pepe's troubles. Had supper with him this evening, and after he had told me his worries we had good talk about a little of everything. I like him better and better" (*Myself and Strangers,* 71). Pepe is José Mut, a friend notable for nothing else to command our attention. And there were the women. In a session on Graves' work held at the Western Historical Association meeting in Fort Worth in fall 2003, Graves described his new book as "raunchy." Here is how raunchy plays out in the narrative. Graves describes one encounter with a Spanish woman as a "purgative, jolly, and guiltless romp" (71). There were other romps. He recounts one longer-term affair with a French woman "who was very good in bed" (54).

To be successful, journal entries have to be about Famous People or be written with the burning intensity of deep feeling, as in, say, Sylvia Plath's journals. But Graves' entries feel stale instead of fresh and penetrating. And they too sometimes echo the unmistakable cadences of Hemingway. Here, for example, is one dated April 14, 1953, on an afternoon at the bullring when the bullfights went poorly: "It all left a rather bad taste. Funny how easy it is, with only a little experience, to know when that stuff is bad" (50). At other times the entries are simply flat, like the ones all of us write when we travel in Europe: "Sitting in the bar Bellver at 10:30 a.m., waiting for your café con leche and croissants, checking the comically moral front page of the newspaper Baleares . . ." (81). At some level Graves knows that his reliance upon old material and obscure actors in a personal drama from fifty years ago is a problem, and so he calls upon "Old John" to comment on what "Young John" was up to, but it's not enough to overcome the datedness of the diary.

But there are quite a few moments of insight too. Several of these have to do with Graves' view of Texas-related authors. In one, for example, he recalls the pleasure of reading John Houghton Allen's *Southwest,* a book about the border country of South Texas published in 1952. It was a reminder that it might be possible to write about Texas, that perhaps the true places of the heart resided there rather than in foreign climes. And yet there is this comment, dated August 21, 1954, on George Sessions Perry's *Hold Autumn in Your Hand:* "It is a good piece of work, and causes me no envy because Texas is not my territory any more." To which "Old John" remarks, in brackets: "This was a *very* major misapprehension, as things turned out, for in the long run Texas was the main territory I did have" (148–149).

A year later, back in the USA, Graves was reading Roy Bedichek's *Adventures with a Texas Naturalist.* In an entry dated October 5 (1955), he declares it "a very pleasant hodgepodge." The rest of his commentary is worth quoting in full:

> Bedichek shares many of my own prejudices against nature-destruction and artificiality, but surely he needs to smile when he says that seeing the vermilion flycatcher for the first time is a major event in one's life. It might even be true, but the smile would help. Altogether, however, he is an even-tempered, sadly amused man of intelligence, taking himself a little seriously, but don't we all? (204)

Here, I think, is a real moment of self-disclosure. Graves is serious to the point of solemn in his most beloved book, *Goodbye to a River.* And he is most observant, as well, of bird life, even re-creating musically one bird's call. Yet, oddly, though Dobie and Webb are both listed in Graves' bibliography for *Goodbye,* Bedichek is not. Whether this is an oversight or an attempt to detach his book from any Bedichekian frame of reference is hard to say. Bedichek, incidentally, died the year Graves was completing *Goodbye to a River.*

Finally, here is Graves' assessment of a famous book by a man who would later be closely associated with Texas writing. The entry is from November 30, 1954, and the book in question is *Tales of the South Pacific:* "Michener to me at present looks like nothing at all—can't write, can't tell a story or even the truth, can't deal with complexity in characters, can only recognize good material and milk it" (174).

By the fall of 1956 Graves had returned to Texas, and by the "drouth-breaking autumn of 1957" he was on the Brazos River, storing up the images and experience that would go into the river book. It was, he writes in his memoir, a "liberation" from the self-doubt of the years in Spain (231, 233). With this act of personal repatriation, Graves had come full circle.

That canoe trip was intended to be both a rediscovery of Texas' past as a subject for serious writing and a valedictory to a river that Graves believed was going to be dammed and thereby forever changed, if not lost. The project reminds one a bit of the impending damming of the much wilder river in James Dickey's *Deliverance,* written a few years later.

The genesis of Graves' book can be gleaned from the Knopf file at the Harry Ransom Humanities Research Center at the University of Texas. Since the time I first looked at these materials, David S. Hamrick has brought out a very useful edition pertaining to this period, in *John Graves and the Making of* Goodbye to a River*: Selected Letters,* 1957–1960. In a letter to his agent, John Schaffner, on September 12, 1957, Graves explained what he wanted to do: "What I mean is that I'd like to set my feelings about that river down now, before they drown it, and the framework for setting them down will be the trip . . . The river has a fine cool melancholy quality in the autumn" (6). The resulting article, "Drifting Down the Brazos," published in *Holiday,* was a shorthand version of the book to come. On May 11, 1959, Graves sent Schaffner a copy of the first draft of Part I. In an accompanying letter he set forth his idea of the book's structure: "Its form is more or less that of a string of beads, the string being the trip-narrative itself and the beads the various digressions in the form of anecdotes, tales, historical commentary, essays, etc." Later in the letter, he returned to his idea of the book:

> It is not to be a "thesis' book"; it has no particular axe to grind, though maybe a tomahawk or two as it stands just now. I think I will be able to give it a real unity apart from that picaresque unity furnished by the trip-background, by bringing the various themes into organic relationship to one another. (14)

By the end of the year he had finished Part II. His editor at Knopf, Harold Strauss, liked the book very much but felt that Part II suffered in comparison with Part I. In a long reply (January 1, 1960), Graves defended Part II, arguing in his quiet but insistent way that its subject matter, the present as compared with the past of Part I, necessitated a different approach. Graves explained,

> The most striking difference is in technique, but when I considered altering the structure of Part II so as to give it the unity of impact that One has, I found that structure—as it usually does—had grown out of subject matter. The "dying fall" had imposed itself. The later time in Brazos history extending into the present, which forms a background for Two as the Indians and the first-coming whites did for One, is for me fragmented and somewhat degenerate. The old monolithic people and things went, and what has replaced them is still chaotic. (Alfred A. Knopf Collection)

The manuscripts reveal that a very high percentage of Parts I and II remained as Graves had written them. There are a few changes worth noting, however, and there were some pitched battles over authorial versus editorial judgment. Graves' dogged conviction that he was right usually carried the day. One of the contested areas was the epigraphs that Graves had placed at the beginning of each chapter. Louis Gannett, an early reader of the galleys who in an oft-quoted blurb, compared Graves with Thoreau, urged the deletion of "fancy" chapter heads as well as omitting many of the literary allusions in the text. He objected in general to what he called "hoity-toity" language and recommended the substitution of more common words to replace some of Graves' recondite diction. Graves stood his ground and explained his position in a letter to Harold Strauss: "I know that in *Goodbye* I attempted a stylistic fusion between colloquial and 'literary' English which would leave me free to run with either hare or hounds as the occasion dictated" (Hamrick, 39). The chapter heads and lofty diction remained intact.

There was discussion about the most minute details. There was, for example, back-and-forth on how to spell "Goodbye," and Graves won that victory too. Near the end of the copyediting process, Strauss wrote Graves a long letter detailing forty-odd queries and proposed changes. These all had to do with diction, phrasing, and punctuation. Graves yielded on some points, but not others. Commas provided the most drama, and in one letter Graves set forth his philosophy of comma punctuation with the zeal of an Oxford grammarian. In the end Graves prevailed, and the book that was published was over 98 percent identical to the original manuscript. Most importantly, Graves retained the structures of Part I (the river's violent human history) and Part II (the present, which threatens the river's existence—pollution, development, dams, etc.) as he had conceived them. In every respect the book was wholly what Graves had wrought—even down to the cryptic encoding of a stylized figure eight on the title page. Although it appears to be nothing more than an impressionistic design, it held a special meaning for Graves, as he wrote Strauss in 1959: "I have a kind of cabalistic brand or good-luck symbol—from what cabala I couldn't tell you—and wouldn't mind seeing it used in the book as a decoration" (Hamrick, 25).

Among the first readers of *Goodbye to a River* none was more important to Graves than J. Frank Dobie, Mr. Texas himself. Earlier in the year Graves had met Dobie at his home in Austin. Although they got on famously, Graves knew that Dobie wouldn't pull any punches about the book, assuming that he decided to read it at all. Dobie was in poor health at the time, but he did read it and wrote Graves in September 1960, telling him: "It's a book I've been waiting for. It could do with fewer Comanche episodes, but every line of interpretation talks to me" (Hamrick, 73). It's interesting that the parts of the book that Dobie seems to have most admired were from Part II, where Graves bemoans the vulgarities and insensitivities of the present. Dobie himself had become quite the critic of modern life. Here he is preaching against the noise and confusion of a vulgar age in a 1944 letter to Bedichek:

> There is something metallic & barren about an awful lot of American citizens. Their minds are puerile, like the funnies, the pictures, and the horseplay humor they feed on. I always take great delight in people of the soil. Otherwise, I find that more & more I want them to be civilized. (Owens, *Three Friends*, 160)

Dobie gave the book a glowing send-off in his syndicated column. His admiration meant much to Graves, who wrote Dobie: "I'm solidly gratified by your letter and your article about my book, and can say without hypocrisy that no other person's approval of that book could mean to me quite what yours does" (Hamrick, 75).

Graves' solemn meditation on an obscure river in Texas certainly did not fit the expectations of what the Northeast thought of Texas-inspired writing. An associate of Graves' publisher, Alfred A. Knopf, told Knopf, who in turn told Graves, that "a book about Texas to be popular has to be very corny" (Hamrick, 32). Or, one might add, it had to be about the very rich—*Giant,* in other words. *Giant* (1952) had been both corny and about the rich. In 1961, a year after *Goodbye,* John Bainbridge published a more typically "Texan" book, *The Super-Americans,* which dealt with ultrarich Texans and their often embarrassing behavior. Yankees loved it.

However completely regional Graves' book is, it should also be seen as part of the national zeitgeist at the tail end of the 1950s. It belongs in the company of *The Organization Man, The Lonely Crowd, The Man in the Gray Flannel Suit,* books that had in common a moral fretting about conformity, mass culture, affluence, American smugness. Each book feared what America was becoming. There was a sense of uneasiness, of malaise. According to this view, America was an arrogant superpowerhouse of consumerism and cultural bloat.

The only antidote in sight was the beat movement. In San Francisco, Allen Ginsberg was inclined to use four-letter words in his poetry and to give readings in the nude. The year Graves rode his canoe down the Brazos, Jack Kerouac published *On the Road,* the ultimate get-away-from-it-all anti-bourgeoisie novel of the era. In Texas things were a lot quieter. Larry McMurtry, for a month or so in 1957, published a little journal at North Texas State called *The Coexistence Review.* It contained beat poems with riffs on what was wrong with everything: "You who believe absolutely every word of / scripture tv commercials / the reader's digest dale carnegie billy gra- / ham and popular songs, / run on to your sleazy heaven and check / the trade in on halos for me, / in case I can't find a flannel suit to match / my SOUL" (quoted in Busby, *Larry McMurtry and the West,* 11).

John Graves of course was no beatnik, but his book does carry a critique of American culture similar to that of the young McMurtry and the Beats in its celebration of solitude and individualism in an era of self-satisfied conformity. By the time Graves nears the completion of his month-long sojourn on the Brazos, made mighty by his imagination, he is by his own account unshaven, a bit ragged-looking, a little ripe, a kind of down-home, extremely well read, back-country figure—all right, a beatnik of sorts—who is almost scary to some of the pampered pilgrims along the shore.

For Graves, the symbol of the new America, to which the lone figure on the river is a living rebuke, is television. Graves sees television as the enemy of lived reality. Near the end of the narrative he describes two old women in an overheated room, their rheumy eyes glued to a television show that, as described, is probably *American Bandstand.* Outside is the river, the weather, the primordial reality of nature. The dichotomy is Emersonian: the preacher inside preaching the dead words, the snowstorm in all its reality and beauty, outside. In Graves' dialectic, television is the simulacrum of experience, a dazed and glazed mass consciousness supplanting whatever perceptions the women might have been able to muster on their own, a sort of invisible frontal lobotomy that television is performing on what used to be their minds.

In his own quiet way, Graves was ahead of his time. In the era of big-finned gas guzzlers, he addressed issues that would later become central to the environmental movement. The word he used was "conservation." Later in the decade, writers like Edward Abbey would heat up the discourse, and new words such as "ecology" would gain hold. Graves was markedly ahead of the curve on these issues, but never strident, never militant in his proclamations. This may be another reason Texans embraced him, preferring a sweet nostalgia to an angry activism.

I want to end with Graves' own description of what he intended to do in his first and most famous book. This was a "Note on the Author" that Graves was asked by his editor to compose for inclusion in the first edition. Only a couple of sentences were used, but the complete version sums up better than anything else what the author himself thought:

> *Goodbye to a River* is in a sense a homecoming book, a reexamination of childhood home things seen through eyes sharpened by years and long absence. Having spent nearly a half of his lifetime away from the Southwest, in places as diverse as New York and Spain and Mexico and Paris and the Canaries, its author says that he never managed to rid himself of an underlying, dozing, provincial consciousness of shotguns and fly rods and cedars and live oaks and mesquites and redbirds and Hereford cattle and people who

> speak with quiet nasal flatness from their palates. When he returned home not long ago, that consciousness came awake. This book is an attempt at its definition. (Hamrick, 38)

In *Goodbye to a River* and his other regional writing, Graves found a way to deal with belatedness—the problem that besets every serious writer. His solution was to abandon the world beyond Texas and make Texas the world—to find a usable tradition in his own hardscrabble backyard of Texas regional writing. Here he could take his place among the Triumvirate or, better yet, supplant them. But there remains a certain limitation as well, a point that is borne out by comparison with two other Texas writers of John Graves' generation. The first is John Howard Griffin, born in Dallas the same year as Graves in Fort Worth—1920. Griffin also lived in Europe, also embraced internationalist culture, and also came back to Texas to write. But his greatest book, *Black Like Me* (1961), was truly a narrative of national significance. Like Graves' river book, it too was the story of a journey, though one of much more consequence. Griffin's harrowing trip on the black side of the color line in the Deep South raised the consciousness of a nation and sold upwards of eleven million copies.

The other instructive comparison is Patricia Highsmith. Born in Graves' hometown one year after him, in 1921, she too was highly Eurocentric in later life, though her first novel, *Strangers on a Train* (1950), dealt in part with a fictionalized version of Fort Worth called Metcalf. Ultimately she would turn away from Texas in her novels, placing them in the various sites where she lived and increasingly in Europe, where she resided as an expatriate for the last decades of her life. She became a national and international writer whose reputation continues to grow more than a decade after her death.

It is interesting that the Fort Worth–Dallas nexus produced three such writers of distinction, all from the same period. The two who constructed national narratives seem destined to live longer in literary annals than the one who chose Texas, past and present, for his narrative. But however things turn out, it seems to have been the right decision for John Graves, and Texas has responded by showering him with honors, awards, and tributes attesting to his lofty standing in the Lone Star State.

Bibliography

Primary Sources: Works of John Graves

BOOKS

Home Place: A Background Sketch in Support of a Proposed Restoration of Pioneer Buildings in Fort Worth, Texas. Fort Worth: Pioneer Texas Heritage Committee, 1958.

Goodbye to a River: A Narrative. New York: Knopf, 1960. Condensed reprint in *Southwestern Writers Anthology.* Austin: Steck-Vaughn, 1967. Other reprints: New York: Sierra Club/Ballantine, 1971. Lincoln: University of Nebraska Press, 1977. Austin: Texas Monthly Press, 1985. New York: Vintage, 2002. Page numbers cited in the text refer to the 1960 edition.

The Creek and the City: Urban Pressures on a Natural Stream. Washington, DC: GPO, 1967.

The Nation's River. Washington, DC: GPO, 1968.

Hard Scrabble: Observations on a Patch of Land. New York: Knopf, 1974. Reprints: Austin: Texas Monthly Press, 1985; Dallas: Southern Methodist University Press, 2002.

Texas Heartland: A Hill Country Year. With photographs by Jim Bones, Jr. College Station: Texas A&M University Press, 1975.

From a Limestone Ledge: Some Essays and Other Ruminations about Country Life in Texas. New York: Knopf, 1980. Reprints: Austin:

Texas Monthly Press, 1985. Dallas: Southern Methodist University Press, 2004.

Blue and Some Other Dogs. Austin: Encino Press, 1981. Originally published as "Ol' Blue," *Texas Monthly,* December 1977. In *From a Limestone Ledge* and *A John Graves Reader* as "Blue and Some Other Dogs." Reprinted in an AKC collection and elsewhere.

Self-Portrait, with Birds. See "Recollections of a Texas Bird Glimpser," under "Essays and Introductions," below.

A John Graves Reader. Austin: University of Texas Press, 1996.

The Meaning of Moonlight. Dallas: Somesuch Press, 1999.

John Graves and the Making of Goodbye to a River*: Selected Letters, 1957–1960.* Ed. David S. Hamrick. Houston: Taylor Wilson Publishing, 2000.

Texas Rivers. With photographs by Wyman Meinzer. Austin: University of Texas Press, 2002.

Texas Hill Country. With photographs by Wyman Meinzer. Austin: University of Texas Press, 2003.

Myself and Strangers: A Memoir of Apprenticeship. New York: Alfred A. Knopf, 2004.

SHORT FICTION

"Quarry." *New Yorker,* November 8, 1947, 89–90.

"The Off-Season." *Stateside,* November 11, 1947, 26–28.

"The Dead Woman." *Stateside,* 1946 or 1947.

"Love vs. Pedro Rakoczy." *Today's Woman,* January 1953.

"The Green Fly." *Town and Country,* 108.4379 (1954): 79, 120, 124–127. Included in the following: *Prize Stories of 1955: The O. Henry Awards,* ed. Paul Engle and Hansford Martin (Garden City, N.J. : Doubleday, 1955), 215–225; *Gringos in Mexico,* ed. Edward Siemens (Fort Worth: Texas Christian University Press, 1988); and *A John Graves Reader.*

"The Laughter from the Western Islands." *Colorado Quarterly* 2.3 (1954): 327–339.

"Mixed Signals at Roaring Valley Institute." *Esquire,* September 1955.

"The Last Running." *Atlantic Monthly* 203.6 (1959): 39–45. Included in the following: *The Best American Short Stories 1960,* ed. Martha Foley (Boston: Houghton Mifflin, 1960; reprint, Austin: Encino

Press, 1974, and New York: Lyons and Burford, 1990); and *A John Graves Reader*. Reprinted a number of times elsewhere. Also published as the book *Last Running* (Austin: Encino Press, 1974; reprint, New York: Lyons and Burford, 1990).

"The Aztec Dog." *Colorado Quarterly* 9.1 (1960): 31–46. Included in the following: *Prize Stories 1962: The O. Henry Awards,* ed. Richard Poirier (Garden City, NJ: Doubleday, 1963); In *A Part of Space: Ten Texas Writers,* ed. Betsy Feagan Colquitt, 113–126 (Fort Worth: Texas Christian University Press, 1969); *Gringos in Mexico,* ed. Edward Siemens (Fort Worth: Texas Christian University Press, 1988); and *A John Graves Reader.*

"In the Absence of Horses." *Escapade* 6.4 (1961). Revised for *A John Graves Reader.*

"The Dreamer." *Readers & Writers,* May–June 1966, 25–32. Revised for *A John Graves Reader.*

ESSAYS AND INTRODUCTIONS

"Controlling Condensation" (by "Alexander Graves"). *Pipe Lovers,* May 1949.

"The Lost Americans." *Holiday,* February 1954.

"U.S. Go Home." *Colorado Quarterly,* Autumn 1955.

Home Place: A Background Sketch in Support of a Proposed Restoration of Pioneer Buildings in Fort Worth. Brochure. Fort Worth: Texas Pioneer Heritage Committee, 1958.

"The Brazos of the Northwest Texas Frontier, Today." *West Texas Historical Association Yearbook* 34 (October 1958).

"Drifting Down the Brazos." *Holiday,* November 1959.

"Carlsbad the Incredible." *Holiday,* September 1961.

"Harry Jackson—a Note." In *Harry Jackson,* program text for sculpture exhibition, Amon Carter Museum, Fort Worth, November 8, 1961.

"On the Desirable Reluctance of Trumpets." *College Composition and Communication* 14.4 (December 1963): 210–214.

"The Overlap Land, Gringo and Mexican Meet in the Rio Grande Valley." *Holiday,* March 1964.

"Rice University: The Pangs of Change." *Holiday,* June 1964.

"The Bright New Waters." *Ford Times,* November 1964.

"A River and a Piece of Country: A Potomac Essay." In *Potomac In-*

terim Report to the President, 51–61. Washington, DC: Department of the Interior, 1966.

"The Thirty Year Fence." In *Why Work.* Palo Alto: Behavioral Research Laboratories, 1966.

Program note. In *Harry Jackson, Susan Pogzeba, Wolfgang Pogzeba.* Exhibition catalog, Amon Carter Museum, Fort Worth, 1969.

"The Old Breed: A Note on John W. Thomason, Jr." Introduction to *A Thomason Sketchbook,* ed. Arnold Rosenfeld. Austin: University of Texas Press, 1969. Reprinted in *Southwest Review* 54.1 (Winter 1969).

"Aunt Clara's Luminous World." *American Heritage,* August 1970.

"Texas: You Ain't Seen Nothing Yet." In *The Water Hustlers,* with Robert H. Boyle and T. H. Watkins, 15–129. New York and San Francisco: Sierra Club, 1971.

Contribution to *Growing Up in Texas: Recollections of Childhood,* by Bertha McKee Dobie et al. Austin: Encino Press, 1972.

"Confessions of a Landowner." *Esquire,* September 1973.

"Living with the Land." *Texas Monthly,* May 1974. Excerpt from *Hard Scrabble.*

"The Region and the Place." Text for *Texas Heartland.*

"The Hard-Used Land." *Atlantic Monthly,* March 1975.

"Amateur Beekeeping in North Central Texas." *Gleanings in Bee Culture,* November 1976.

"Tribute to George Williams." *Sallyport,* November 15, 1976. Included in *A John Graves Reader.*

"A Handful of Ideas on Beekeeping." *Gleanings in Bee Culture,* 1977.

"Coping." *Texas Monthly,* February 1977. Included in *From a Limestone Ledge* as "Notes of an Uncertain Bluecollar Man."

"Good as Gold." *Texas Monthly,* April 1977. Included in *From a Limestone Ledge* as "Coronado's Stepchildren."

"Goats Need Love Too." *Texas Monthly,* June 1977. Included in *From a Limestone Ledge* as "A Few Words in Favor of Goats."

"Of Bees and Men." *Texas Monthly,* August 1977. Included in *From a Limestone Ledge,* with same title.

"Meat." *Texas Monthly,* September 1977. Included in *From a Limestone Ledge,* with same title.

"The World to Wine." *Texas Monthly,* October 1977. Included in *From a Limestone Ledge* as "Vin du Pays."

"Ol' Blue." See *Blue and Some Other Dogs.*

"Texas as Maybe a Place." Essay for *A Texas Portfolio,* photographs by Jim Bones. Austin, Encino Press, 1978.

"Poultry in Motion." *Texas Monthly,* January 1978. Included in *From a Limestone Ledge* as "Some Chickens I Have Known."

"Fencing Myself In." *Texas Monthly,* March 1978. Included in *From a Limestone Ledge* as "More Than Most People Probably Want to Know about Fences."

"Stayin' Alive." *Texas Monthly,* April 1978.

"Building Fever." *Texas Monthly,* July 1978. Included in *From a Limestone Ledge,* with same title.

"The Loser." *Texas Monthly,* August 1978. Included in *From a Limestone Ledge* and in *A John Graves Reader* as "A Loser."

"The Snuff of Dreams." *Texas Monthly,* October 1978. Included in *From a Limestone Ledge* as "Tobacco without Smoke I: Dippers."

"The Chew Road to Knowledge." *Texas Monthly,* November 1978. Included in *From a Limestone Ledge* as "Tobacco without Smoke II: Chewers."

"Sacred Cows." *Texas Monthly,* December 1978. Included in *From a Limestone Ledge* and *A John Graves Reader* as "Nineteen Cows."

"Through All Kinds of Weather." *Texas Monthly,* February 1979. Included in *From a Limestone Ledge* as "Weather between East and West."

"All That Litters." *Texas Monthly,* May 1979. Included in *From a Limestone Ledge* as "Trash as Treasure."

"Range Goats." *The New Farm,* July/August 1979.

"Kindred Spirits." *Texas Monthly,* November 1979. Included in *From a Limestone Ledge* and *A John Graves Reader,* with same title.

Introduction to *Landscapes of Texas: Photographs from Texas Highways Magazine.* College Station: Texas A&M University Press, 1980.

Preface to *Digging into South Texas Prehistory: A Guide for Amateur Archaeologists,* by Thomas R. Hester. San Antonio: Corona Publishing Co., 1980.

"One Man's Music." *Texas Monthly,* March 1980. Included in *From a Limestone Ledge* as "Noticing."

"Whose Woods Are These?" *Texas Monthly,* June 1980. Included in *From a Limestone Ledge* as "One's Own Sole Ground."

"The Heat Treatment." *Texas Monthly,* September 1980.

"The Southwest as the Cradle of the Writer." In *The American Southwest: Cradle of Literary Art,* ed. Robert W. Walts, 5–20. San Marcos: Southwest Texas State University Press, 1981.

"Going Under." *Texas Monthly,* March 1981. Reprinted in *The Ultimate Fishing Book* (Boston: Houghton Mifflin, 1981) and *A John Graves Reader* as "Fishing the Run."

"Lord of the Flies." *Texas Monthly,* September 1981.

"Cowboys: A Few Thoughts from the Sidelines." Introduction to *Cowboy Life on the Texas Plains: The Photographs of Ray Rector,* ed. Margaret Rector. College Station: Texas A&M University Press, 1982. Included in *A John Graves Reader.*

"Drinking." *Texas Monthly,* March 1982. Included in *A John Graves Reader* as "The Water of Life."

"Big River." *Texas Monthly,* June 1982. Commissioned piece on the Rio Grande canyons.

"The Old Guard: Dobie, Webb, and Bedichek." In *The Texas Literary Tradition: Fiction, Folklore, History,* ed. Don Graham, James W. Lee, and William T. Pilkington, 16–25. Austin: College of Liberal Arts of the University of Texas and the Texas State Historical Association, 1983.

Foreword to *The Other Texas Frontier,* by Harry Huntt Ransom. Austin: University of Texas Press, 1984.

"Dead Oaks." *Texas Monthly,* October 1984. Environment department.

"Folklore and Me." In *Sonovagun Stew: A Folklore Miscellany,* ed. Frances Edward Abernethy, 2–11. Dallas: Southern Methodist University Press, 1985.

"Recollections of a Texas Bird Glimpser: An Essay." Introduction to *Of Birds and Texas,* folio of paintings by Stuart and Scott Gentling. Fort Worth: Gentling Editions, 1986. Later revised and republished alone as *Self-Portrait, with Birds: Some Semi-Ornithological Recollections* (Dallas: Chama Press, 1991). This revision, with slight further alterations, is in *A John Graves Reader.*

"The Exhausted Land." *Texas Monthly,* January 1986. Included in the anthology *Texas, Our Texas* (Austin: Texas Monthly Press, 1986).

Introduction to reissue of *This Stubborn Soil,* by William A. Owens. New York: Nick Lyons Books, 1986.

Foreword to *Gringos in Mexico: One Hundred Years of Mexico in the American Short Story.* Ed. Edward Simmen. Fort Worth: Texas Christian University Press, 1988.

Introduction to *William D. Wittliff and the Encino Press.* A bibliography by Gould Whaley, Jr. Dallas: Still Point Press, 1989.

"My Favorite Place." *Texas Monthly,* May 1989.

Untitled. *Southern Living,* January 1990.

Introduction to *Gulf Coast Cooking,* by Virginia Elverson. Fredericksburg, TX: Shearer Publishing, 1991.

Introduction to reissue of *Cynthia Ann Parker,* by James T. DeShields. Dallas: Chama Press, 1991.

"Quiet Haven in Easy Reach." *Southern Living,* May 1991. Essay on Krause Springs.

"State of Nature: A 50th Anniversary Celebration." *Texas Parks and Wildlife,* December 1992.

Afterword to *Barton Springs Eternal,* by Turk Pipkin and Marshall Frech. Austin: Softshoe Publishing, 1993.

Dedicatory speech delivered at Southwest Texas State University on October 5, 1993. Published in *The Southwestern Writers Collection Dedication.* Southwestern Writers Collection, Southwest Texas State University, San Marcos, 1993.

"Watching the Gulf." *Travel Holiday,* December 1994/January 1995. Article on Padre Island.

Foreword to *Born of the River,* by Turk Pipkin. Austin: Softshoe Publishing, 1995.

Introduction to *Oil Notes,* by Rick Bass. Dallas: Southern Methodist University Press, 1995.

"John Graves on Birds." *Texas Parks and Wildlife,* April 1995. Excerpt from *Self-Portrait, with Birds.*

"Notes of a Back-Country Bumbler." In *West of Key West,* ed. John Cole and Hawk Pollard. Mechanicsburg, PA: Stackpole Books, 1996.

"Paw Prints." *Texas Monthly,* December 1996.

"Our Own Piece of the Country." *CITE 39: Texas Places.* Special double issue, *CITE: The Architectural and Design Review of Houston* 39 (Fall 1997).

Foreword to *Texas Bound, Book II: 22 Texas Stories.* Dallas: Southern Methodist University Press, 1998.

Introduction to *Texas Sky,* photographs by Wyman Meinzer. Austin: University of Texas Press, 1998.

Squib sandwich recipe in *Stirring Prose: Cooking with Texas Authors,* by Deborah Douglas. College Station: Texas A&M University Press, 1998.

"Sandhill Crane." In *Great Texas Birds,* paintings by John P. O'Neill, ed. Suzanne Winckler. Austin: University of Texas Press, 1999.

"The Canadian." *Texas Parks and Wildlife,* March 1999.

"Texas Hill Country." *National Geographic,* April 1999.

"The Pecos." *Texas Parks and Wildlife,* December 1999.

"The Llano." *Texas Parks and Wildlife,* November 2000.

Introduction to *Vaquero: Genesis of the Texas Cowboy,* by Bill Wittliff. Austin: University of Texas Press, 2004.

Secondary Sources

BOOKS AND PERIODICALS

Abbey, Edward. *Beyond the Wall.* New York: Henry Holt and Co., 1984.

Adams, Timothy Dow. "John Graves." In *Dictionary of Literary Biography Yearbook:* 1983, ed. Mary Bruccoli and Jean W. Ross. Detroit: Gale, 1984.

Austin, J. L. *How to Do Things with Words.* Cambridge, MA: Harvard University Press, 1962.

Bass, Rick. Review of *The Last Running. Dallas Morning News,* April 8, 1990, sec. J, 7.

Basso, Keith. *Wisdom Sits in Places: Landscape and Language among the Western Apache.* Albuquerque: University of New Mexico Press, 1996.

Bennett, Patrick. "John Graves: A Hard Scrabble World," in *Talking with Texas Writers: Twelve Interviews.* College Station: Texas A&M Press, 1980.

———. "Laura Furman, Beverly Lowry, and Shelby Hearon." In *Texas Women Writers: A Tradition of Their Own,* ed. Sylvia Ann Grider and Lou Halsell Rodenberger, 153–154. College Station: Texas A&M University Press, 1997.

Bogie, T. M. Review of *Goodbye to a River: A Narrative. Library Journal* (September 15, 1960).

———. Review of *Hard Scrabble: Observations on a Patch of Land. Library Journal* (April 1, 1974).

Bradford, M. E. "Arden Up the Brazos: John Graves and the Uses of the Pastoral." *Southern Review* 57 (1972).

———. "In Keeping with the Way: John Graves' *Hard Scrabble.*" *Southwest Review* 60 (1975).

———. "John Graves." In *Fifty Western Writers: A Bio-Bibliographical Sourcebook,* ed. Fred Erisman and Richard W. Etulain. Westport, CT.: Greenwood Press, 1982.

Buell, Lawrence. *The Environmental Imagination: Thoreau, Nature Writing, and the Formation of American Culture.* Cambridge, MA: Harvard University Press, 1995.

———. *Writing for an Endangered World: Literature, Culture, and Environment in the U.S. and Beyond.* Cambridge, MA: Harvard University Press, 2001.

Busby, Mark. *Larry McMurtry and the West: An Ambivalent Relationship.* Denton: University of North Texas Press, 1995.

———. "John Graves." In *American Nature Writers,* ed. John Elder. New York: Scribner's, 1996.

Callaway, Evelyn G. Review of *From a Limestone Ledge: Some Essays and Other Ruminations about Country Life in Texas. Library Journal* (November 15, 1980).

Carson, Rachel. *Silent Spring.* New York: Houghton Mifflin, 1962.

Cheshire, Ashley. "John Graves: Life and Letters at Hard Scrabble." *Dallas Times Herald Sunday Magazine,* August 1, 1976, 1–3, 20–21.

Clifford, Craig. "John Graves." In *Updating the Literary West,* ed. Thomas J. Lyon, 571–579. Fort Worth: Texas Christian University Press, 1997.

Cronon, William. "A Place for Stories: Nature, History, and Narrative." *Journal of American History* 78 (1992): 1347–1376.

———. "The Trouble with Wilderness; or, Getting Back to the Wrong Nature." In *Uncommon Ground: Rethinking the Human Place in Nature,* ed. William Cronon, 69–90. New York: Norton, 1996.

Crume, Paul. "A Man and His River." *Dallas Morning News Sunday Magazine,* February 20, 1972.

Davenport, Priscilla. "A Literary Trek from Hong Kong to the Kitchen Sink." *Dallas Morning News,* May 3, 1961, sec. G, 6.

Elledge, Scott. *E. B. White: A Biography.* New York: W. W. Norton and Co., 1984.

Endress, Clifford. "Texas Literature: The Twists and Turns of an Enigmatic Tradition." *Texas Humanist* (1983).

Erisman, Fred. "Western Writers and the Literary Historian." *North Dakota Review* (Autumn 1979): 64–69.

Eyrich, Claire. "John Graves: 'Texas Thoreau' Celebrates Life Anew in Print." *Fort Worth Star-Telegram,* November 16, 1980, sec. C, 18.

Gard, Wayne. "A World of Its Own." *New York Times Book Review,* October 9, 1960, 6.

Glotfelty, Cheryl. Introduction to *Ecocriticism Reader*, ed. Glotfelty and Harold Fromm. Athens: University of Georgia Press, 1996.

Graham, Don. *Giant Country: Essays on Texas*. Fort Worth: Texas Christian University Press, 1998.

Grant, Lyman. Review of *From a Limestone Ledge: Some Essays and Other Ruminations about Country Life in Texas. Texas Humanist* (1981).

Greene, A. C. *The Fifty Best Books on Texas*. Dallas: Pressworks, 1982.

Grover, Dorys Crow. *John Graves*. Western Writers Series. Boise: Boise State University Press, 1989.

Gunter, Pete A. Y., and Max Oelschlaeger. *Texas Land Ethics*. Austin: University of Texas Press, 1997.

Hamrick, David S., ed. *John Graves and the Making of "Goodbye to a River": Selected Letters*, 1957–1960. Houston: Taylor Wilson Publishing, 2000.

Hendrick, Kimmis. "Last Look at a Frontier." Review of *Goodbye to a River, A Narrative. Christian Science Monitor*, November 10, 1960.

Hoagland, Edward. Review of *Hard Scrabble: Observations on a Patch of Land. New York Times Book Review*, May 19, 1974, 2.

Hollandsworth, Skip. "John Graves: The Thoreau of Texas." *Dallas Morning News*, April 29, 1979, sec. G, 6.

Holley, Joe. "John Graves: A Master of Details and Ruminations." *Texas Humanist* (1984).

Horgan, Paul. *Great River: The Rio Grande in North American History*. New York: Holt, 1954.

———. "A Sort of Love Letter to the Brazos." Review of *Goodbye to a River. New York Herald Tribune Book Review*, October 9, 1960, 8.

Johnstone, Barbara. *Stories, Community, and Place: Narratives from Middle America*. Bloomington: Indiana University Press, 1990.

La Vere, David. *Life among the Texas Indians: The WPA Narratives*. College Station: Texas A&M University Press, 1998.

Lenhart, Maria. "Making the Mundane Not So Dull." Review of *From a Limestone Ledge: Some Essays and Other Ruminations about Country Life in Texas. Christian Science Monitor*, January 14, 1981, 17.

Leopold, Aldo. *A Sand County Almanac: With Essays on Conservation from Round River*. San Francisco: Sierra Club Books, 1949.

Limerick, Patricia Nelson. *Something in the Soil: Legacies and Reckonings in the New West*. New York: Norton, 2000.

Lopez, Barry. *Arctic Dreams.* New York: Vintage Books, 1986.

Love, Glen. "Revaluing Nature: Toward an Ecological Criticism." In *The Ecocriticism Reader: Landmarks in Literary Ecology,* ed. Cheryll Glotfelty and Harold Fromm, 225–240. Athens: University of Georgia Press, 1996.

Lowry, Beverly. *The Perfect Sonya.* New York: Viking, 1987. Reprint, Fort Worth: Texas Christian University Press, 2004. Page numbers cited in the text are from the 1987 edition.

Lyon, Thomas J. "The Nature Essay in the West." In *A Literary History of the American West,* ed. J. Golden Taylor and Thomas J. Lyon. Fort Worth: Texas Christian University Press, 1987.

McMurtry, Larry. "Ever a Bridegroom: Reflections of the Failure of Texas Literature." *Texas Observer,* October 23, 1981. Reprinted in *Range Wars: Heated Debates, Sober Reflections, and Other Assessments of Texas Writing,* ed. Craig Clifford and Tom Pilkington (Dallas: SMU Press, 1989).

Medina, David D. "When the Work Comes Right." *Sallyport: The Magazine of Rice University,* Spring 1995, 18–25.

Momaday, N. Scott. *The Way to Rainy Mountain.* Albuquerque: University of New Mexico Press, 1969.

Murphy, Patrick D. *Farther Afield in the Study of Nature-Oriented Literature.* Charlottesville: University Press of Virginia, 2000.

Old Texas. Silent film, directed by Wiswall Brothers. 1916; DVD, Lindley-Ockander International Television, 2004.

Owens, William A. *Three Friends: Roy Bedichek, J. Frank Dobie, Walter Prescott Webb.* Garden City, NY: Doubleday, 1969. Reprint, Austin: University of Texas Press, 1975. Page numbers cited in the text refer to the 1975 edition.

Perrin, Noel. "Rediscovering *Goodbye to a River,* by John Graves." *Georgia Review* (Winter 1993).

Pilkington, Tom. *State of Mind: Texas Literature and Culture.* College Station: Texas A&M Press, 1998.

Pilkington, William T[om]. *Imagining Texas: The Literature of the Lone Star State.* Boston: American Press, 1981.

Ritchey, Mike. "Giants of Texas Letters Probe State's Literary Tradition." *Fort Worth Star-Telegram,* April 3, 1983, sec. E, 7.

Rosaldo, Renato. *Culture and Truth: The Remaking of Social Analysis.* Boston: Beacon Press, 1989.

Ryden, Kent C. *Landscape with Figures.* Iowa City: University of Iowa Press, 2001.

———. *Mapping the Invisible Landscape: Folklore, Writing, and the Sense of Place.* Iowa City: University of Iowa Press, 1993.

Slotkin, Richard. *Regeneration through Violence: The Mythology of the American Frontier,* 1600–1860. Middletown, CT: Wesleyan University Press, 1973.

Slovic, Scott. *Seeking Awareness in American Nature Writing.* Salt Lake City: University of Utah Press, 1992.

Smith, Evan. "Great Expectations." *Texas Monthly,* August 2000, 9–10.

Strunk, William, Jr. *Elements of Style.* With revisions, an introduction, and a chapter on writing by E. B. White. New York: Macmillan, 1979.

Terry, Marshall. "The Republic of Texas Letters." In *Range Wars: Heated Debates, Sober Reflections, and Other Assessments of Texas Writing,* ed. Craig Clifford and Tom Pilkington, 137–154. Dallas: Southern Methodist University Press, 1989.

"Texas Monthly Awards." http://www.texasmonthly.com/mag/awards.php.

Thoreau, Henry David. *Walking.* New York: Penguin, 1955.

———. *Walden.* Boston: Beacon Press, 1997.

Tinkle, Lon. Review of *Goodbye to a River: A Narrative. Chicago Sunday Tribune,* October 16, 1960, 3.

Tuan, Yi-Fu. *Space and Place: The Perspective of Experience.* Minneapolis: University of Minnesota Press, 1977.

Weeks, Edward. "Biography of a River." Review of *Goodbye to a River: A Narrative. Atlantic Monthly,* April 1961.

White, E. B. *One Man's Meat.* New York: Harper and Row, 1982.

Whitney, Gordon G. *From Coastal Wilderness to Fruited Plain: A History of Environmental Change in Temperate North America from* 1500 *to the Present.* Cambridge: Cambridge University Press, 1994.

Woolley, Bryan. "No Goodbye." *Dallas Life Magazine, Dallas Morning News,* June 7, 1992.

Young, Mallory. "On Reading John Graves, Slowly." *Texas Books in Review* (1984).

OTHER RESOURCES

"About the Magazine." http://www.texasmonthly.com/mag.

Alfred A. Knopf Collection. Harry Ransom Humanities Research Center, University of Texas at Austin.

Arlen, Michael J. "Notes on the New Journalism." *Atlantic Monthly,* May 1972, 61–71. http://www.theatlantic.com/issues/72may/new-journalism-p2.htm.

Broyles, William. "John Graves Tribute." Author's party, Texas Book Festival, Austin, November 11, 2000.

"Comanche Indians." The Handbook of Texas Online. http://www.tsha.utexas.edu/handbook/online/articles/view/CC/bmc72.html.

Curtis, Greg. "Great Days." *Texas Monthly,* February 1993. http://www.epnet.com.

———. "The Uncertain Sage." *Texas Monthly,* March 1994. http://www.epnet.com.

John Graves Collection. Southwestern Writers Collection, Texas State University–San Marcos.

Moyers, Bill. "John Graves, the Head Varmint of Hard Scrabble." Transcript of *Bill Moyers Journal,* PBS special, July 23, 1979.

Sherman, Scott. "'New' Journalism." *Columbia Journalism Review* 40.4 (November/December 2001): 59. http://www.epnet.com.

Sultzman, Lee. "Comanche History." In *First Nations Histories.* http://www.tolatsga.org/ComancheOne.html.

"The *Texas Monthly* Days." Panel discussion with John Graves, Jan Reid, and Suzanne Winckler and moderated by Stephen Harrigan, September 7, 2002. Videocassette. Southwestern Writers Collection, Alkek Library, Texas State University–San Marcos.

"*Texas Monthly:* Thirty Years." Southwestern Writers Collection, Texas State University–San Marcos. http://www.library.txstate.edu/swwc/exhibits/tm.html.

"Urban and Rural Population: 1900 to 1990." U.S. Census Bureau. Released October 1995. http://www.census.gov/population/censusdata/urpop0090.txt.

"Vocabulary." In *A Teacher's Guide to the Holocaust.* Florida Center for Instructional Technology, College of Education, University of South Florida, 2001. http://fcit.coedu.usf.edu/holocaust/people/VICTIMS2.htm.

"Writer Archives." http://www.texasmonthly.com/mag/issues/authors/index.php. See also "Texas Monthly Archives," http://www.texasmonthly.com/mag/archive.php.

Notes on Contributors

Editors

MARK BUSBY is director of the Southwest Regional Humanities Center and a professor of English at Texas State University–San Marcos. A native of Ennis, Texas, he is author of *Larry McMurtry and the West: An Ambivalent Relationship* and *Ralph Ellison* and editor of *The Greenwood Encyclopedia of American Regional Cultures: The Southwest* and *New Growth/2: Contemporary Short Stories by Texas Writers.* He is coeditor (with Dick Heaberlin) of *From Texas to the World and Back: Essays on the Journeys of Katherine Anne Porter* and the journals *Southwestern American Literature* and *Texas Books in Review.* He has also published *Preston Jones* and *Lanford Wilson* in the Western Writers Series at Boise State University, coedited *The Frontier Experience and the American Dream,* and was a contributing editor of *Taking Stock: A Larry McMurtry Casebook.* He has published in *Western American Literature, MELUS, New Mexico Humanities Review, A Literary History of the American West,* and elsewhere. His first novel, *Fort Benning Blues,* was published by TCU Press in 2001.

TERRELL DIXON teaches Literature and the Environment in the English Department at the University of Houston Central Campus. He served as chair of the English Department at the University of

Houston throughout the 1980s and for the first half of the 1990s, and he currently holds a Martha Gano Houstoun Research Grant in that department. He also served as a founding director of the University of Houston's Scholars' Community from 1996 to 1998. He is a founding member of the Association for the Study of Literature and Environment, and he served as president of that group in 2002. He has edited *City Wilds: Essays and Stories about Urban Nature* (University of Georgia Press, 2002), and he served as coeditor (with Scott Slovic) of an early ecocomposition text *Being in the World: An Environmental Reader for Writers* (1993). He is the author of numerous articles and essays on environmental literature, urban nature, and the city of Houston.

Contributors

RICK BASS was born in Fort Worth, grew up in Houston, and now lives in the Yaak Valley in Montana. He is the author of *The Deer Pasture* (1985), *Wild to the Heart* (1987), *Oil Notes* (1989), *Winter* (1991), *The Ninemile Wolves* (1992), *The New Wolves* (1998), *Brown Dog of the Yaak: Essays on Art and Activism* (1999), *Colter: The True Story of the Best Dog I Ever Had* (2000), and *The Roadless Yaak: Reflections and Observations about One of Our Last Great Wilderness Areas* (2002). His collection of short stories, *The Watch,* was published in 1989, and *The Hermit's Story: Stories* in 2002. Bass published his first novel, *Where the Sea Used to Be,* in 1998 and his second, *The Diezmo: A Novel,* in 2005. His most recent work is *The Lives of Rocks* (2006). Among his awards are a PEN/Nelson Algren Award Special Citation for fiction, the General Electric Younger Writers Award, and a National Endowment for the Arts Creative Writing Fellowship.

BETSY BERRY is a lecturer in American and British literature at the University of Texas at Austin. She is a creative writer as well, and her poetry and prose have been published in numerous journals and anthologies, including *Lone Star Literature.* Her latest short story, "Human Sexuality," will appear in the forthcoming book *Literary Austin.*

WILLIAM BROYLES, JR., was the founding editor of *Texas Monthly* magazine, where he initiated John Graves' regular column. Broyles created and wrote the Emmy Award–winning television series *China Beach* as well as the highly regarded Vietnam War memoir, *Brothers in Arms.* Broyles is also an accomplished screenwriter, nominated for an Academy Award for the screenplay for *Apollo* 13 (co-written with Al Reinert). He also wrote the screenplays for *Jarhead, The Polar Express, Unfaithful, Planet of the Apes, Cast Away,* and *Entrapment.*

BARBARA J. COOK currently teaches Native American literature and literature and the environment as well as other American literature courses at Mount Aloysius College in Cresson, Pennsylvania. She taught previously at Eastern Kentucky University. Cook earned a PhD from the University of Oregon, MA from Utah State University, and BA from Texas State University–San Marcos. Her recent publications include *From the Center of Tradition: Critical Perspectives on Linda Hogan* (editor); "Enclosed by Racist Politics: Space, Place, and Power Dynamics in the Slave Narrative of Harriet Jacobs and in Environmental Justice Activism," in *Restoring the Connection to the Natural World: Essays on the African American Environmental Imagination,* edited by Sylvia Mayer; "*La Llorona* and A Call For Environmental Justice in the Borderlands: Ana Castillo's *So Far from God,*" in *Northwest Review;* and "A Tapestry of History and Reimagination: Women's Place in James Welch's *Fools Crow,*" in *American Indian Quarterly.*

DON GRAHAM is the J. Frank Dobie Regents Professor of American and English Literature at the University of Texas at Austin. He is the author of a number of works, including *Kings of Texas: The 150-Year Saga of an American Ranching Empire,* winner of the Texas Institute of Letters Carr P. Collins Award; *Giant Country: Essays on Texas,* which won the Violet Crown Award from the Austin Writers' League; and *No Name on the Bullet: A Biography of Audie Murphy.* He is editor of *Lone Star Literature: A Texas Anthology* and is a writer-at-large for *Texas Monthly.*

DAVE HAMRICK is the editor of *John Graves and the Making of* Goodbye to a River, the 2004–2006 president of the Texas Institute of Letters, and an assistant director and the sales and marketing manager for the University of Texas Press at Austin.

BILL HARVEY was born and raised in John Graves' hometown, Fort

Worth, and spent much of his youth on the Brazos River fishing, canoeing, wandering, and wondering. He received a BS and a PhD from Texas A&M and a master's in public policy from the LBJ School at the University of Texas at Austin. A veteran of the U.S. Navy, Bill worked for the Texas Parks and Wildlife Department for twenty years and is currently with the Texas Cooperative Extension Service. An avid student of Texas history, as well as an outdoorsman, fly fisherman, and photographer, he is the author of *Texas Cemeteries: The Resting Places of Famous, Infamous, and Just Plain Interesting Texans* (2003). He is currently working on a photography book and a book about fishing.

DICKIE MAURICE HEABERLIN is the immediate past Jesse H. and Mary Gibbs Jones Professor of Southwestern Studies at the Southwest Regional Humanities Center, located on the campus of Texas State University–San Marcos and is a professor of English. He coedited (with Mark Busby) *From Texas to the World and Back: Essays on the Journeys of Katherine Anne Porter* (2001). His forthcoming book is *Rivers of Oil: A History of the Oil Field Novel.*

DAVE HICKEY received a BA in 1961 from Texas Christian University, where he was John Graves' student, and an MA in 1963 from the University of Texas at Austin. He currently teaches in the creative writing program at the University of Nevada, Las Vegas. Hickey is the recipient of a National Endowment for the Arts grant (1969) and the College Art Association's Frank Jewett Mather Award for Distinction in Art or Architectural Criticism (1993). In 2002 he received one of the prestigious MacArthur Foundation "genius" grants. He served as executive editor of *Art in America* magazine and as contributing editor to the *Village Voice.* He has written for most major American cultural publications, including *Rolling Stone, Art News, Art in America, Artforum, Interview, Harper's, Vanity Fair, Nest,* the *New York Times,* and the *Los Angeles Times.* He now serves as contributing editor to *Art issues* magazine in Los Angeles. Hickey's critical essays on art have been collected in two volumes: *The Invisible Dragon: Four Essays on Beauty* (1993) and *Air Guitar: Essays on Art and Democracy* (1998). His most recent book, *Stardumb* (1999), is a collection of stories with drawings by John DeFazio.

ALEX HUNT is assistant professor of American literature at West Texas A&M University. He has published articles on Cormac McCarthy, Leslie Marmon Silko, Rudolfo Anaya, and other topics in Southwestern literary, cultural, and environmental studies. He is at work on a book on contemporary Southwestern literatures and landscapes.

SAMUEL HYNES is Woodrow Wilson Professor of Literature Emeritus at Princeton University. He and John Graves were students together at Columbia. He is the author of several major works of literary criticism, including *The Auden Generation, Edwardian Occasions,* and *The Edwardian Turn of Mind.* Hynes is also the author of a memoir based on his wartime experiences as a Marine Corps pilot, *Flights of Passage.* His book about soldiers' narratives of the two world wars and Vietnam, *The Soldiers' Tale,* won a Robert F. Kennedy Book Award.

JAMES LANGSTON received his master's degree in literature from the University of Houston. He is a member of the English faculty at Houston Community College and is currently working on a manuscript about Texas writers.

JAMES WARD LEE, emeritus professor of English at the University of North Texas, recently retired as acquisitions editor at Texas Christian University Press. Lee is coeditor, with Judy Alter, of *Literary Fort Worth.* His latest book is *Adventures with a Texas Humanist.* He is currently working on *Literary West Texas* and now lives in Fort Worth.

CORY LOCK is an assistant professor of University Programs at St. Edward's University, where she teaches courses in writing, literature, and American culture. Her recent article on Southwestern writers appears in *The Greenwood Encyclopedia of American Regional Cultures: The Southwest.* She has also published articles on Texas literature, music, and dance in such publications as *The Journal of Texas Music History* and *ATQ: 19th-Century American Literature and Culture.*

LISA SLAPPEY received her PhD in English from Rice University in Houston, where she currently teaches courses on environmental literature and Native American literature. Through Rice's Glasscock School of Continuing Studies, she also team-teaches a class on Persian rugs.

BILL WITTLIFF and his wife, Sally, founded Encino Press, which has published Southwestern works of note since the early 1960s, including a number of John Graves' works. An accomplished photographer, Wittliff's photographs documenting the life of the Mexican vaquero (taken 1969–1971) were published as *Vaquero* in 2003. In 1985, with the donation of their lifelong collection of original manuscripts and books, Bill and Sally founded the Southwestern Writers Collection at Texas State University–San Marcos. In 1996 the Wittliffs also established the Wittliff Gallery of Southwestern and Mexican Photography at Texas State. Wittliff's movie credits as a screenwriter include *Thaddeus Rose and Eddie, The Black Stallion, Honeysuckle Rose, Raggedy Man, The Cowboy Way, The Perfect Storm,* and others. He also was executive producer of the television series *Lonesome Dove,* for which he adapted the script from Larry McMurtry's novel.

Index